7589 27

P9-CNC-917

WITHDRAWN

ARGUING *with* ZOMBIES

ARGUING *with* ZOMBIES

Economics, Politics, and the Fight for a Better Future

Paul Krugman

W. W. NORTON & COMPANY
Independent Publishers Since 1923

Since this page cannot legibly accommodate all the copyright notices, pages 415–16 constitute an extension of the copyright page.

For information about special discounts for bulk purchases, please contact W. W. Norton Special Sales at specialsales@wwnorton.com or 800-233-4830

Manufacturing by LSC Communications, Harrisonburg
Book design by Daniel Lagin Design
Production manager: Julia Druskin

Library of Congress Cataloging-in-Publication Data

Names: Krugman, Paul R., author.
Title: Arguing with zombies : economics, politics, and the fight for
    a better future / Paul Krugman.
Description: New York, NY : W. W. Norton & Company, [2020] |
    Includes index.
Identifiers: LCCN 2019032129 | ISBN 9781324005018 (hardcover) |
    ISBN 9781324005025 (epub)
Subjects: LCSH: Economics—Popular works. | United States—Economic
    conditions—21st century—Popular works. | Common fallacies.
Classification: LCC HC106.84 .K78 2020 | DDC 330.973—dc23
LC record available at https://lccn.loc.gov/2019032129

W. W. Norton & Company, Inc., 500 Fifth Avenue, New York, N.Y. 10110
www.wwnorton.com

W. W. Norton & Company Ltd., 15 Carlisle Street, London W1D 3BS

1 2 3 4 5 6 7 8 9 0

To the memory of my late colleague and friend Uwe Reinhart, who did more than anyone to advance the discussion of health care economics and helped me in particular avoid making a fool of myself.

CONTENTS

Acknowledgments   xv

INTRODUCTION: The Good Fight   1

1. SAVING SOCIAL SECURITY

Essay: After the Khaki Election   13

Social Security Scares   16
Inventing a Crisis   19
Buying into Failure   22
Social Security Lessons   25
Privatization Memories   28
Where Government Excels   30

2. THE ROAD TO OBAMACARE

Essay: Developing a Positive Agenda   35

Ailing Health Care   38
Health Care Confidential   41
Health Care Terror   44
The Waiting Game   47
Health Care Hopes   50
Fear Strikes Out   53
Obamacare Fails to Fail   56
Imaginary Health Care Horrors   59

3. THE ATTACK ON OBAMACARE

Essay: The Cruelty Caucus   65

Three Legs Good, No Legs Bad   67
Obamacare's Very Stable Genius   70
Get Sick, Go Bankrupt, and Die   73
How Democrats Can Deliver on Health Care   76

4. BUBBLE AND BUST

Essay: The Sum of All Fears   81

Running Out of Bubbles   83
That Hissing Sound   86
Innovating Our Way to Financial Crisis   89
The Madoff Economy   92
The Ignoramus Strategy   95
Nobody Understands Debt   97

5. CRISIS MANAGEMENT

Essay: The Triumph of Macroeconomics   103

Depression Economics Returns   106
IS-LMentary   109
Stimulus Arithmetic (Wonkish but Important)   113
The Obama Gap   115
The Stimulus Tragedy   118

6. THE CRISIS IN ECONOMICS

Essay: The Cost of Bad Ideas   123

The Mythical Seventies   126
That Eighties Show   128
How Did Economists Get It So Wrong?   130
Bad Faith, Pathos, and G.O.P. Economics   149
What's Wrong with Functional Finance? (Wonkish)   152

7. AUSTERITY

Essay: Very Serious People   157

Myths of Austerity   160
The Excel Depression   163
Jobs and Skills and Zombies   166
Structural Humbug   169

8. THE EURO

Essay: A Bridge Too Far   175

The Spanish Prisoner   178
Crash of the Bumblebee   181
Europe's Impossible Dream   184
What's the Matter with Europe?   187

9. FISCAL PHONIES

Essay: The Gullibility of the Deficit Scolds   193

The Flimflam Man   195
The Hijacked Commission   198
What's in the Ryan Plan?   201
Melting Snowballs and the Winter of Debt   203
Democrats, Debt, and Double Standards   207
On Paying for a Progressive Agenda   210

10. TAX CUTS

Essay: The Ultimate Zombie   215

The Twinkie Manifesto   218
The Biggest Tax Scam in History   221
The Trump Tax Scam, Phase 2   224
Why Was Trump's Tax Cut a Fizzle?   227
The Trump Tax Cut: Even Worse Than You've Heard   230
The Economics of Soaking the Rich   234
Elizabeth Warren Does Teddy Roosevelt   238

11. TRADE WARS

Essay: Globaloney and the Backlash   *243*

Oh, What a Trumpy Trade War!   246
A Trade War Primer   249
Making Tariffs Corrupt Again   254

12. INEQUALITY

Essay: The Skewing of America   *259*

The Rich, the Right, and the Facts   261
Graduates versus Oligarchs   282
Money and Morals   285
Don't Blame Robots for Low Wages   288
What's the Matter with Trumpland?   291

13. CONSERVATIVES

Essay: Movement Conservatism   *297*

Same Old Party   299
Eric Cantor and the Death of a Movement   302
The Great Center-Right Delusion   305
The Empty Quarters of U.S. Politics   308

14. EEK! SOCIALISM!

Essay: Red-Baiting in the 21st Century   *313*

Capitalism, Socialism, and Unfreedom   315
Something Not Rotten in Denmark   319
Trump versus the Socialist Menace   322

15. CLIMATE

Essay: The Most Important Thing   *327*

Donald and the Deadly Deniers   329
The Depravity of Climate-Change Denial   332
Climate Denial Was the Crucible for Trumpism   335
Hope for a Green New Year   338

16. TRUMP

Essay: Why Not the Worst?   *343*

The Paranoid Style in G.O.P. Politics   345
Trump and the Aristocracy of Fraud   348
Stop Calling Trump a Populist   351
Partisanship, Parasites, and Polarization   354
Why It Can Happen Here   358
Who's Afraid of Nancy Pelosi?   361
Truth and Virtue in the Age of Trump   364
Conservatism's Monstrous Endgame   367
Manhood, Moola, McConnell, and Trumpism   370

17. ON THE MEDIA

Essay: Beyond Fake News   *375*

Bait-and-Switch   377
Triumph of the Trivial   380
Is There Any Point to Economic Analysis?   383
The Year of Living Stupidly   385
Hillary Clinton Gets Gored   387

18. ECONOMIC THOUGHTS

Essay: The Dismal Science   *393*

How I Work   395
The Instability of Moderation   407
Transaction Costs and Tethers: Why I'm a Crypto Skeptic   411

Credits   415
Index   417

ACKNOWLEDGMENTS

Most of the articles in this book were originally published as newspaper columns, and the nature of column-writing almost by definition prevents real-time consultation or even collaboration. You get up, have some coffee, decide what you're going to write about—planning ahead almost never works, because it gets trumped by events—and turn something in by 5 p.m. Blog posts, which can go from vague idea to the public domain in a matter of an hour or less, offer even less chance for discussion. In most cases the only person I could turn to for productive critiques and review was my wife, Robin Wells, who often provided invaluable feedback.

Column-writing does, however, rest on a background of ongoing discussion of issues. I drew on the wisdom of many people over the course of the fifteen years' work chronicled here. I'll try to name a few of them, in the full awareness that it's a hugely incomplete list—I literally wrote thousands of columns and blog posts over that period, and often can't even remember who I leaned on for the necessary expertise—and unfairly neglects many.

On health care, I got a lot of help from Uwe Reinhardt, to whom this book is dedicated, and Jonathan Gruber.

Dean Baker helped convince me that we had a huge housing-bubble problem.

Brad DeLong and I sort of double-teamed the call for a Keynesian response to the crisis.

My account of the problems with efficient-market finance drew heavily on work by Justin Fox.

Mike Konczal helped me understand the bad logic of austerian economics, and Simon Wren-Lewis helped me grasp why that bad logic was prevailing in the U.K.

Richard Kogan was, I think, the first person to alert me to the nonexistence of a snowballing-debt problem.

Emmanuel Saez and Gabriel Zucman, aside from teaching all of us a huge amount about taxation, helped me out a lot in understanding new Democratic proposals, especially the Warren wealth tax.

Chad Bown talked me through what was happening with Trump's tariffs.

Larry Mishel taught me most of what I know about the relationship or lack thereof between technology and inequality. More generally, I've often relied on my Stone Center colleague Janet Gornick to understand what inequality data mean.

Most of what I know about movement conservatism comes from Rick Perlstein.

Another Stone Center colleague, Leslie McCall, helped me get the political science of voter attitudes on taxes and spending right (or at least less wrong).

Correspondence with the inimitable Michael Mann helped me understand the nasty politics of climate science.

Finally, a word of thanks to Norton's Drake McFeely, who has been publishing my trade books—making them vastly better than they would otherwise have been—since long before I began writing for the *Times*.

ARGUING *with* ZOMBIES

INTRODUCTION

The Good Fight

Punditry was never part of the plan.

When I finished graduate school in 1977, I envisioned a life devoted to teaching and research. If I ended up playing any role in public debate, I assumed it would be as a technocrat—someone dispassionately providing policymakers with information about what worked and what didn't.

And if you look at my most cited research, most of it is pretty apolitical. The list is dominated by papers on economic geography and international trade. These papers aren't just apolitical; they're mostly not even about policy. Instead, they're attempts to make sense of global patterns of trade and the location of industries. They are, to use the economics jargon, "positive economics"—analysis of how the world works—not "normative economics"—prescriptions for how it should work.

But in 21st-century America, everything is political. In many cases, accepting what the evidence says about an economic question will be seen as a partisan act. For example, will inflation surge if the Federal Reserve buys a lot of government bonds? The clear empirical answer is "no" if the economy is depressed: the Fed bought $3 trillion in bonds after the 2008 financial crisis, and inflation stayed low. But assertions that Fed policy was dangerously inflationary became, in effect, the official Republican view, so simply recognizing reality became seen as a liberal position.

Indeed, in some cases even asking certain questions is seen as a partisan act. If you ask what is happening to income inequality, quite a few conservatives will denounce you as un-American. As they see it, even bringing up the distribution of income, or comparing the growth in middle-class incomes with those of the rich, is "Marxist talk."

And it's not just economics, of course. If anything, we economists have it easy compared to climate scientists, who face persecution for reaching conclusions powerful interests don't want anyone to hear about. Or consider social scientists studying the causes of gun violence: from 1996 to 2017 the Centers for Disease Control were literally forbidden to fund research into firearm injuries and deaths.

So what's a would-be scholar to do? One response is to ignore the political heat and just keep doing your research. That's a choice I can respect, and for most scholars, even in economics, it's the right choice.

But we also need public intellectuals: people who will understand and respect the research, but are willing to jump into the political fray.

This book is a collection of articles, mostly written for *The New York Times*, in which I tried to play that role. I'll talk later about how I got into that position, and what I'm trying to do with it. First, though, let's ask a different question: What's all the politicization about?

THE ROOTS OF POLITICIZATION

There are many issues in politics, and you could imagine people staking out a wide variety of positions that don't correspond to a simple left-right axis. You could, for example, envision voters who are strongly in favor of gun control, demand aggressive policies to fight global warming, but want to see Social Security and Medicare privatized if not eliminated.

In practice, however, politics in modern America really is pretty much one-dimensional. This is especially true among elected representatives. Tell me where a member of Congress stands on issues like universal health care, and you can predict where he or she stands on climate policy—and vice versa.

What defines this single political dimension? It's basically the traditional left-right continuum: How much role do you believe public policy should have in reducing the risks and inequalities of a market economy? Do you want society to be like modern Denmark, with its high taxes, strong social safety net, and extensive worker protections, or like America in the Gilded Age, when laissez-faire ruled?

At one level, this axis of contention is about values. People on the left tend to have a concept of social justice along the lines formalized by the philosopher John Rawls: they believe that people should advocate the society they'd choose if they didn't know who they would be, which role they would play. Basically, this moral position is "There but for the grace of God go I," although often without the God part.

People on the right, by contrast, view (or claim to view) government intervention to reduce inequality and risk as immoral. Taxing the rich to help the poor, as they see it, is a form of theft, no matter how laudable the purpose.

Economics can't tell you what values to have. It can, however, shed light on what to expect from policy that reflects any particular set of values. That, however, is where the politicization comes in. In particular, opponents of a larger role for government want to argue that such a role is not just immoral but counterproductive, even destructive. And if the evidence doesn't agree, they attack both the evidence and those producing it.

In principle, this kind of politicization could come from the left as well as the right. Indeed, there have been times and places where powerful players refuse to acknowledge, for example, that price controls ever cause shortages, or that printing money ever causes inflation—see Venezuela, recent history of. Even in America, there are some people on the left who will attack you (O.K., me) as a shill for corporate interests for pointing out that there are multiple ways to achieve universal health coverage, that it can be done while preserving a significant role for private insurance.

But given the realities of money and power, in modern America most of the politicization of everything reflects pressures from the right.

After all, while there is a philosophical case for a low-tax, minimal government society, modern conservatism relies less on philosophical persuasion than on the fact there are people who would gain a lot personally if we were to retrace our steps toward the Gilded Age. There may not be many of those people, but they're extremely rich. It's very much in their interest to promote the view that moving in their preferred direction would be good for everyone. And monetary support from right-wing billionaires is a powerful force propping up zombie ideas—ideas that should have been killed by contrary evidence, but instead keep shambling along, eating people's brains.

The most persistent such zombie is the insistence that taxing the wealthy is hugely destructive to the economy as a whole, so that cutting taxes on high incomes will produce miraculous economic growth. This doctrine keeps failing in practice, but if anything has gained an ever-stronger hold over the Republican Party.

There are other zombies, too. If you want a low-tax, low-benefit state, you want to claim that safety-net programs are harmful and unworkable. So a lot of effort goes into insisting that providing universal health coverage is impossible, even though every advanced country besides the U.S. somehow manages to achieve just that.

You get the idea. But while it's easy to understand the politicization of tax and spending analysis, why does the politicization extend to areas that don't so obviously correspond to class interests? Even billionaires need a livable planet, so why has climate change become such a left-right issue? Recessions hurt everyone, so why do conservatives oppose printing money to fight slumps? And why are racial attitudes so closely correlated with positions on taxing and spending?

A lot of the answer is that political players believe—I think rightly—that there is a kind of halo effect that links all forms of government activism. If people are persuaded that we need a public policy to reduce emissions of greenhouse gases, they become more receptive to the idea that we need public policies to reduce inequality. If they are persuaded that monetary policy can fight recessions, they're more likely to support policies that expand access to health care.

This has always been true. Back in the forties and fifties the U.S. right fought fiercely against Keynesian economics, to the point of trying to prevent it from being taught in universities, even though John Maynard Keynes correctly described it as a "moderately conservative" doctrine—a way to preserve capitalism, not replace it. Why? Because they saw it as the thin edge of the wedge for bigger government in general. But we're much more politically polarized now than we were then, so the politicization extends further.

Beyond the halo effect, there's also the effect of political strategizing. You see, politics in America used to have two dimensions, not one—there was a left-right axis, but also a racial equality/segregation axis. And to this day there are a significant number of voters who like big government for themselves but don't like people with darker skins. (The opposite, libertarian position—small government with racial tolerance—is logically coherent, but doesn't seem to have any supporters beyond a few dozen guys in bow ties.) But there are almost no racist big-government politicians. Instead, the economic right has sought to win over working-class whites, even as it attacks programs they depend on, by catering to their racial animosity. So racial tolerance, and other forms of social liberalism like gender equality and LGBTQ rights, have been caught up in the same political divide as everything else.

The result of all this is, as I said, that everything is political. "Everyone is entitled to his own opinion, but not to his own facts," Daniel Patrick Moynihan famously declared; but in modern America a lot of people do believe that they're entitled to their own facts. This means that the technocratic dream—the idea of being a politically neutral analyst helping policymakers govern more effectively—is, for now at least, dead. But that's not the only role available to scholars who care about where we're going as a society.

PUNDITRY IN A TIME OF POLARIZATION

Suppose that you're someone who knows a fair bit about a technical subject like economics, but also wants to have an effect on public discourse—that is, the way people who don't know or care about the technical issues discuss that subject. Obviously that describes my status, but it also applies to a number of other people. There are other economists who have moved into the public sphere—people like Joseph Stiglitz, a great economist who has reinvented himself as a public intellectual, or Britain's Simon Wren-Lewis. There are also a growing number of journalists with good backgrounds in economics, like the *Times*'s David Leonhardt or *The Washington Post*'s Catherine Rampell. What does it take to play that role effectively?

The final section of this book contains an essay I wrote in 1991, "How I Work," that lays out four rules for research. So let me similarly lay out my four rules for punditry, which inform almost everything in this book. The first two rules should be noncontroversial; the remaining rules, I suspect, less so. Here's the list:

Stay with the easy stuff
Write in English
Be honest about dishonesty
Don't be afraid to talk about motives

Staying with the easy stuff: There are many hard questions in economics—questions on which serious, honest researchers disagree. How should pundit-economists deal with these questions?

My answer is that for the most part they should stay away from these questions wherever possible. The truth is that the vast majority of real-world economics disputes are about easy questions—questions for which there is a clearly right answer, but one that powerful interests don't want to accept. You can improve public discourse by focusing on these questions, and trying to get the right answers across. The hard questions won't go away, but the op-ed page isn't a good place to argue about them.

For example, when it comes to the effects of government debt, what the public needs to know is that trying to balance the budget in a depressed economy makes the depression deeper, and that fears of a runaway debt spiral are vastly exaggerated. There are other, harder issues, like the question of which interest rate should be used in assessing infrastructure spending. But the easy questions provide plenty of material to write about.

Writing in English: When I say that economist-pundits should write in English, of course I don't mean that literally. In fact, the world would be in better shape if we had more people explaining basic economic concepts in German. What I mean, instead, is that to be an effective pundit, you have to use plain language and not presume that people already understand unfamiliar concepts.

To see what I mean, consider my most cited paper, "Increasing Returns and Economic Geography." During my research-only years (the paper was published in 1991), I had a reputation among economists as a lucid writer, good at providing intuition and keeping the math level down. Yet in that paper, the equations aside, you find statements like this: "In the presence of imperfect competition and increasing returns, pecuniary externalities matter." Would even one percent of my *Times* readership have any idea what that's all about?

Staying away from jargon is harder than it sounds. That's partly because most jargon serves a purpose—that quote says something important to its intended audience, and it would take a lot of space and time, hundreds if not thousands of words, to make the same point without the terms of art. It's also because after spending years immersed in a technical subject it can be hard to remember how normal human beings, even smart, well-educated people, actually talk.

I've been writing at the *Times* for two decades, yet I still get occasional queries from copy editors about passages they don't understand (and which readers won't understand) because I've carelessly assumed that general readers will use words the same way economists do. For example, when economists say "investment" they usually mean construction of new factories and office buildings, yet they need to spell this out if they don't want readers thinking that they're talking about buying stocks.

This doesn't mean that you should imagine that your readers are stupid. You just have to think hard about how to communicate. In fact, in 2019 I published a column, "Getting Real About Rural America," that was in part a sort of stealth restatement of the arguments in that 1991 paper. And I think most readers understood what I was getting at, even if I made many of them angry.

Being honest about dishonesty: now we get into the more controversial aspects of punditry. As I've explained, these days everything is political. And as a result, many public arguments, in economics and everything else, are being made in bad faith.

To take the most obvious example, people arguing that we should cut taxes on the rich may pretend to have arrived at that position by looking at the evidence, but that's not true: there is no evidence that would persuade them to change their view. In practice, they deal with contrary evidence by shifting goalposts—for example, the same people who predicted that Bill Clinton's tax hike would cause a depression now claim that the Clinton-era boom was part of the long-run payoff to Ronald Reagan's 1981 tax cuts. Or they simply lie, making up numbers and other supposed facts.

So how should an economist-pundit deal with this reality? One answer, which I know appeals to many economists, is to continue acting as if we were having a good-faith debate: to lay out the evidence, explain why it means one view is right and the other is wrong, and stop there.

My view, as you might guess, is that this isn't enough, that it's actually unfair to readers. When you're confronting bad-faith arguments, the public should be informed not just that these arguments are wrong, but that they are in fact being made in bad faith. It is, to take another example, important to point out that the people who predicted runaway inflation from the Fed's bond-buying were wrong. But it's also important to point out that none of them have been willing to admit that they were wrong, let alone explain what led them astray—and that some of them abruptly reversed position as soon as there was a Republican in the White House.

In other words, we should be honest about the dishonesty that pervades political debate. Often, the mendacity is the message. Which brings me to my final rule.

Don't be afraid to talk about motives: I wish we lived in a world in which one could normally assume that policy arguments are made in good faith. And some are. For example, there is a real debate about how effective "quantitative easing"—bond purchases by the Fed—actually is in boosting the economy. I'm on the skeptical side, but I can respect the optimists, and both sides, I believe, are open to persuasion.

But in most of the important policy debates in 21st-century America, one side consistently argues in bad faith. I've already made the point that this needs to be pointed out, that you should tell readers not just that extravagant claims about the power of tax cuts are false, but that those making such claims are knowingly being dishonest. Let me go a step further, and argue that being fair with readers means explaining why they're dishonest.

For the most part, that means talking about the nature of modern U.S. conservatism, about the interlocking network of media organizations and think tanks that serves the interests of right-wing billionaires, and has effectively taken over the G.O.P. This network—"movement conservatism"—is what keeps zombie ideas, like belief in the magic of tax cuts, alive. If you're having a real, good-faith debate, impugning the other side's motives is a bad thing. If you're debating bad-faith opponents, acknowledging their motives is just a matter of being honest about what's going on.

I wish the world weren't like this. There are times when I long for the naïveté of my professional youth, when I was simply trying to get the right answer and could normally assume that the people I was debating with were engaged in the same enterprise. But if you're going to be an effective public intellectual, you deal with the world you have, not the one you want.

ABOUT THIS BOOK

I began writing for the *Times* in 2000. For several years prior I had written monthly columns for *Fortune* and *Slate*, but I was still mainly a research economist. In fact, I wrote what I personally consider possibly my best academic paper, "It's Baaack: Japan's Slump and the Return of the Liquidity Trap," in 1998.

The *Times* expected me to write almost entirely about business and economics. But I found myself in a position neither they nor I expected. The administration of George W. Bush was dishonest to a degree never before seen in U.S. politics (though now surpassed by the Trumpists), and it was obviously, it seemed to me, taking us to war on false pretenses. Yet nobody else with a column in a major newspaper seemed willing to point this out. As a result, I felt I had to do the job.

The best writing I did during that period, however, was published in my 2003 columns collection, *The Great Unraveling*. So it's not an era I feel the need to revisit.

Instead, with a few exceptions, this volume picks up in 2004, after Bush was reelected. By then many other people had taken on the fraudulent march to war, leaving me free to focus on issues that were much more up my alley, like the attempt to privatize Social Security and the efforts to expand health insurance coverage.

More than a third of this book is devoted to various aspects of the 2008 financial crisis and its aftermath. Nobody really predicted that crisis, other than people who also predicted many other crises that never happened. I myself recognized that we had a huge housing bubble, but was shocked at the damage the burst bubble inflicted, mainly because I hadn't realized how vulnerable our financial system had become thanks to the growth of unregulated "shadow" banking.

Once the crash happened, however, economists who had studied these things found themselves in familiar territory. We know a lot about financial crises, from both theory and history. We also know a lot about how economies work in the aftermath of crises: that 1998 paper was about what happens when even a zero interest rate isn't enough to restore full employment, a condition that went from being a uniquely Japanese problem to the norm across the Western world.

For me, then, the five or so years following the 2008 crisis were both the best and the worst of times. They were the best of times in the sense that my role as newspaper columnist and my academic research converged almost perfectly, so that I was in a position to say a lot about what policymakers should be doing. They were the worst of times in the sense that policymakers insistently refused to use the knowledge we had, choosing instead to obsess over budget deficits based on bad, often bad-faith arguments, and inflicting vast unnecessary suffering as a result.

The rest of the book is mainly about what the title says: arguing with zombies, from the tax-cut zombie to climate-change denial, and also about the movement conservatism that keeps those zombies shambling along. Yes, there's also quite a lot about Donald Trump, but I see Trump not as a departure from the past so much as the culmination of where movement conservatism has been taking us for decades.

I finish the book with some lighter reading—well, not actually, but stuff that puts me in a better mood. The last section offers a selection of relatively economistic pieces that go back to my intellectual roots. They're a bit harder and more jargony than my *Times* columns, but I hope some readers make the effort to see how I actually think about issues.

This book, then, tells a story of the fight for truth, justice, and the anti-zombie way. I don't know if that fight can ever be fully won, although it can be lost. But it's definitely a cause worth fighting for.

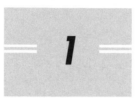

Saving Social Security

AFTER THE KHAKI ELECTION

ELECTION NIGHT 2004 WASN'T AS MUCH OF A SHOCK AS ELECTION NIGHT 2016, but it came as a bitter disappointment to American liberals. George W. Bush's image has improved in retrospect; people see him, correctly, as better than Donald Trump, and forget about the enormities that took place on his watch. Above all, he took America to war on false pretenses, and hundreds of thousands died as a result. Seeing voters reward that vileness was not a happy thing.

Furthermore, there were plenty of commentators who saw the election not just as a one-time event, but as a harbinger of permanent conservative rule. If you watched the TV networks—this was a time when people still watched the regular networks—they were full of people pronouncing the death of American liberalism, the confirmation that we were a basically conservative nation.

But a closer look told a different story. The 2004 election wasn't a ratification of conservative policies, because it was notable for the absence of policy discussion—partly because policy issues couldn't break through the trivialization imposed by much of the news media. For example, at one point I went through a month of network news transcripts to see what viewers had been told about the health care proposals of the two candidates, which were in fact very different. The answer was, nothing. There had been a couple of reports on how health proposals were playing politically, but not a word about what was actually in those proposals.

The election was fought, instead, on images and perception. Bush was still basking in the post-9/11 glow and the illusion of victory in Iraq; many Americans still saw him as a heroic icon of national security, making it what the British call a "khaki election." A lesser but still significant theme involved traditional values: some advocates had begun pushing for legalization of gay marriage, and there was a nasty backlash.

So Bush won reelection, as I used to joke, by posing as America's defender against gay married terrorists. But as soon as the election was over, he declared that he had a mandate to . . . privatize Social Security, converting it into a system of individual investment accounts.

Why did Bush and his advisers imagine that this would fly politically? Part of the answer is that, like many well-off people, they had no idea just how essential Social Security is to most Americans.

If you're a well-paid political consultant, journalist, think-tank pundit, whatever, you probably have a significant private retirement plan and expect to have considerable assets when you reach 65. But most retirees depend on Social Security for the majority of their income, and for around a third it's almost their only source of income. Once people began to realize that Bush really wanted to undermine the program, they were not happy.

But Bush and company didn't just fail to appreciate how beloved Social Security is among voters at large. They also relied too much on elite consensus.

Things may be changing lately, but during the period covered by this book there were, at any given time, things that everyone inside the Beltway who wanted to seem wise and well-informed "knew"—not because those things were true, but because they were what everyone else in the elite was saying. And one of these things was that Social Security was in crisis and had to be drastically reformed. People who said this hadn't themselves looked into how America's retirement system works or the arithmetic of its future; they just knew that it was what they were expected to say. As I wrote at one point, calling Social Security a crisis demanding benefit cuts was a "badge of seriousness."

The desire to sound serious went along with a desire to sound trendy and with it. Social Security was already 70 years old when the privatization debate took place, and a fair number of commentators took its very age as a reason it needed to be changed, converted into something 21st-century sounding.

After all, corporate pensions had changed drastically: the old-fashioned "defined benefit" pension that paid you a fixed amount each month had given way to "defined contribution" plans that put money into an investment account. Why not do the same for Social Security? Actually, there were very good reasons. In fact, the new riskiness of private retirement plans meant that it became even more important that people have a stable guaranteed income, in case their investments go bad. But this wasn't obvious to people not accustomed to thinking hard about the economics of retirement.

Which is where I (and a number of progressive policy wonks) came in.

Social Security was saved from privatization mainly by two things: the immense opposition of the general public once it realized what was happening, and the determined stand by Democratic leaders, especially Nancy Pelosi, against elite nonsense. (Pelosi, asked when she would present her own plan for Social Security, responded "Never. Is never good enough for you?") But there was a role, which seemed important at the time, for people like me in puncturing the nonsense—showing that the supposed crisis wasn't real, that privatization wasn't an answer to any real problem, that providing basic support in retirement is one of those things the government should do, and can do better than the private sector.

And an amazing thing happened. For the first time since I had become a *New York Times* columnist, my side in a policy debate actually won.

SOCIAL SECURITY SCARES

March 5, 2004

The annual report of the Social Security system's trustees reveals a system in pretty good financial shape. In fact, it would take only modest injections of money to maintain that system's current benefit levels for at least the next seventy-five years. Other reports, however, appear to portray a system in deep financial trouble. For example, a 2002 Treasury study, described on Tuesday in *The New York Times*, claims that Social Security and Medicare are $44 trillion in the red. What's the truth?

Here's a hint: while even right-wing politicians insist in public that they want to save Social Security, the ideologues shaping their views are itching for an excuse to dismantle the system. So you have to read alarming reports generated by people who work at ideologically driven institutions—a list that now, alas, includes the U.S. Treasury—with great care.

First, two words—"and Medicare"—make a huge difference. According to the Treasury study, only 16 percent of that $44 trillion shortfall comes from Social Security. Second, the supposed shortfall in both programs comes mainly from projections about the distant future; 62 percent of the combined shortfall comes after 2077.

So does the Treasury report show a looming Social Security crisis? No.

Social Security's problem, such as it is, is a matter of demography: as the population ages, the number of retirees will rise faster than the number of workers. As a result, benefit costs will rise by about 2 percent of G.D.P. over the next thirty years, and creep up slowly thereafter. By comparison, making the Bush tax cuts permanent would reduce revenue by at least 2.5 percent of G.D.P., starting now. That—combined with the fact that Social Security, unlike the rest of the federal government, is currently running a surplus—is why the Bush tax cuts are a much bigger problem for the nation's fiscal future than the Social Security shortfall.

Medicare, though often lumped in with Social Security, is a different program facing different problems. The projected rise in Medicare expenses is mainly driven not by demography, but by the rising cost of medical care, which in turn mainly reflects medical progress, which allows doctors to treat a wider range of conditions.

If this trend continues—which is by no means certain when we are considering the very long run—we may face a real long-term dilemma that involves all medical care, not just care for retirees, and is as much moral as economic. It may eventually be the case that providing all Americans with the full advantages of modern medicine will force the government to raise much more money than it now does. Yet not providing that care will mean watching poor and middle-class Americans die early or suffer a greatly reduced quality of life because they can't afford full medical treatment.

But this dilemma will be there regardless of what we do to Social Security. It's not even clear that we should try to resolve the dilemma now. I'm all for taking the long view; when the administration makes budget projections for only five years to hide known costs just a few years further out, that's an outrage. By all means, let's plan ahead. But let's set some limits. When people issue ominous warnings about the cost of Medicare after 2077, my question is, Why should fiscal decisions today reflect the possible cost of providing generations not yet born with medical treatments not yet invented?

The biggest risk now facing Social Security is political. Will those who hate the system use scare tactics and fuzzy math to bring it down?

After Alan Greenspan's call for cuts in Social Security benefits, Republican members of Congress declared that the answer is to create private retirement accounts. It's amazing that they are still peddling this snake oil; it's even more amazing that journalists continue to let them get away with it. Yesterday in *The Wall Street Journal*, a writer judiciously declared that "personal accounts alone won't cure Social Security's ills." I guess that's true;

similarly, eating doughnuts alone won't cause you to lose weight. Why is it so hard to say clearly that privatization would worsen, not improve, Social Security's finances?

Should we consider modest reforms that reduce the expenses or widen the revenue base of Social Security? Sure. But beware of those who claim that we must destroy the system in order to save it.

INVENTING A CRISIS

December 7, 2004

Privatizing Social Security—replacing the current system, in whole or in part, with personal investment accounts—won't do anything to strengthen the system's finances. If anything, it will make things worse. Nonetheless, the politics of privatization depend crucially on convincing the public that the system is in imminent danger of collapse, that we must destroy Social Security in order to save it.

I'll have a lot to say about all this when I return to my regular schedule in January. But right now it seems important to take a break from my break, and debunk the hype about a Social Security crisis.

There's nothing strange or mysterious about how Social Security works: it's just a government program supported by a dedicated tax on payroll earnings, just as highway maintenance is supported by a dedicated tax on gasoline.

Right now the revenues from the payroll tax exceed the amount paid out in benefits. This is deliberate, the result of a payroll tax increase—recommended by none other than Alan Greenspan—two decades ago. His justification at the time for raising a tax that falls mainly on lower- and middle-income families, even though Ronald Reagan had just cut the taxes that fall mainly on the very well-off, was that the extra revenue was needed to build up a trust fund. This could be drawn on to pay benefits once the baby boomers began to retire.

The grain of truth in claims of a Social Security crisis is that this tax increase wasn't quite big enough. Projections in a recent report by the Congressional Budget Office (which are probably more realistic than the very cautious projections of the Social Security Administration) say that the trust fund will run out in 2052. The system won't become "bankrupt" at that point; even after the trust fund is gone, Social Security revenues will cover 81 percent of the promised benefits. Still, there is a long-run financing problem.

But it's a problem of modest size. The report finds that extending the life of the trust fund into the 22nd century, with no change in benefits, would require additional revenues equal to only 0.54 percent of G.D.P. That's less than 3 percent of federal spending—less than we're currently spending in Iraq. And it's only about one-quarter of the revenue lost each year because of President Bush's tax cuts—roughly equal to the fraction of those cuts that goes to people with incomes over $500,000 a year.

Given these numbers, it's not at all hard to come up with fiscal packages that would secure the retirement program, with no major changes, for generations to come.

It's true that the federal government as a whole faces a very large financial shortfall. That shortfall, however, has much more to do with tax cuts—cuts that Mr. Bush nonetheless insists on making permanent—than it does with Social Security.

But since the politics of privatization depend on convincing the public that there is a Social Security crisis, the privatizers have done their best to invent one.

My favorite example of their three-card-monte logic goes like this: first, they insist that the Social Security system's current surplus and the trust fund it has been accumulating with that surplus are meaningless. Social Security, they say, isn't really an independent entity—it's just part of the federal government.

If the trust fund is meaningless, by the way, that Greenspan-sponsored tax increase in the 1980s was nothing but an exercise in class warfare: taxes on working-class Americans went up, taxes on the affluent went down, and the workers have nothing to show for their sacrifice.

But never mind: the same people who claim that Social Security isn't an independent entity when it runs surpluses also insist that late next decade, when the benefit payments start to exceed the payroll tax receipts, this will represent a crisis—you see, Social Security has its own dedicated financing, and therefore must stand on its own.

There's no honest way anyone can hold both these positions, but very little about the privatizers' position is honest. They come to bury Social Security, not to save it. They aren't sincerely concerned about the possibility that the system will someday fail; they're disturbed by the system's historic success.

For Social Security is a government program that works, a demonstration that a modest amount of taxing and spending can make people's lives better and more secure. And that's why the right wants to destroy it.

BUYING INTO FAILURE

December 17, 2004

As the Bush administration tries to persuade America to convert Social Security into a giant 401(k), we can learn a lot from other countries that have already gone down that road.

Information about other countries' experience with privatization isn't hard to find. For example, the Century Foundation, at www.tcf.org, provides a wide range of links.

Yet, aside from giving the Cato Institute and other organizations promoting Social Security privatization the space to present upbeat tales from Chile, the U.S. news media have provided their readers and viewers with little information about international experience. In particular, the public hasn't been let in on two open secrets:

Privatization dissipates a large fraction of workers' contributions on fees to investment companies.

It leaves many retirees in poverty.

Decades of conservative marketing have convinced Americans that government programs always create bloated bureaucracies, while the private sector is always lean and efficient. But when it comes to retirement security, the opposite is true. More than 99 percent of Social Security's revenues go toward benefits, and less than 1 percent for overhead. In Chile's system, management fees are around twenty times as high. And that's a typical number for privatized systems.

These fees cut sharply into the returns individuals can expect on their accounts. In Britain, which has had a privatized system since the days of Margaret Thatcher, alarm over the large fees charged by some investment companies eventually led government regulators to impose a "charge cap." Even so, fees continue to take a large bite out of British retirement savings.

A reasonable prediction for the real rate of return on personal accounts in the U.S. is 4 percent or less. If we introduce a system with British-level management fees, net returns to workers will be reduced by more than a quarter. Add in deep cuts in guaranteed benefits and a big increase in risk, and we're looking at a "reform" that hurts everyone except the investment industry.

Advocates insist that a privatized U.S. system can keep expenses much lower. It's true that costs will be low if investments are restricted to low-overhead index funds—that is, if government officials, not individuals, make the investment decisions. But if that's how the system works, the suggestions that workers will have control over their own money—two years ago, Cato renamed its Project on Social Security Privatization by replacing "privatization" with "choice"—are false advertising.

And if there are rules restricting workers to low-expense investments, investment industry lobbyists will try to get those rules overturned.

For the record, I don't think giving financial corporations a huge windfall is the main motive for privatization; it's mostly an ideological thing. But that windfall is a major reason Wall Street wants privatization, and everyone else should be very suspicious.

Then there's the issue of poverty among the elderly.

Privatizers who laud the Chilean system never mention that it has yet to deliver on its promise to reduce government spending. More than twenty years after the system was created, the government is still pouring in money. Why? Because, as a Federal Reserve study puts it, the Chilean government must "provide subsidies for workers failing to accumulate enough capital to provide a minimum pension." In other words, privatization would have condemned many retirees to dire poverty, and the government stepped back in to save them.

The same thing is happening in Britain. Its Pensions Commission warns that those who think Mrs. Thatcher's privatization solved the pension problem are living in a "fool's paradise." A lot of additional government spending will be required to avoid the return of widespread poverty among the elderly—a problem that Britain, like the U.S., thought it had solved.

Britain's experience is directly relevant to the Bush administration's plans. If current hints are an indication, the final plan will probably claim to save money in the future by reducing guaranteed Social Security benefits. These savings will be an illusion: twenty years from now, an American version of Britain's commission will warn that big additional government spending is needed to avert a looming surge in poverty among retirees.

So the Bush administration wants to scrap a retirement system that works, and can be made financially sound for generations to come with modest reforms. Instead, it wants to buy into failure, emulating systems that, when tried elsewhere, have neither saved money nor protected the elderly from poverty.

SOCIAL SECURITY LESSONS

August 15, 2005

S ocial Security turned 70 yesterday. And to almost everyone's surprise, the nation's most successful government program is still intact.

Just a few months ago the conventional wisdom was that President Bush would get his way on Social Security. Instead, Mr. Bush's privatization drive flopped so badly that the topic has almost disappeared from national discussion.

But I'd like to revisit Social Security for a moment, because it's important to remember what Mr. Bush tried to get away with.

Many pundits and editorial boards still give Mr. Bush credit for trying to "reform" Social Security. In fact, Mr. Bush came to bury Social Security, not to save it. Over time, the Bush plan would have transformed Social Security from a social insurance program into a mutual fund, with nothing except a name in common with the system F.D.R. created.

In addition to misrepresenting his goals, Mr. Bush repeatedly lied about the current system. Oh, I'm sorry—was that a rude thing to say? Still, the fact is that Mr. Bush repeatedly said things that were demonstrably false and that his staff must have known were false. The falsehoods ranged from his claim that Social Security is unfair to African-Americans to his claim that "waiting just one year adds $600 billion to the cost of fixing Social Security."

Meanwhile, the administration politicized the Social Security Administration and used taxpayer money to promote a partisan agenda. Social Security officials participated in what were in effect taxpayer-financed political rallies, from which skeptical members of the public were excluded.

I'm writing about this in the past tense, but some of it is still going on. Last week Jo Anne Barnhart, the commissioner of Social Security, published an op-ed article claiming that Social Security as we know it was designed for a society in which people didn't live long enough to collect a lot of benefits. "The number of older Americans living now," wrote Ms. Barnhart, "is greater than anyone could have imagined in 1935."

Now, it turns out that an article on the Social Security Administration's Web site, "Life Expectancy for Social Security," specifically rejects the idea the Social Security was originally "designed in such a way that few people would collect the benefits," and the related idea that the system faces problems from "a supposed dramatic increase in life expectancy in recent years."

And the current number of older Americans as a share of the population is just about what the founders of Social Security expected. The 1934 report of F.D.R.'s Commission on Economic Security, which laid the groundwork for the Social Security Act, projected that 12.7 percent of Americans would be 65 or older by the year 2000. The actual number was 12.4 percent.

Despite Ms. Barnhart's efforts, however, privatization seems to be dead for the time being. The Democratic leadership in Congress defied the punditocracy—which was very much in favor of privatization—by refusing to cave in, and the American people made it clear that they like Social Security the way it is.

But the campaign for privatization provided an object lesson in how the administration sells its policies: by misrepresenting its goals, lying about the facts, and abusing its control of government agencies. These were the same tactics used to sell both tax cuts and the Iraq war.

And there are two reasons to study that lesson. One is to be prepared for whatever comes next on Mr. Bush's agenda. Despite the tough talk about Iran, I don't think he can propose another war—there aren't enough troops to fight the wars we already have. But there's still room for another big domestic initiative, probably tax reform.

Forewarned is forearmed: the real goals of reform won't be as advertised, the administration will say things about the current system that aren't true, and the Treasury Department will function in a purely partisan capacity.

The other is that the public's visceral rejection of privatization, together with growing dismay over the debacle in Iraq, offers Democrats an opportunity to make an issue of the administration's pattern of deception. The question is whether they will dare to seize that opportunity, when for some of them it means admitting that they, too, were fooled.

PRIVATIZATION MEMORIES

New York Times *Blog*

March 28, 2015

D ave Weigel has one of the more interesting Harry Reid retrospectives, focusing on his role in fighting back Bush's attempt to privatize Social Security—and in particular on the way he forged an alliance with liberal bloggers.

I remember that episode very well, for several reasons. One was that I, too, was writing a lot, debunking one bad argument for privatization after another. It wasn't the first time I had done that kind of thing, but this was different in two ways: it was really intense, and for once my side of the argument won the political fight.

It was also a formative period for my perceptions of how policy arguments actually play out in modern America. There are always three sides here: the right, which isn't interested in facts or logic; the left (which isn't very leftist in this country—they're really center-left by anyone else's standards); and self-proclaimed centrists, who have very little in the way of a constituency in the country at large but have a lot of influence inside the Beltway.

And what you learned early on in the Social Security debate was that centrists desperately want to believe that there is symmetry between the left and the right, that Democrats and Republicans are equally extreme in their own way. And this means that they are always looking for ways to say nice things about Republicans and their policy proposals, no matter how bad those proposals are. That's how Paul Ryan ended up getting an award for fiscal responsibility.

So back in 2005, Bush was making a dubious claim coupled with a complete non sequitur. First, the claim that Social Security was in crisis; second, that privatization was the answer, even though it would do nothing at all to help the system's finances. How could centrists say nice things about such a crude bait-and-switch?

Well, here's Joe Klein in 2005:

> I agree with Paul [Krugman] in that private accounts have nothing to do with solvency and solvency is the issue. I disagree with Paul because I think private accounts [are] a terrific policy and that in the information age, you're going to need different kinds of structures in the entitlement area than you had in the industrial age. But it is very hard to do that kind of change under these political circumstances where you have the parties at such loggerheads.
>
> The Democrats have for the last 10 or 15 years blatantly, shamelessly demagogued this issue. They've offered nothing positive on Social Security or on Medicare or on Medicaid, and it's time for them to compromise here.

Say what? To his credit, Klein later admitted that he was all wrong here. But the point is that what we saw here was the instinct to come up with something, anything, that would let centrists pretend symmetry between the parties.

Incidentally, about Democrats doing nothing about Medicare and Medicaid: it's interesting to look at budget projections made around the time of the Social Security debate. Back then CBO projected that by fiscal 2014 Medicare spending would rise to $708 billion and Medicaid spending to $361 billion. The actual numbers for 2014 were 600 and 301, respectively, despite the Medicaid expansion under Obamacare. At least some of this unexpectedly low cost can be attributed to measures included in the Affordable Care Act. And strange to say, this was achieved without destroying or privatizing the programs.

But back to 2005: what Harry Reid realized was that it was time to stop courting the Very Serious People and instead make an alliance with the DFHs—which isn't quite shorthand for Dirty Foolish Hippies—who, unlike the VSPs, were actually making sense on both the policy and the politics. It was an important turning point.

WHERE GOVERNMENT EXCELS

April 10, 2015

As Republican presidential hopefuls trot out their policy agendas—which always involve cutting taxes on the rich while slashing benefits for the poor and middle class—some real new thinking is happening on the other side of the aisle. Suddenly, it seems, many Democrats have decided to break with Beltway orthodoxy, which always calls for cuts in "entitlements." Instead, they're proposing that Social Security benefits actually be expanded.

This is a welcome development in two ways. First, the specific case for expanding Social Security is quite good. Second, and more fundamentally, Democrats finally seem to be standing up to anti-government propaganda and recognizing the reality that there are some things the government does better than the private sector.

Like all advanced nations, America mainly relies on private markets and private initiatives to provide its citizens with the things they want and need, and hardly anyone in our political discourse would propose changing that. The days when it sounded like a good idea to have the government directly run large parts of the economy are long past.

Yet we also know that some things more or less must be done by government. Every economics textbook talks about "public goods" like national defense and air traffic control that can't be made available to anyone without being made available to everyone, and which profit-seeking firms, therefore, have no incentive to provide. But are public goods the only area where the government outperforms the private sector? By no means.

One classic example of government doing it better is health insurance.

Yes, conservatives constantly agitate for more privatization—in particular, they want to convert Medicare into nothing more than vouchers for the purchase of private insurance—but all the evidence says this would move us in precisely the wrong direction. Medicare and Medicaid are substantially cheaper and more efficient than private insurance; they even involve less bureaucracy. Internationally, the American health system is unique in the extent to which it relies on the private sector, and it's also unique in its incredible inefficiency and high costs.

And there's another major example of government superiority: providing retirement security.

Maybe we wouldn't need Social Security if ordinary people really were the perfectly rational, farsighted agents economists like to assume in their models (and right-wingers like to assume in their propaganda). In an idealized world, 25-year-old workers would base their decisions about how much to save on a realistic assessment of what they will need to live comfortably when they're in their 70s. They'd also be smart and sophisticated in how they invested those savings, carefully seeking the best trade-offs between risk and return.

In the real world, however, many and arguably most working Americans are saving much too little for their retirement. They're also investing these savings badly. For example, a recent White House report found that Americans are losing billions each year thanks to investment advisers trying to maximize their own fees rather than their clients' welfare.

You might be tempted to say that if workers save too little and invest badly, it's their own fault. But people have jobs and children, and they must cope with all the crises of life. It's unfair to expect them to be expert investors, too. In any case, the economy is supposed to work for real people leading real lives; it shouldn't be an obstacle course only a few can navigate.

And in the real world of retirement, Social Security is a shining example of a system that works. It's simple and clean, with low operating costs and minimal bureaucracy. It provides older Americans who worked hard all their lives with a chance of living decently in retirement, without requiring that they show an inhuman ability to think decades ahead and be investment whizzes as well. The only problem is that the decline of private pensions, and their replacement with inadequate 401(k)-type plans, has left a gap that Social Security isn't currently big enough to fill. So why not make it bigger?

Needless to say, suggestions along these lines are already provoking near-hysterical reactions, not just from the right, but from self-proclaimed centrists. As I wrote some years ago, calling for cuts to Social Security has long been seen inside the Beltway as a "badge of seriousness, a way of showing how statesmanlike and tough-minded you are." And it's only a decade since former president George W. Bush tried to privatize the program, with a lot of centrist support.

But true seriousness means looking at what works and what doesn't. Privatized retirement schemes work very badly; Social Security works very well. And we should build on that success.

The Road to Obamacare

DEVELOPING A POSITIVE AGENDA

I'M NOT A REAL HEALTH CARE ECONOMIST, BUT I PLAY ONE ON TV—AND, more important, on the *Times* op-ed page. And I studied to play that role, learning from the best of the real health care economists, especially my late Princeton colleague Uwe Reinhardt.

Why health care? After the hugely invigorating victory against Social Security privatization, progressive policy wonks faced a challenge. We'd shown what we were against, but what were we for? What changes to U.S. policy did we want to see happen?

The obvious answer, to anyone familiar with the differences among advanced countries, was that we should try to do what everyone else does: provide essential health care to everyone. America was unique among wealthy nations as being a place where people who didn't have good jobs or suffered from pre-existing medical conditions couldn't get health insurance, and faced financial ruin or even premature death if they needed expensive treatment. So why not make an effort to join the civilized world?

But in the mid-2000s Democrats were still living in the shadow of the failed 1993 Clinton health reform. Bill Clinton tried a massive overhaul of health care; his plan crashed and burned (kind of like the Bush Social Security push). Was there any chance of a successful do-over?

Yes, there was. The Affordable Care Act, aka Obamacare, was an incomplete and imperfect reform, but it nonetheless extended essential health care to tens of millions of Americans. But getting there was anything but easy.

Timing was crucial: the A.C.A. was enacted during the very brief period, in 2009–2010, when Democrats had unified control of Congress and the White House, control that came largely from the economic catastrophe that unfolded at the end of the Bush administration. Political leadership was also crucial. If Nancy Pelosi—the same leader who defeated the attack on Social

Security—hadn't held Democrats' feet to the fire, the opportunity would have slipped away.

Yet hard thinking was also crucial. The reason Democrats were relatively ready to move on health care was that advocates and policy wonks had spent the preceding years preparing the ground: making the case for health reform, and laying out a policy and political strategy for getting there.

A central piece of that strategy was that Democratic reform plans deliberately left as much as possible of the existing health care system in place.

The crucial thing to understand about modern health care is that it must be paid for mainly by some kind of health insurance. Why? Because health costs strike unevenly, but are huge when they happen. Routine doctors' visits and over-the-counter drugs don't cost much; the big money is in dialysis, open-heart surgery, and so on. In any given year, most people don't face those major expenses; as a result, at any given time, a small fraction of the population accounts for the great bulk of health costs. But you don't know whether you'll be one of those unlucky people, and if you are, you won't be able to afford treatment unless you're immensely wealthy—or you have good insurance.

So how do people get insurance? In the mid-2000s, and to a large extent even now, the U.S. system was a crazy quilt with some big holes in it. Senior citizens are covered by Medicare, and many though not all of the poor are covered by Medicaid—government programs that directly pay the bills. Most of the rest of us get insurance through our employers, thanks to a combination of tax advantages and rules that force companies to cover all their employees if they offer coverage at all. But millions of people fall through the cracks: they're too young for Medicare, not quite poor enough for Medicaid, and their jobs aren't good enough to come with health benefits.

How could these holes be filled? The economics aren't hard: we could easily extend Medicare-like coverage to everyone. After all, that's what lots of other countries do—including our neighbor Canada. And most of the health policy wonks I know would be perfectly happy with such a "single-payer" system.

The trouble is getting there from here. In particular, transitioning to a single-payer system would mean replacing employer-based insurance with a government program. And that's a very heavy political lift, for two reasons.

The lesser of those reasons is the power of special interests. Yes, that's the smaller problem—although hardly trivial. When Bill Clinton tried to pass major health reform in 1993, opposition from insurance companies, who financed a lavish advertising campaign smearing his plan, was an important factor in his failure.

But even aside from industry interests, a push to transform everything into single-payer would mean telling 156 million Americans—half the population—that they have to give up the insurance they now have. True, it would be replaced with another form of coverage; and you could argue, with justice, that the new program would be better for the great majority of those currently covered by their employers. But would they believe you? How many would be swayed by the attacks of conservative opponents of reform?

What happened in the period from 2005 to 2008 was that progressive policy wonks and politicians alike converged on a second-best solution: leave employer-based coverage in place, but rely on a mix of regulation and subsidies to extend coverage to the uninsured. We knew from experience abroad that this can work—Switzerland, for example, uses a decentralized system along these lines to achieve universal coverage. And it looked far closer to political feasibility than Medicare for All.

Hence the Affordable Care Act, aka Obamacare. The columns in this section document how the argument evolved, how the plan went, and what happened when Obamacare went into effect.

AILING HEALTH CARE

April 11, 2005

Those of us who accuse the administration of inventing a Social Security crisis are often accused, in return, of do-nothingism, of refusing to face up to the nation's problems. I plead not guilty: America does face a real crisis—but it's in health care, not Social Security.

Well-informed business executives agree. A recent survey of chief financial officers at major corporations found that 65 percent regard immediate action on health care costs as "very important." Only 31 percent said the same about Social Security reform.

But serious health care reform isn't on the table, and in the current political climate it probably can't be. You see, the health care crisis is ideologically inconvenient.

Let's start with some basic facts about health care.

Notice that I said "health care reform," not "Medicare reform." The rising cost of Medicare may loom large in political discussion, because it's a government program (and because it's often, wrongly, lumped together with Social Security by the crisis-mongers), but this isn't a story of runaway government spending. The costs of Medicare and of private health plans are both rising much faster than G.D.P. per capita, and at about the same rate per enrollee.

So what we're really facing is rapidly rising spending on health care generally, not just the part of health care currently paid for by taxpayers.

Rising health care spending isn't primarily the result of medical price inflation. It's primarily a response to innovation: the range of things that medicine can do keeps increasing. For example, Medicare recently started paying for implanted cardiac devices in many patients with heart trouble, now that research has shown them to be highly effective. This is good news, not bad.

So what's the problem? Why not welcome medical progress, and consider its costs money well spent? There are three answers.

First, America's traditional private health insurance system, in which workers get coverage through their employers, is unraveling. The Kaiser Family Foundation estimates that in 2004 there were at least five million fewer jobs providing health insurance than in 2001. And health care costs have become a major burden on those businesses that continue to provide insurance coverage: General Motors now spends about $1,500 on health care for every car it produces.

Second, rising Medicare spending may be a sign of progress, but it still must be paid for—and right now few politicians are willing to talk about the tax increases that will be needed if the program is to make medical advances available to all older Americans.

Finally, the U.S. health care system is wildly inefficient. Americans tend to believe that we have the best health care system in the world. (I've encountered members of the journalistic elite who flatly refuse to believe that France ranks much better on most measures of health care quality than the United States.) But it isn't true. We spend far more per person on health care than any other country—75 percent more than Canada or France—yet rank near the bottom among industrial countries in indicators from life expectancy to infant mortality.

This last point is, in a way, good news. In the long run, medical progress may force us to make a harsh choice: if we don't want to become a society in which the rich get life-saving medical treatment and the rest of us don't, we'll have to pay much higher taxes. The vast waste in our current system means, however, that effective reform could both improve quality and cut costs, postponing the day of reckoning.

To get effective reform, however, we'll need to shed some preconceptions—in particular, the ideologically driven belief that government is always the problem and market competition is always the solution.

The fact is that in health care, the private sector is often bloated and bureaucratic, while some government agencies—notably the Veterans Administration system—are lean and efficient. In health care, competition and personal choice can and do lead to higher costs and lower quality. The United States has the most privatized, competitive health system in the advanced world; it also has by far the highest costs, and close to the worst results.

HEALTH CARE CONFIDENTIAL

January 27, 2006

A merican health care is desperately in need of reform. But what form should change take? Are there any useful examples we can turn to for guidance?

Well, I know about a health care system that has been highly successful in containing costs, yet provides excellent care. And the story of this system's success provides a helpful corrective to anti-government ideology. For the government doesn't just pay the bills in this system—it runs the hospitals and clinics.

No, I'm not talking about some faraway country. The system in question is our very own Veterans Health Administration, whose success story is one of the best-kept secrets in the American policy debate.

In the 1980s and early 1990s, says an article in *The American Journal of Managed Care*, the V.H.A. "had a tarnished reputation of bureaucracy, inefficiency and mediocre care." But reforms beginning in the mid-1990s transformed the system, and "the V.A.'s success in improving quality, safety and value," the article says, "have allowed it to emerge as an increasingly recognized leader in health care."

Last year customer satisfaction with the veterans' health system, as measured by an annual survey conducted by the National Quality Research Center, exceeded that for private health care for the sixth year in a row. This high level of quality (which is also verified by objective measures of performance) was achieved without big budget increases. In fact, the veterans' system has managed to avoid much of the huge cost surge that has plagued the rest of U.S. medicine.

How does the V.H.A. do it?

The secret of its success is the fact that it's a universal, integrated system. Because it covers all veterans, the system doesn't need to employ legions of administrative staff to check patients' coverage and demand payment from their insurance companies. Because it covers all aspects of medical care, it has been able to take the lead in electronic record-keeping and other innovations that reduce costs, ensure effective treatment, and help prevent medical errors.

Moreover, the V.H.A., as Phillip Longman put it in the *Washington Monthly*, "has nearly a lifetime relationship with its patients." As a result, it "actually has an incentive to invest in prevention and more effective disease management. When it does so, it isn't just saving money for somebody else. It's maximizing its own resources. In short, it can do what the rest of the health care sector can't seem to, which is to pursue quality systematically without threatening its own financial viability."

Oh, and one more thing: the veterans' health system bargains hard with medical suppliers, and pays far less for drugs than most private insurers.

I don't want to idealize the veterans' system. In fact, there's reason to be concerned about its future: will it be given the resources it needs to cope with the flood of wounded and traumatized veterans from Iraq? But the transformation of the V.H.A. is clearly the most encouraging health policy story of the past decade. So why haven't you heard about it?

The answer, I believe, is that pundits and policymakers don't talk about the veterans' system because they can't handle the cognitive dissonance. (One prominent commentator started yelling at me when I tried to describe the system's successes in a private conversation.) For the lesson of the V.H.A.'s success story—that a government agency can deliver better care at lower cost than the private sector—runs completely counter to the pro-privatization, anti-government conventional wisdom that dominates today's Washington.

The dissonance between the dominant ideology and the realities of health care is one reason the Medicare drug legislation looks as if someone went down a checklist of things that the veterans' system does right, and in each case did the opposite. For example, the V.H.A. avoids dealing with insurance companies; the drug bill shoehorns insurance companies into the program even though they serve no real function. The V.H.A. bargains effectively on drug prices; the drug bill forbids Medicare from doing the same.

Still, ideology can't hold out against reality forever. Cries of "socialized medicine" didn't, in the end, succeed in blocking the creation of Medicare. And farsighted thinkers are already suggesting that the Veterans Health Administration, not President Bush's unrealistic vision of a system in which people go "comparative shopping" for medical care the way they do when buying tile (his example, not mine), represents the true future of American health care.

HEALTH CARE TERROR

July 9, 2007

T hese days terrorism is the first refuge of scoundrels. So when British authorities announced that a ring of Muslim doctors working for the National Health Service was behind the recent failed bomb plot, we should have known what was coming.

"National healthcare: Breeding ground for terror?" read the on-screen headline, as the Fox News host Neil Cavuto and the commentator Jerry Bowyer solemnly discussed how universal health care promotes terrorism.

While this was crass even by the standards of Bush-era political discourse, Fox was following in a long tradition. For more than sixty years, the medical-industrial complex and its political allies have used scare tactics to prevent America from following its conscience and making access to health care a right for all its citizens.

I say conscience, because the health care issue is, most of all, about morality.

That's what we learn from the overwhelming response to Michael Moore's *Sicko*. Health care reformers should, by all means, address the anxieties of middle-class Americans, their growing and justified fear of finding themselves uninsured or having their insurers deny coverage when they need it most. But reformers shouldn't focus only on self-interest. They should also appeal to Americans' sense of decency and humanity.

What outrages people who see *Sicko* is the sheer cruelty and injustice of the American health care system—sick people who can't pay their hospital bills literally dumped on the sidewalk, a child who dies because an emergency room that isn't a participant in her mother's health plan won't treat her, hard-working Americans driven into humiliating poverty by medical bills.

Sicko is a powerful call to action—but don't count the defenders of the status quo out. History shows that they're very good at fending off reform by finding new ways to scare us.

These scare tactics have often included over-the-top claims about the dangers of government insurance. *Sicko* plays part of a recording Ronald Reagan once made for the American Medical Association, warning that a proposed program of health insurance for the elderly—the program now known as Medicare—would lead to totalitarianism.

Right now, by the way, Medicare—which did enormous good, without leading to a dictatorship—is being undermined by privatization.

Mainly, though, the big-money interests with a stake in the present system want you to believe that universal health care would lead to a crushing tax burden and lousy medical care.

Now, every wealthy country except the United States already has some form of universal care. Citizens of these countries pay extra taxes as a result—but they make up for that through savings on insurance premiums and out-of-pocket medical costs. The overall cost of health care in countries with universal coverage is much lower than it is here.

Meanwhile, every available indicator says that in terms of quality, access to needed care, and health outcomes, the U.S. health care system does worse, not better, than other advanced countries—even Britain, which spends only about 40 percent as much per person as we do.

Yes, Canadians wait longer than insured Americans for elective surgery. But overall, the average Canadian's access to health care is as good as that of the average insured American—and much better than that of uninsured Americans, many of whom never receive needed care at all.

And the French manage to provide arguably the best health care in the world, without significant waiting lists of any kind. There's a scene in *Sicko* in which expatriate Americans in Paris praise the French system. According to the hard data they're not romanticizing. It really is that good.

All of which raises the question Mr. Moore asks at the beginning of *Sicko*: who are we?

"We have always known that heedless self-interest was bad morals; we know now that it is bad economics." So declared F.D.R. in 1937, in words that apply perfectly to health care today. This isn't one of those cases where we face painful trade-offs—here, doing the right thing is also cost-efficient. Universal health care would save thousands of American lives each year, while actually saving money.

So this is a test. The only things standing in the way of universal health care are the fear-mongering and influence-buying of interest groups. If we can't overcome those forces here, there's not much hope for America's future.

THE WAITING GAME

July 16, 2007

Being without health insurance is no big deal. Just ask President Bush. "I mean, people have access to health care in America," he said last week. "After all, you just go to an emergency room."

This is what you might call callousness with consequences. The White House has announced that Mr. Bush will veto a bipartisan plan that would extend health insurance, and with it such essentials as regular checkups and preventive medical care, to an estimated 4.1 million currently uninsured children. After all, it's not as if those kids really need insurance—they can just go to emergency rooms, right?

O.K., it's not news that Mr. Bush has no empathy for people less fortunate than himself. But his willful ignorance here is part of a larger picture: by and large, opponents of universal health care paint a glowing portrait of the American system that bears as little resemblance to reality as the scare stories they tell about health care in France, Britain, and Canada.

The claim that the uninsured can get all the care they need in emergency rooms is just the beginning. Beyond that is the myth that Americans who are lucky enough to have insurance never face long waits for medical care.

Actually, the persistence of that myth puzzles me. I can understand how people like Mr. Bush or Fred Thompson, who declared recently that "the poorest Americans are getting far better service" than Canadians or the British, can wave away the desperation of uninsured Americans, who are often poor and voiceless. But how can they get away with pretending that insured Americans always get prompt care, when most of us can testify otherwise?

A recent article in *Business Week* put it bluntly: "In reality, both data and anecdotes show that the American people are already waiting as long or longer than patients living with universal health-care systems."

A cross-national survey conducted by the Commonwealth Fund found that America ranks near the bottom among advanced countries in terms of how hard it is to get medical attention on short notice (although Canada was slightly worse), and that America is the worst place in the advanced world if you need care after hours or on a weekend.

We look better when it comes to seeing a specialist or receiving elective surgery. But Germany outperforms us even on those measures—and I suspect that France, which wasn't included in the study, matches Germany's performance.

Besides, not all medical delays are created equal. In Canada and Britain, delays are caused by doctors trying to devote limited medical resources to the most urgent cases. In the United States, they're often caused by insurance companies trying to save money.

This can lead to ordeals like the one recently described by Mark Kleiman, a professor at U.C.L.A., who nearly died of cancer because his insurer kept delaying approval for a necessary biopsy. "It was only later," writes Mr. Kleiman on his blog, "that I discovered why the insurance company was stalling; I had an option, which I didn't know I had, to avoid all the approvals by going to 'Tier II,' which would have meant higher co-payments."

He adds, "I don't know how many people my insurance company waited to death that year, but I'm certain the number wasn't zero."

To be fair, Mr. Kleiman is only surmising that his insurance company risked his life in an attempt to get him to pay more of his treatment costs. But there's no question that some Americans who seemingly have good insurance nonetheless die because insurers are trying to hold down their "medical losses"—the industry term for actually having to pay for care.

On the other hand, it's true that Americans get hip replacements faster than Canadians. But there's a funny thing about that example, which is used constantly as an argument for the superiority of private health insurance over a government-run system: the large majority of hip replacements in the United States are paid for by, um, Medicare.

That's right: the hip-replacement gap is actually a comparison of two government health insurance systems. American Medicare has shorter waits

than Canadian Medicare (yes, that's what they call their system) because it
has more lavish funding—end of story. The alleged virtues of private insurance have nothing to do with it.

The bottom line is that the opponents of universal health care appear
to have run out of honest arguments. All they have left are fantasies: horror
fiction about health care in other countries, and fairy tales about health care
here in America.

HEALTH CARE HOPES

September 21, 2007

A ll the evidence suggests that it has finally become politically possible to give Americans what citizens of every other advanced nation already have: guaranteed health insurance. The economics of universal health care are sound, and polls show strong public support for guaranteed care. The only thing we have to fear is fear itself.

Unfortunately, there's a lot of that around.

True, one kind of fear seems, provisionally, to have been overcome: the timidity of Democratic politicians scarred by the failure of the original Clinton health plan.

To see how much things have changed, consider Hillary Clinton's evolution. Just fifteen months ago, *The New York Times* reported that "her plans to expand coverage are tempered and incremental," and that "she continues to shy from the ultimate challenge: describing what a comprehensive Democratic health care plan would look like."

Indeed, when she was asked how costs might be controlled, she demurred: "It depends on what kind of system you're devising. And that's still not at all clear to me, what the body politic will bear."

But that was then.

John Edwards broke the issue of health care reform open in February, when he proposed a smart and serious plan for universal health insurance—and bravely announced his willingness to pay for the plan by letting some of the Bush tax cuts expire. Suddenly, universal health care went from being a distant progressive dream to something you could actually envision happening in the next administration.

Senator Clinton delayed a long time before coming out with her own plan—a delay that created a lot of anxiety among health care reformers, and may, as I'll explain in a minute, be a bad omen for the future. Still, this week she did deliver a plan, and it's as strong as the Edwards plan—because unless you get deep into the fine print, the Clinton plan basically *is* the Edwards plan.

That's not a criticism; it's much more important that a politician get health care right than that he or she score points for originality. Senator Clinton may be politically cautious, but she does understand health care economics and she knows a good thing when she sees it.

The Edwards and Clinton plans as well as the slightly weaker but similar Obama plan achieve universal-or-near-universal coverage through a well-thought-out combination of insurance regulation, subsidies, and public-private competition. These plans may disappoint advocates of a cleaner, simpler single-payer system. But it's hard to see how Medicare for All could get through Congress any time in the near future, whereas Edwards-type plans offer a reasonable second best that you can actually envision being enacted by a Democratic Congress and signed by a Democratic president just two years from now.

To get there, however, would require overcoming a lot more fear.

There won't be a serious Republican alternative. The health care plans of the leading Republican candidates, such as they are, are the same old, same old: they principally rely on tax breaks that go mainly to the well-off, but will supposedly conjure up the magic of the market. As Ezra Klein of *The American Prospect* cruelly but accurately puts it: "The Republican vision is for a world in which the sick and dying get to deduct some of the cost of health insurance that they don't have—and can't get—on their taxes."

But the G.O.P. nominee, whoever he is, won't be trying to persuade the public of the merits of his own plan. Instead, he'll try to scare the dwindling fraction of Americans who still have good health insurance by claiming that the Democrats will take it away.

The smear-and-fear campaign has already started. The Democratic plans all bear a strong resemblance to the health care plan that Mitt Romney signed into law as governor of Massachusetts, differing mainly in offering Americans additional choices. But that didn't stop Mr. Romney from denouncing the Clinton plan as "European-style socialized medicine." And Fred Thompson claims that the Clinton plan denies choice—which it actually offers in abundance—and relies on "punishment" instead.

These attacks probably won't be effective enough to prevent a Democrat from winning next year. But that won't be the end of the story: even if the Democrats take the White House and expand their Congressional majorities, the insurance and drug lobbies will try to bully them into backing down on their campaign promises.

That's why the long delay before Senator Clinton announced her health care plan made supporters of universal care, myself included, so nervous—a nervousness that is not completely assuaged by the fact that she finally did deliver. It's good to know that whoever gets the Democratic nomination will run on a very good health care plan. What remains is the question of whether he or she will have the determination to turn that plan into reality.

FEAR STRIKES OUT

March 21, 2010

The day before Sunday's health care vote, President Obama gave an unscripted talk to House Democrats. Near the end, he spoke about why his party should pass reform: "Every once in a while a moment comes where you have a chance to vindicate all those best hopes that you had about yourself, about this country, where you have a chance to make good on those promises that you made. . . . And this is the time to make true on that promise. We are not bound to win, but we are bound to be true. We are not bound to succeed, but we are bound to let whatever light we have shine."

And on the other side, here's what Newt Gingrich, the Republican former speaker of the House—a man celebrated by many in his party as an intellectual leader—had to say: if Democrats pass health reform, "They will have destroyed their party much as Lyndon Johnson shattered the Democratic Party for 40 years" by passing civil rights legislation.

I'd argue that Mr. Gingrich is wrong about that: proposals to guarantee health insurance are often controversial before they go into effect—Ronald Reagan famously argued that Medicare would mean the end of American freedom—but always popular once enacted.

But that's not the point I want to make today. Instead, I want you to consider the contrast: on one side, the closing argument was an appeal to our better angels, urging politicians to do what is right, even if it hurts their careers; on the other side, callous cynicism. Think about what it means to condemn health reform by comparing it to the Civil Rights Act. Who in modern America would say that L.B.J. did the wrong thing by pushing for racial equality? (Actually, we know who: the people at the Tea Party protest who hurled racial epithets at Democratic members of Congress on the eve of the vote.)

And that cynicism has been the hallmark of the whole campaign against reform.

Yes, a few conservative policy intellectuals, after making a show of thinking hard about the issues, claimed to be disturbed by reform's fiscal implications (but were strangely unmoved by the clean bill of fiscal health from the Congressional Budget Office) or to want stronger action on costs (even though this reform does more to tackle health care costs than any previous legislation). For the most part, however, opponents of reform didn't even pretend to engage with the reality either of the existing health care system or of the moderate, centrist plan—very close in outline to the reform Mitt Romney introduced in Massachusetts—that Democrats were proposing.

Instead, the emotional core of opposition to reform was blatant fearmongering, unconstrained either by the facts or by any sense of decency.

It wasn't just the death panel smear. It was racial hate-mongering, like a piece in *Investor's Business Daily* declaring that health reform is "affirmative action on steroids, deciding everything from who becomes a doctor to who gets treatment on the basis of skin color." It was wild claims about abortion funding. It was the insistence that there is something tyrannical about giving young working Americans the assurance that health care will be available when they need it, an assurance that older Americans have enjoyed ever since Lyndon Johnson—whom Mr. Gingrich considers a failed president—pushed Medicare through over the howls of conservatives.

And let's be clear: the campaign of fear hasn't been carried out by a radical fringe, unconnected to the Republican establishment. On the contrary, that establishment has been involved and approving all the way. Politicians like Sarah Palin—who was, let us remember, the G.O.P.'s vice-presidential candidate—eagerly spread the death panel lie, and supposedly reasonable, moderate politicians like Senator Chuck Grassley refused to say that it was untrue. On the eve of the big vote, Republican members of Congress warned that "freedom dies a little bit today" and accused Democrats of "totalitarian tactics," which I believe means the process known as "voting."

Without question, the campaign of fear was effective: health reform went from being highly popular to wide disapproval, although the numbers have been improving lately. But the question was, would it actually be enough to block reform?

And the answer is no. The Democrats have done it. The House has passed the Senate version of health reform, and an improved version will be achieved through reconciliation.

This is, of course, a political victory for President Obama, and a triumph for Nancy Pelosi, the House speaker. But it is also a victory for America's soul. In the end, a vicious, unprincipled fear offensive failed to block reform. This time, fear struck out.

EDITORS' NOTE: March 23, 2010

The Paul Krugman column on Monday, about the health care bill, quoted Newt Gingrich as saying that "Lyndon Johnson shattered the Democratic Party for 40 years" by passing civil rights legislation. The quotation originally appeared in *The Washington Post*, which reported after the column went to press that Mr. Gingrich said it referred to Johnson's Great Society policies, not to the 1964 Civil Rights Act.

OBAMACARE FAILS TO FAIL

July 13, 2014

How many Americans know how health reform is going? For that matter, how many people in the news media are following the positive developments?

I suspect that the answer to the first question is "Not many," while the answer to the second is "Possibly even fewer," for reasons I'll get to later. And if I'm right, it's a remarkable thing—an immense policy success is improving the lives of millions of Americans, but it's largely slipping under the radar.

How is that possible? Think relentless negativity without accountability. The Affordable Care Act has faced nonstop attacks from partisans and right-wing media, with mainstream news also tending to harp on the act's troubles. Many of the attacks have involved predictions of disaster, none of which have come true. But absence of disaster doesn't make a compelling headline, and the people who falsely predicted doom just keep coming back with dire new warnings.

Consider, in particular, the impact of Obamacare on the number of Americans without health insurance. The initial debacle of the federal Web site produced much glee on the right and many negative reports from the mainstream press as well; at the beginning of 2014, many reports confidently asserted that first-year enrollments would fall far short of White House projections.

Then came the remarkable late surge in enrollment. Did the pessimists face tough questions about why they got it so wrong? Of course not. Instead, the same people just came out with a mix of conspiracy theories and new predictions of doom. The administration was "cooking the books," said Senator John Barrasso of Wyoming; people who signed up wouldn't actually pay their premiums, declared an array of "experts"; more people were losing insurance than gaining it, declared Senator Ted Cruz of Texas.

But the great majority of those who signed up did indeed pay up, and we now have multiple independent surveys—from Gallup, the Urban Institute, and the Commonwealth Fund—all showing a sharp reduction in the number of uninsured Americans since last fall.

I've been seeing some claims on the right that the dramatic reduction in the number of uninsured was caused by economic recovery, not health reform (so now conservatives are praising the Obama economy?). But that's pretty lame, and also demonstrably wrong.

For one thing, the decline is too sharp to be explained by what is at best a modest improvement in the employment picture. For another, that Urban Institute survey shows a striking difference between the experience in states that expanded Medicaid—which are also, in general, states that have done their best to make health care reform work—and those that refused to let the federal government cover their poor. Sure enough, the decline in uninsured residents has been three times as large in Medicaid-expansion states as in Medicaid-expansion rejecters. It's not the economy; it's the policy, stupid.

What about the cost? Last year there were many claims about "rate shock" from soaring insurance premiums. But last month the Department of Health and Human Services reported that among those receiving federal subsidies—the great majority of those signing up—the average net premium was only $82 a month.

Yes, there are losers from Obamacare. If you're young, healthy, and affluent enough that you don't qualify for a subsidy (and don't get insurance from your employer), your premium probably did rise. And if you're rich enough to pay the extra taxes that finance those subsidies, you have taken a financial hit. But it's telling that even reform's opponents aren't trying to highlight these stories. Instead, they keep looking for older, sicker, middle-class victims, and keep failing to find them.

Oh, and according to Commonwealth, the overwhelming majority of the newly insured, including 74 percent of Republicans, are satisfied with their coverage.

You might ask why, if health reform is going so well, it continues to poll badly. It's crucial, I'd argue, to realize that Obamacare, by design, by and large doesn't affect Americans who already have good insurance. As a result, many people's views are shaped by the mainly negative coverage in the news media. Still, the latest tracking survey from the Kaiser Family Foundation shows that a rising number of Americans are hearing about reform from family and friends, which means that they're starting to hear from the program's beneficiaries.

And as I suggested earlier, people in the media—especially elite pundits—may be the last to hear the good news, simply because they're in a socioeconomic bracket in which people generally have good coverage.

For the less fortunate, however, the Affordable Care Act has already made a big positive difference. The usual suspects will keep crying failure, but the truth is that health reform is—gasp!—working.

IMAGINARY HEALTH CARE HORRORS

March 30, 2015

There's a lot of fuzzy math in American politics, but Representative Pete Sessions of Texas, the chairman of the House Rules Committee, recently set a new standard when he declared the cost of Obamacare "unconscionable." If you do "simple multiplication," he insisted, you find that the coverage expansion is costing $5 million per recipient. But his calculation was a bit off—namely, by a factor of more than a thousand. The actual cost per newly insured American is about $4,000.

Now, everyone makes mistakes. But this wasn't a forgivable error. Whatever your overall view of the Affordable Care Act, one indisputable fact is that it's costing taxpayers much less than expected—about 20 percent less, according to the Congressional Budget Office. A senior member of Congress should know that, and he certainly has no business making speeches about an issue if he won't bother to read budget office reports.

But that is, of course, how it's been all along with Obamacare. Before the law went into effect, opponents predicted disaster on all levels. What has happened instead is that the law is working pretty well. So how have the prophets of disaster responded? By pretending that the bad things they said would happen have, in fact, happened.

Costs aren't the only area where enemies of reform prefer to talk about imaginary disasters rather than real success stories. Remember, Obamacare was also supposed to be a huge job-killer. In 2011, the House even passed a bill called the Repealing the Job-Killing Health Care Law Act. Health reform, opponents declared, would cripple the economy and in particular cause businesses to force their employees into part-time work.

Well, Obamacare went into effect fully at the beginning of 2014—and private-sector job growth actually accelerated, to a pace we haven't seen since the Clinton years. Meanwhile, involuntary part-time employment—the number of workers who want full-time work but can't get it—has dropped sharply. But the usual suspects talk as if their dire predictions came true. Obamacare, Jeb Bush declared a few weeks ago, is "the greatest job suppressor in the so-called recovery."

Finally, there's the never-ending hunt for snarks and boojums—for ordinary, hard-working Americans who have suffered hardship thanks to health reform. As we've just seen, Obamacare opponents by and large don't do math (and they're sorry when they try). But all they really need are a few sob stories, tales of sympathetic individuals who have been impoverished by some aspect of the law.

Remarkably, however, they haven't been able to find those stories. Early last year, Americans for Prosperity, a Koch brothers–backed group, ran a series of ads featuring alleged Obamacare victims—but not one of those tales of woe stood up to scrutiny. More recently, Representative Cathy McMorris Rodgers of Washington State took to Facebook to ask for Obamacare horror stories. What she got instead was a torrent of testimonials from people whose lives have been improved, and in some cases saved, by health reform.

In reality, the only people hurt by health reform are Americans with very high incomes, who have seen their taxes go up, and a relatively small number of people who have seen their premiums rise because they're young and healthy (so insurers previously saw them as good risks) and affluent (so they don't qualify for subsidies). Neither group supplies suitable victims for attack ads.

In short, when it comes to the facts, the attack on health reform has come up empty-handed. But the public doesn't know that. The good news about costs hasn't made it through at all: according to a recent poll by Vox.com, only 5 percent of Americans know that Obamacare is costing less than predicted, while 42 percent think the government is spending more than expected.

And the favorable experiences of the roughly 16 million Americans who have gained insurance so far have had little effect on public perceptions. Partly that's because the Affordable Care Act, by design, has had almost no effect on those who already had good health insurance: Before the act, a large majority of Americans were already covered by their employers, by Medicare, or by Medicaid, and they have seen no change in their status.

At a deeper level, however, what we're looking at here is the impact of post–truth politics. We live in an era in which politicians and the supposed experts who serve them never feel obliged to acknowledge uncomfortable facts, in which no argument is ever dropped, no matter how overwhelming the evidence that it's wrong.

And the result is that imaginary disasters can overshadow real successes. Obamacare isn't perfect, but it has dramatically improved the lives of millions. Someone should tell the voters.

3

The Attack on Obamacare

THE CRUELTY CAUCUS

WHERE WERE YOU IN JUNE 2012, WHEN THE SUPREME COURT HANDED down its crucial decision on the constitutionality of Obamacare? If you have no idea, you're not a health policy nerd. I, on the other hand, am. I was on vacation in England, sitting in a pub with my wife—and with wifi access—hanging on the reports.

The first reporting was garbled, making it seem as if the court had killed health reform. Happily, it hadn't. And once it was clear that reform had, in fact, survived, there was only one thing to do: I ordered a double scotch, and drank it rapidly.

While reform survived, however, the court did impose one limit on the Affordable Care Act: it made one piece of the law, the expansion of Medicaid to everyone up to 133 percent of the poverty line, optional for states.

You might think that this would make little difference. After all, under the act, the federal government would initially pick up the entire tab; after a few years this would drop to 90 percent, but it was still an incredible deal. I mean, what kind of state government would turn down an offer to provide health insurance to large numbers of its residents at virtually no cost, while also bringing in federal dollars that would boost the state economy?

The answer was, almost every state government controlled by Republicans. Some eventually changed their minds, but as of mid-2019 there are still fourteen states that have refused to provide essential medical care to some of their most vulnerable citizens even though it wouldn't cost them anything.

At first you could possibly have rationalized refusal to expand Medicaid as a strategic move, an attempt to discredit Obamacare as a whole. But the A.C.A. has been in effect for a long time now; if refusing to expand Medicaid was going to do it in, that would have happened already. So at this point we have to accept that there's something even uglier going on.

I mean, it's one thing to balk at plans to tax the rich and help the poor. You could justify that position either on the grounds that taxing the rich will discourage job creators or something like that, or simply because you care more about the rich than the poor. But refusing free money that would help the poor is something else—it's cruelty for its own sake.

Well, what we've learned about U.S. politics since 2012 is that there are a lot of people who share that particular brand of cruelty. It's still, I believe, a relatively small part of the electorate. But it's a much bigger share of the G.O.P. base, and a solid majority of professional Republican politicians.

Which brings me to the campaign against Obamacare after the 2016 election once again briefly gave the G.O.P. unified control of Congress and the White House. Republicans finally had the chance to undo Barack Obama's most important domestic initiative, repealing the whole Affordable Care Act. Doing so would have made some sense from their point of view, since repeal of the whole act would have meant repealing the taxes on high incomes that paid for the Medicaid expansion and the subsidies to middle-income families. But once it became apparent that repeal would take coverage away from tens of millions, even the G.O.P. balked at the prospect.

What was left was a campaign of sabotage: trying to undermine Obamacare by striking at its provisions in ways that didn't too obviously take away people's health insurance, but made insurance harder to get, more expensive, or both. The reason this was possible was the very set of compromises Democrats made to get health reform passed in the first place: because the Affordable Care Act is a hybrid public-private system rather than a simple government insurance program, it has a number of moving parts, and it's not too hard to throw sand in its gears.

The thing about this campaign of sabotage was that it didn't directly benefit anyone—the wealthy still had to pay the same taxes. So, like refusing the Medicaid expansion, it was purely about hurting the act's beneficiaries, and in some cases actually cost more money than leaving the act intact.

The good news was that Obamacare's architects built better than many, including myself, had realized. The law was hardly immune to sabotage, but it proved more robust than many had feared. In the columns collected in this section, I describe the attack on the law, and the way it has mostly survived.

THREE LEGS GOOD, NO LEGS BAD

July 10, 2017

W ill fifty Republican senators be willing to inflict grievous harm on their constituents in the name of party loyalty? I have no idea.

But this seems like a good moment to review why Republicans can't come up with a non-disastrous alternative to Obamacare. It's not because they're stupid (although they have become stunningly anti-intellectual). It's because you can't change any major element of the Affordable Care Act without destroying the whole thing.

Suppose you want to make health coverage available to everyone, including people with pre-existing conditions. Most of the health economists I know would love to see single-payer—Medicare for All. Realistically, however, that's too heavy a lift for the time being.

For one thing, the insurance industry would not take kindly to being eliminated, and has a lot of clout. Also, a switch to single-payer would require a large tax increase. Most people would gain more from the elimination of insurance premiums than they would lose from the tax hike, but that would be a hard case to make in an election campaign.

Beyond that, most Americans under 65 are covered by their employers, and are reasonably happy with that coverage. They would understandably be nervous about any proposal to replace that coverage with something else, no matter how truthfully you assured them that the replacement would be better.

So the Affordable Care Act went for incrementalism—the so-called three-legged stool.

It starts by requiring that insurers offer the same plans, at the same prices, to everyone, regardless of medical history. This deals with the problem of pre-existing conditions. On its own, however, this would lead to a "death spiral": healthy people would wait until they got sick to sign up, so those who did sign up would be relatively unhealthy, driving up premiums, which would in turn drive out more healthy people, and so on.

So insurance regulation has to be accompanied by the individual mandate, a requirement that people sign up for insurance, even if they're currently healthy. And the insurance must meet minimum standards: buying a cheap policy that barely covers anything is functionally the same as not buying insurance at all.

But what if people can't afford insurance? The third leg of the stool is subsidies that limit the cost for those with lower incomes. For those with the lowest incomes, the subsidy is 100 percent, and takes the form of an expansion of Medicaid.

The key point is that all three legs of this stool are necessary. Take away any one of them, and the program can't work.

But does it work even with all three legs? Yes.

To understand what's happened with the A.C.A. so far, you need to realize that as written (and interpreted by the Supreme Court), the law's functioning depends a lot on cooperation from state governments. And where states have in fact cooperated, expanding Medicaid, operating their own insurance exchanges, and promoting both enrollment and competition among insurers, it has worked pretty darn well.

Compare, for example, the experience of Kentucky and its neighbor Tennessee. In 2013, before full implementation of the A.C.A., Tennessee had slightly fewer uninsured, 13 percent versus 14 percent. But by 2015 Kentucky, which implemented the law in full, had cut its uninsured rate to just 6 percent, while Tennessee was at 11.

Or consider the problem of counties with only one (or no) insurer, meaning no competition. As one recent study points out, this is almost entirely a red-state problem. In states with G.O.P. governors, 21 percent of the population lives in such counties; in Democratic-governor states, less than 2 percent.

So Obamacare is, though nobody will believe it, a well-thought-out law that works where states want it to work. It could and should be made to work better, but Republicans show no interest in making that happen. Instead, all their ideas involve sawing off one or more legs of that three-legged stool.

First, they're dead set on repealing the individual mandate, which is unpopular with healthy people but essential to making the system work for those who need it.

Second, they're determined to slash subsidies—including making savage cuts to Medicaid—in order to free up money that they can use to cut taxes on the wealthy. The result would be a drastic rise in net premiums for most families.

Finally, we're now hearing a lot about the Cruz amendment, which would let insurers offer bare-bones plans with minimal coverage and high deductibles. These would be useless to people with pre-existing conditions, who would find themselves segregated into a high-cost market—effectively sawing off the third leg of the stool.

So which parts of their plan would Republicans have to abandon to avoid a huge rise in the number of uninsured? The answer is, all of them.

After all these years of denouncing Obamacare, then, Republicans have no idea how to do better. Or, actually, they have no ideas at all.

OBAMACARE'S VERY STABLE GENIUS

April 9, 2018

Front pages continue, understandably, to be dominated by the roughly 130,000 scandals currently afflicting the Trump administration. But polls suggest that the reek of corruption, intense as it is, isn't likely to dominate the midterm elections. The biggest issue on voters' minds appears, instead, to be health care.

And you know what? Voters are right. If Republicans retain control of both houses of Congress, we can safely predict that they'll make another try at repealing Obamacare, taking health insurance away from 25 million or 30 million Americans. Why? Because their attempts to sabotage the program keep falling short, and time is running out.

I'm not saying that sabotage has been a complete failure. The Trump administration has succeeded in driving insurance premiums sharply higher—and yes, I mean "succeeded," because that was definitely the goal.

Enrollment on the Affordable Care Act's insurance exchanges has also declined since 2016—with almost all the decline taking place in Trump administration–run exchanges, rather than those run by states—and the overall number of Americans without health insurance, after declining dramatically under Obama, has risen again.

But what Republicans were hoping and planning for was a "death spiral" of declining enrollment and soaring costs. And while constant claims that such a death spiral is underway have had their effect—a majority of the public believes that the exchanges are collapsing—it isn't. In fact, the program has been remarkably stable when you bear in mind that it's being administered by people trying to make it fail.

What's the secret of Obamacare's stability? The answer, although nobody will believe it, is that the people who designed the program were extremely smart. Political reality forced them to build a Rube Goldberg device, a complex scheme to achieve basically simple goals; every progressive health expert I know would have been happy to extend Medicare to everyone, but that just wasn't going to happen. But they did manage to create a system that's pretty robust to shocks, including the shock of a White House that wants to destroy it.

Originally, Obamacare was supposed to rest on a "three-legged stool." Private insurers were barred from discriminating based on pre-existing conditions; individuals were required to buy insurance meeting minimum standards—the "individual mandate"—even if they were currently healthy; and subsidies were provided to make insurance affordable.

Republicans have, however, done their best to saw off one of those legs; even before they repealed the mandate, they drastically reduced outreach efforts in an attempt to discourage healthy Americans from enrolling.

The result has been that the population actually signing up for coverage is both smaller and sicker than it would otherwise have been, forcing insurers to charge higher premiums.

But that's where the subsidies come in.

Under the A.C.A., the poorest Americans are covered by Medicaid, so private premiums don't matter. Meanwhile, many of those with higher incomes—up to 400 percent of the poverty line, or more than $95,000 for a family of four—are eligible for subsidies. That's 59 percent of the population, but because many of those with higher incomes get insurance through their employers, it's 83 percent of those signing up on the exchanges. And here's the thing: Those subsidies aren't fixed. Instead, the formula sets the subsidy high enough to put a limit on how high premium payments can go as a percentage of income.

What this means is that of the 27 million Americans who have either gained coverage through the Medicaid expansion or purchased insurance on the exchanges, only about two million are exposed to those Trump-engineered premium hikes. That's still a lot of people, but it's not enough to get a death spiral going. In fact, for complicated reasons ("silver-loading"—don't ask), after-subsidy premiums have actually gone down for many people.

And that leaves the G.O.P. very, very frustrated.

From the beginning, Republicans hated Obamacare not because they expected it to fail, but because they feared that it would succeed, and thereby demonstrate that government actually can do things to make people's lives better. And their nightmare is gradually coming true: although it took a long time, the Affordable Care Act is finally becoming popular, and the public's concern that the G.O.P. will kill it is becoming an important political liability.

What this says to me is that if Republicans manage to hold on to Congress, they will make another all-out push to destroy the act—because they'll know that it's probably their last chance. Indeed, if they don't kill Obamacare soon, the next step will probably be an enhanced program that lets Americans of all ages buy into Medicare.

So voters are right to believe that health care is very much an issue in the midterm elections. It may not be the most important thing at stake—there's a good case to be made that the survival of American democracy is on the line. But it's a very big deal.

GET SICK, GO BANKRUPT, AND DIE

September 3, 2018

L et's be honest: despite his reputation as a maverick, John McCain spent most of his last decade being a very orthodox Republican, toe-ing the party line no matter how irresponsible it became. Think of the way he abandoned his onetime advocacy of action to limit climate change.

But he redeemed much of that record with one action: he cast the crucial vote against G.O.P. attempts to repeal the Affordable Care Act. That single "nay" saved health care for tens of millions of Americans, at least for a while.

But now McCain is gone, and with him, as far as we can tell, the only Republican in Congress with anything resembling a spine. As a result, if Republicans hold Congress in November, they will indeed repeal Obamacare. That's not a guess: it's an explicit promise, made by Vice President Mike Pence last week.

But what about the problems that sank the repeal effort in 2017? Surely Republicans have spent the past year rethinking their policy ideas, trying to come up with ways to undo the A.C.A. without inflicting enormous harm on ordinary Americans, especially those with pre-existing medical condi-tions. Right?

See, I made a joke.

Of course, Republicans haven't rethought their ideas on health care (or, actually, anything else). Partly that's because the modern G.O.P. doesn't do policy analysis. Democrats have a network of think tanks and sympathetic independent experts who look hard at evidence, try to devise solutions to real problems, and sometime affect actual legislative proposals. Republicans have nothing comparable; their tame "experts" are basically in the business of saying whatever their political masters want to hear.

In the case of health care, however, there's an even deeper problem: the G.O.P. can't come up with an alternative to the Affordable Care Act because no such alternative exists. In particular, if you want to preserve protection for people with pre-existing conditions—the health issue that matters most to voters, including half of Republicans—Obamacare is the *most conservative* policy that can do that. The only other options are things like Medicare for All that would involve moving significantly to the left, not the right.

Health economists have explained this point many times over the years; but as always, it's difficult to get a man to understand something when his salary depends on his not understanding it. Still, let's try one more time.

If you want private insurers to cover people with pre-existing conditions, you have to ban discrimination based on medical history. But that in itself isn't enough, because if policies cost the same for everyone, those who sign up will be sicker than those who don't, creating a bad risk pool and forcing high premiums. That was the case in New York, where premiums for individual policies were very high before the A.C.A.—and promptly fell by half when Obamacare went into effect.

For what Obamacare did was provide incentives to get healthy people to sign up, too. On one side there was a penalty for not having insurance (the individual mandate). On the other, there were subsidies designed to limit health expenses as a share of income. Republicans have tried to sabotage health care by doing away with the mandate, and have succeeded in driving premiums higher; but the system is still standing thanks to those subsidies.

The point, again, is that Obamacare is the most conservative option for covering pre-existing conditions, and if Republicans really cared about the scores of millions of Americans with such conditions, they would support and indeed try to strengthen the A.C.A.

Instead, they're going to kill it if they hold on in two months. But covering pre-existing conditions is popular; therefore, they're pretending that they'll do that, while offering proposals that would, in fact, do no such thing.

Why do they imagine they can get away with such brazen fraud, because that's what it is? Do they imagine that voters are stupid?

Well, yes. In recent rallies Donald Trump has been declaring that Democrats want to "raid Medicare to pay for socialism."

But the more important target is the news media, many members of which still haven't learned to cope with the pervasive bad faith of modern conservatism.

When someone like, say, Senator Dean Heller of Nevada co-sponsors a bill that purports to protect pre-existing conditions but actually doesn't, what he hopes for are headlines that say "Heller Announces Plan to Protect Americans With Pre-existing Conditions," with the key fact—that his bill wouldn't do that at all—buried in the seventeenth paragraph.

Or better yet, from his point of view, that seventeenth paragraph would state only that "some Democrats" say his bill is a fraud, while Republicans disagree. Both sides, you know.

So if you're an American who suffers from a pre-existing medical condition, or fear that you might develop such a condition in the future, you need to be clear about the reality: Republicans are coming for your health care. If they hold the line in November, health insurance at an affordable price—maybe at any price—will be gone in a matter of months.

HOW DEMOCRATS CAN DELIVER ON HEALTH CARE

November 22, 2018

New Jersey shows the way. You got a problem with that?

"Democrats need to have a positive agenda, not just be against Donald Trump." How many times did you hear pundits say something like that during the midterm campaigns? In fact, you're still hearing it from people like Seth Moulton, who's leading the (apparently failing) effort to block Nancy Pelosi from returning as House speaker.

What makes this lazy accusation so annoying is that it's demonstrably, arithmetically wrong. Yes, Trump was on everyone's mind, but he was remarkably absent from Democratic messaging. A tally by the Wesleyan Media Project found that the 2018 elections stand out not for how much Democrats talked about the tweeter in chief, but for how little: not since 2002 has an opposition party run so few ads attacking the occupant of the White House.

So what did the campaigns that led to a blue wave talk about? Above all, health care, which featured in more than half of Democrats' ads. Which raises the question: Now that Democrats have had their big House victory and a lot of success in state-level races, can they do anything to deliver on their key campaign issue?

Yes, they can.

Actually, just by capturing the House Democrats achieved one big goal—taking repeal of the Affordable Care Act off the table. True, the G.O.P. lawsuit against the act's protection of pre-existing conditions is still awaiting a ruling—the long silence of the Republican-leaning judge in that case is getting increasingly strange. But there won't be any more legislative attempts to dismantle the law.

On the other hand, with Republicans still controlling the Senate and White House, major new federal legislation on health care isn't going to happen. Democrats may debate about their future agenda, which seems likely to include offering some form of Medicare buy-in option for Americans under 65. And it's important that they have this debate: one reason they were able to achieve major health reform in 2009–2010 was that, unlike 2017 Republicans, who had put no thought into the actual implications of repeal, they had hashed out key issues over the previous two years. But for now, at least, Washington will be gridlocked (which is better than where we were!).

There can, however, be action at the state level.

The A.C.A. didn't, strictly speaking, create a national program. Instead, it set rules and provided financing for fifty state-level programs. States were encouraged to create their own health insurance marketplaces, although they had the option to use healthcare.gov, the federal site. A 2012 Supreme Court decision also let states opt out of Medicaid expansion, and many did choose to refuse federal dollars and deprive their own residents of health care.

This has created a divergence in health care destinies, depending on states' political orientation. In 2013, before the A.C.A. went into effect, California had an above-average rate of uninsurance: 17.2 percent of its population was uncovered. North Carolina did somewhat better, with "only" 15.6 percent uninsured. But as of last year, the uninsured rate in California had fallen ten points, to 7.2 percent, while North Carolina's rate was still above 10 percent.

What made the difference? Solid-blue California, with a Democratic governor and Legislature, did all it could to make Obamacare work: It expanded Medicaid, operated its own marketplace, and made major efforts to get people signed up. North Carolina, under Republican rule, did none of these things.

And the importance of state-level action has only increased in the past two years, as the Trump administration and its congressional allies, unable to fully repeal the A.C.A., have nonetheless done all they can to sabotage it. They eliminated the individual mandate, which pushed people to sign up while they were still healthy; they eliminated reinsurance that helped insurance companies manage their own risk; they cut back drastically on outreach.

All of these measures acted to drive premiums up and enrollment down. But states can, if they choose, fill the Trump-size hole.

The most dramatic example of how this can be done is New Jersey, where Democrats gained full control at the end of 2017 and promptly created state-level versions of both the mandate and reinsurance. The results were impressive: New Jersey's premiums for 2019 are 9.3 percent lower than for 2018, and are now well below the national average. Undoing Trumpian sabotage seems to have saved the average buyer around $1,500 a year.

Now that Democrats have won control of multiple states, they can and should emulate New Jersey's example, and move beyond it if they can. Why not, for example, introduce state-level public options—actuarially sound government plans—as alternatives to private insurance?

The point is that while the new House majority won't be able to do much beyond defending Obamacare, at least for now, its allies in the states can do much more, and in the process deliver on the agenda the whole party ran on this year. As they say in New Jersey, you got a problem with that?

4

Bubble and Bust

THE SUM OF ALL FEARS

DOES ANYONE STILL REMEMBER THE ASIAN FINANCIAL CRISIS OF THE late 1990s? With everything that has happened since, it can seem like ancient history. Yet for those who followed it, it was a deeply frightening event, not just for its immediate consequences—trillions of dollars were lost, tens of millions of people saw their lives disrupted—but as an omen.

Circa 1996, the great majority of economists, myself included, believed that while the world was full of risks, one particular kind of risk, that of a 1930s-type depression, had been eliminated by the progress of economic knowledge. Such things have, after all, happened to other social ills. Back in 1854 Dr. John Snow realized that a cholera outbreak in London was tied to just one public pump; once epidemiologists realized that tainted water spread the disease, cholera epidemics became a thing of the past.

Similarly, in 1936 John Maynard Keynes realized that inadequate spending and cascading bank failures were the cause of mass unemployment, and once policymakers came to understand that diagnosis, Great Depression–style slumps also became a thing of the past.

Recessions, even nasty ones, didn't stop happening; the U.S. unemployment rate hit almost 11 percent in 1982. But that recession, like most slumps after World War II, was more like shock therapy than a heart attack: it was more or less deliberately imposed by policymakers to cool off what they feared was about to become runaway inflation. Nobody expected the return of old-style "panics," with bank runs and businesses going under because people were hiding their savings under mattresses.

But that's what happened in Thailand, Malaysia, Indonesia, South Korea in the late 1990s. A slower-motion crisis, a sustained malaise, came to Japan, which just a few years before had been widely seen as an emerging economic superpower. And while some observers—all too many Western economists,

I'm sorry to say—were inclined to dismiss these crises as aberrations with nothing to teach the rest of us, others of us were deeply shaken.

After all, some of these nations were relatively modern and sophisticated, and while their policymakers weren't ideal (whose are?), they weren't being run by idiots. Japan, in particular, looked at a fundamental level a lot like us: a big, rich, educated, technologically advanced, politically stable nation with competent if not brilliant monetary and fiscal authorities. If Japan could find itself caught in a "lost decade" of stagnation and deflation, couldn't the same thing happen here?

I wrote about these concerns at the time, notably in a 1998 academic paper ("It's Baaack: Japan's Slump and the Return of the Liquidity Trap") that has, I think, stood the test of time pretty well, and a 1999 book, *The Return of Depression Economics*. Others raised similar alarms, including a then-Princeton professor by the name of Ben Bernanke. But it wasn't a message many wanted to hear.

But the parallels between ourselves and Japan grew stronger over time. By 2005 or so I and many (but not enough) others had grown concerned about what looked like an immense housing bubble. It seemed obvious that bad things would happen when that bubble burst. As it turned out, it was far worse than almost anyone realized. Years of financial deregulation and financial "innovation" (which often amounted to finding ways to evade regulation) had created a banking system that was, in a modern, high-tech way, just as vulnerable to panics as the banking system on the eve of the Great Depression.

And the panic came.

The columns in this section describe the growing fear I and others felt that something was going terribly wrong, and the wall of misconception we had to climb when the things we feared might happen, did. The question then became what to do. But more about that in the next section.

RUNNING OUT OF BUBBLES

May 27, 2005

Remember the stock market bubble? With everything that's happened since 2000, it feels like ancient history. But a few pessimists, notably Stephen Roach of Morgan Stanley, argue that we have not yet paid the price for our past excesses.

I've never fully accepted that view. But looking at the housing market, I'm starting to reconsider.

In July 2001, Paul McCulley, an economist at Pimco, the giant bond fund, predicted that the Federal Reserve would simply replace one bubble with another. "There is room," he wrote, "for the Fed to create a bubble in housing prices, if necessary, to sustain American hedonism. And I think the Fed has the will to do so, even though political correctness would demand that Mr. Greenspan deny any such thing."

As Mr. McCulley predicted, interest rate cuts led to soaring home prices, which led in turn not just to a construction boom but to high consumer spending, because homeowners used mortgage refinancing to go deeper into debt. All of this created jobs to make up for those lost when the stock bubble burst.

Now the question is what can replace the housing bubble.

Nobody thought the economy could rely forever on home buying and refinancing. But the hope was that by the time the housing boom petered out, it would no longer be needed.

But although the housing boom has lasted longer than anyone could have imagined, the economy would still be in big trouble if it came to an end. That is, if the hectic pace of home construction were to cool, and consumers were to stop borrowing against their houses, the economy would slow down sharply. If housing prices actually started falling, we'd be looking at a very nasty scene, in which both construction and consumer spending would plunge, pushing the economy right back into recession.

That's why it's so ominous to see signs that America's housing market, like the stock market at the end of the last decade, is approaching the final, feverish stages of a speculative bubble.

Some analysts still insist that housing prices aren't out of line. But someone will always come up with reasons why seemingly absurd asset prices make sense. Remember *Dow 36,000*? Robert Shiller, who argued against such rationalizations and correctly called the stock bubble in his book *Irrational Exuberance*, has added an ominous analysis of the housing market to the new edition, and says the housing bubble "may be the biggest bubble in U.S. history."

In parts of the country there's a speculative fever among people who shouldn't be speculators that seems all too familiar from past bubbles—the shoeshine boys with stock tips in the 1920s, the beer-and-pizza joints showing CNBC, not ESPN, on their TV sets in the 1990s.

Even Alan Greenspan now admits that we have "characteristics of bubbles" in the housing market, but only "in certain areas." And it's true that the craziest scenes are concentrated in a few regions, like coastal Florida and California.

But these aren't tiny regions; they're big and wealthy, so that the national housing market as a whole looks pretty bubbly. Many home purchases are speculative; the National Association of Realtors estimates that 23 percent of the homes sold last year were bought for investment, not to live in. According to *Business Week*, 31 percent of new mortgages are interest only, a sign that people are stretching to their financial limits.

The important point to remember is that the bursting of the stock market bubble hurt lots of people—not just those who bought stocks near their peak. By the summer of 2003, private-sector employment was three million below its 2001 peak. And the job losses would have been much worse if the stock bubble hadn't been quickly replaced with a housing bubble.

So what happens if the housing bubble bursts? It will be the same thing all over again, unless the Fed can find something to take its place. And it's hard to imagine what that might be. After all, the Fed's ability to manage the economy mainly comes from its ability to create booms and busts in the housing market. If housing enters a post-bubble slump, what's left?

Mr. Roach believes that the Fed's apparent success after 2001 was an illusion, that it simply piled up trouble for the future. I hope he's wrong. But the Fed does seem to be running out of bubbles.

THAT HISSING SOUND

August 8, 2005

This is the way the bubble ends: not with a pop, but with a hiss.

Housing prices move much more slowly than stock prices. There are no Black Mondays, when prices fall 23 percent in a day. In fact, prices often keep rising for a while even after a housing boom goes bust.

So the news that the U.S. housing bubble is over won't come in the form of plunging prices; it will come in the form of falling sales and rising inventory, as sellers try to get prices that buyers are no longer willing to pay. And the process may already have started.

Of course, some people still deny that there's a housing bubble. Let me explain how we know that they're wrong.

One piece of evidence is the sense of frenzy about real estate, which irresistibly brings to mind the stock frenzy of 1999. Even some of the players are the same. The authors of the 1999 best seller *Dow 36,000* are now among the most vocal proponents of the view that there is no housing bubble.

Then there are the numbers. Many bubble deniers point to average prices for the country as a whole, which look worrisome but not totally crazy. When it comes to housing, however, the United States is really two countries, Flatland and the Zoned Zone.

In Flatland, which occupies the middle of the country, it's easy to build houses. When the demand for houses rises, Flatland metropolitan areas, which don't really have traditional downtowns, just sprawl some more. As a result, housing prices are basically determined by the cost of construction. In Flatland, a housing bubble can't even get started.

But in the Zoned Zone, which lies along the coasts, a combination of high population density and land-use restrictions—hence "zoned"—makes it hard to build new houses. So when people become willing to spend more on houses, say because of a fall in mortgage rates, some houses get built, but the prices of existing houses also go up. And if people think that prices will continue to rise, they become willing to spend even more, driving prices still higher, and so on. In other words, the Zoned Zone is prone to housing bubbles.

And Zoned Zone housing prices, which have risen much faster than the national average, clearly point to a bubble.

In the nation as a whole, housing prices rose about 50 percent between the first quarter of 2000 and the first quarter of 2005. But that average blends results from Flatland metropolitan areas like Houston and Atlanta, where prices rose 26 and 29 percent respectively, with results from Zoned Zone areas like New York, Miami, and San Diego, where prices rose 77, 96, and 118 percent.

Nobody would pay San Diego prices without believing that prices will continue to rise. Rents rose much more slowly than prices: the Bureau of Labor Statistics index of "owners' equivalent rent" rose only 27 percent from late 1999 to late 2004. *Business Week* reports that by 2004 the cost of renting a house in San Diego was only 40 percent of the cost of owning a similar house—even taking into account low interest rates on mortgages. So it makes sense to buy in San Diego only if you believe that prices will keep rising rapidly, generating big capital gains. That's pretty much the definition of a bubble.

Bubbles end when people stop believing that big capital gains are a sure thing. That's what happened in San Diego at the end of its last housing bubble: after a rapid rise, house prices peaked in 1990. Soon there was a glut of houses on the market, and prices began falling. By 1996, they had declined about 25 percent after adjusting for inflation.

And that's what's happening in San Diego right now, after a rise in house prices that dwarfs the boom of the 1980s. The number of single-family houses and condos on the market has doubled over the past year. "Homes that a year or two ago sold virtually overnight—in many cases triggering bidding wars—are on the market for weeks," reports the *Los Angeles Times*. The same thing is happening in other formerly hot markets.

Meanwhile, the U.S. economy has become deeply dependent on the housing bubble. The economic recovery since 2001 has been disappointing in many ways, but it wouldn't have happened at all without soaring spending on residential construction, plus a surge in consumer spending largely based on mortgage refinancing. Did I mention that the personal savings rate has fallen to zero?

Now we're starting to hear a hissing sound, as the air begins to leak out of the bubble. And everyone—not just those who own Zoned Zone real estate—should be worried.

INNOVATING OUR WAY TO FINANCIAL CRISIS

December 3, 2007

The financial crisis that began late last summer, then took a brief vacation in September and October, is back with a vengeance.

How bad is it? Well, I've never seen financial insiders this spooked—not even during the Asian crisis of 1997–1998, when economic dominoes seemed to be falling all around the world.

This time, market players seem truly horrified—because they've suddenly realized that they don't understand the complex financial system they created.

Before I get to that, however, let's talk about what's happening right now.

Credit—lending between market players—is to the financial markets what motor oil is to car engines. The ability to raise cash on short notice, which is what people mean when they talk about "liquidity," is an essential lubricant for the markets, and for the economy as a whole.

But liquidity has been drying up. Some credit markets have effectively closed up shop. Interest rates in other markets—like the London market, in which banks lend to each other—have risen even as interest rates on U.S. government debt, which is still considered safe, have plunged.

"What we are witnessing," says Bill Gross of the bond manager Pimco, "is essentially the breakdown of our modern-day banking system, a complex of leveraged lending so hard to understand that Federal Reserve Chairman Ben Bernanke required a face-to-face refresher course from hedge fund managers in mid-August."

The freezing up of the financial markets will, if it goes on much longer, lead to a severe reduction in overall lending, causing business investment to go the way of home construction—and that will mean a recession, possibly a nasty one.

Behind the disappearance of liquidity lies a collapse of trust: market players don't want to lend to each other, because they're not sure they'll be repaid.

In a direct sense, this collapse of trust has been caused by the bursting of the housing bubble. The run-up of home prices made even less sense than the dot-com bubble—I mean, there wasn't even a glamorous new technology to justify claims that old rules no longer applied—but somehow financial markets accepted crazy home prices as the new normal. And when the bubble burst, a lot of investments that were labeled AAA turned out to be junk.

Thus, "super-senior" claims against subprime mortgages—that is, investments that have first dibs on whatever mortgage payments borrowers make, and were therefore supposed to pay off in full even if a sizable fraction of these borrowers defaulted on their debts—have lost a third of their market value since July.

But what has really undermined trust is the fact that nobody knows where the financial toxic waste is buried. Citigroup wasn't supposed to have tens of billions of dollars in subprime exposure; it did. Florida's Local Government Investment Pool, which acts as a bank for the state's school districts, was supposed to be risk-free; it wasn't (and now schools don't have the money to pay teachers).

How did things get so opaque? The answer is "financial innovation"—two words that should, from now on, strike fear into investors' hearts.

O.K., to be fair, some kinds of financial innovation are good. I don't want to go back to the days when checking accounts didn't pay interest and you couldn't withdraw cash on weekends.

But the innovations of recent years—the alphabet soup of C.D.O.s and S.I.V.s, R.M.B.S., and A.B.C.P.—were sold on false pretenses. They were promoted as ways to spread risk, making investment safer. What they did instead—aside from making their creators a lot of money, which they didn't have to repay when it all went bust—was to spread confusion, luring investors into taking on more risk than they realized.

Why was this allowed to happen? At a deep level, I believe that the problem was ideological: policymakers, committed to the view that the market is always right, simply ignored the warning signs. We know, in particular, that Alan Greenspan brushed aside warnings from Edward Gramlich, who was a member of the Federal Reserve Board, about a potential subprime crisis.

And free-market orthodoxy dies hard. Just a few weeks ago Henry Paulson, the Treasury secretary, admitted to *Fortune* magazine that financial innovation got ahead of regulation—but added, "I don't think we'd want it the other way around." Is that your final answer, Mr. Secretary?

Now, Mr. Paulson's new proposal to help borrowers renegotiate their mortgage payments and avoid foreclosure sounds in principle like a good idea (although we have yet to hear any details). Realistically, however, it won't make more than a small dent in the subprime problem.

The bottom line is that policymakers left the financial industry free to innovate—and what it did was to innovate itself, and the rest of us, into a big, nasty mess.

THE MADOFF ECONOMY

December 19, 2008

T he revelation that Bernard Madoff—brilliant investor (or so almost everyone thought), philanthropist, pillar of the community—was a phony has shocked the world, and understandably so. The scale of his alleged $50 billion Ponzi scheme is hard to comprehend.

Yet surely I'm not the only person to ask the obvious question: How different, really, is Mr. Madoff's tale from the story of the investment industry as a whole?

The financial services industry has claimed an ever-growing share of the nation's income over the past generation, making the people who run the industry incredibly rich. Yet, at this point, it looks as if much of the industry has been destroying value, not creating it. And it's not just a matter of money: the vast riches achieved by those who managed other people's money have had a corrupting effect on our society as a whole.

Let's start with those paychecks. Last year, the average salary of employees in "securities, commodity contracts, and investments" was more than four times the average salary in the rest of the economy. Earning a million dollars was nothing special, and even incomes of $20 million or more were fairly common. The incomes of the richest Americans have exploded over the past generation, even as wages of ordinary workers have stagnated; high pay on Wall Street was a major cause of that divergence.

But surely those financial superstars must have been earning their millions, right? No, not necessarily. The pay system on Wall Street lavishly rewards the appearance of profit, even if that appearance later turns out to have been an illusion.

Consider the hypothetical example of a money manager who leverages up his clients' money with lots of debt, then invests the bulked-up total in high-yielding but risky assets, such as dubious mortgage-backed securities. For a while—say, as long as a housing bubble continues to inflate—he (it's almost always a he) will make big profits and receive big bonuses. Then, when the bubble bursts and his investments turn into toxic waste, his investors will lose big—but he'll keep those bonuses.

O.K., maybe my example wasn't hypothetical after all.

So, how different is what Wall Street in general did from the Madoff affair? Well, Mr. Madoff allegedly skipped a few steps, simply stealing his clients' money rather than collecting big fees while exposing investors to risks they didn't understand. And while Mr. Madoff was apparently a self-conscious fraud, many people on Wall Street believed their own hype. Still, the end result was the same (except for the house arrest): the money managers got rich; the investors saw their money disappear.

We're talking about a lot of money here. In recent years the finance sector accounted for 8 percent of America's G.D.P., up from less than 5 percent a generation earlier. If that extra 3 percent was money for nothing—and it probably was—we're talking about $400 billion a year in waste, fraud, and abuse.

But the costs of America's Ponzi era surely went beyond the direct waste of dollars and cents.

At the crudest level, Wall Street's ill-gotten gains corrupted and continue to corrupt politics, in a nicely bipartisan way. From Bush administration officials like Christopher Cox, chairman of the Securities and Exchange Commission, who looked the other way as evidence of financial fraud mounted, to Democrats who still haven't closed the outrageous tax loophole that benefits executives at hedge funds and private equity firms (hello, Senator Schumer), politicians have walked when money talked.

Meanwhile, how much has our nation's future been damaged by the magnetic pull of quick personal wealth, which for years has drawn many of our best and brightest young people into investment banking, at the expense of science, public service, and just about everything else?

Most of all, the vast riches being earned—or maybe that should be "earned"—in our bloated financial industry undermined our sense of reality and degraded our judgment.

Think of the way almost everyone important missed the warning signs of an impending crisis. How was that possible? How, for example, could Alan Greenspan have declared, just a few years ago, that "the financial system as a whole has become more resilient"—thanks to derivatives, no less? The answer, I believe, is that there's an innate tendency on the part of even the elite to idolize men who are making a lot of money, and assume that they know what they're doing.

After all, that's why so many people trusted Mr. Madoff.

Now, as we survey the wreckage and try to understand how things can have gone so wrong, so fast, the answer is actually quite simple: what we're looking at now are the consequences of a world gone Madoff.

THE IGNORAMUS STRATEGY

New York Times *Blog*

April 27, 2013

A while back Noah Smith described one common strategy for arguing against Keynesian economics, and yours truly in particular: "Relentlessly pretend to be an ignorant simpleton." Of course, as always, this strategy is most effective if you aren't pretending, and really are an ignorant simpleton.

Which brings me to this rant by Ken Langone, in which he answers my arguments by saying, "Let's stop all this crap with all of these high falutin' thoughts and ideas. You know what happens to people, their eyes glaze over, I don't know what the hell he's saying."

This may, by the way, be the first time I've ever heard anyone say "high falutin'" outside of an old Western.

Anyway, this wounds my vanity. I like to imagine that I'm pretty good at making economic arguments as simple as possible, and stating them in plain English. True, I never get to the simplicity of "People are having to tighten their belts, so the government should tighten its belt too." But that's because the world isn't that simple, and some lines sound good but are just wrong.

Now, I don't know if Langone is really as dumb as he sounds; my guess is, probably not—the attempt to sound like a regular guy, while actually sounding like an actor in a 1950s B-movie, is a giveaway. Still, maybe this is an occasion to restate what is really going on in the economy, and why I advocate the things I do.

So, in order:

1. The economy isn't like an individual family that earns a certain amount and spends some other amount, with no relationship between the two. My spending is your income and your spending is my income. If we both slash spending, both of our incomes fall.

2. We are now in a situation in which many people have cut spending, either because they chose to or because their creditors forced them to, while relatively few people are willing to spend more. The result is depressed incomes and a depressed economy, with millions of willing workers unable to find jobs.

3. Things aren't always this way, but when they are, *the government is not in competition with the private sector.* Government purchases don't use resources that would otherwise be producing private goods, they put unemployed resources to work. Government borrowing doesn't crowd out private borrowing, it puts idle funds to work. As a result, now is a time when the government should be spending more, not less. If we ignore this insight and cut government spending instead, the economy will shrink and unemployment will rise. In fact, even private spending will shrink, because of falling incomes.

4. This view of our problems has made correct predictions over the past four years, while alternative views have gotten it all wrong. Budget deficits haven't led to soaring interest rates (and the Fed's "money-printing" hasn't led to inflation); austerity policies have greatly deepened economic slumps almost everywhere they have been tried.

5. Yes, the government must pay its bills in the long run. But spending cuts and/or tax increases should wait until the economy is no longer depressed, and the private sector is willing to spend enough to produce full employment.

Is this impossibly complicated? I don't think so. Now, I suppose that someone like Langone will just respond that it's all gibberish he can't understand. But unless he really is stupid, which as I said I doubt, that's only because he doesn't want to understand.

NOBODY UNDERSTANDS DEBT

February 9, 2015

Many economists, including Janet Yellen, view global economic troubles since 2008 largely as a story about "deleveraging"—a simultaneous attempt by debtors almost everywhere to reduce their liabilities. Why is deleveraging a problem? Because my spending is your income, and your spending is my income, so if everyone slashes spending at the same time, incomes go down around the world.

Or as Ms. Yellen put it in 2009, "Precautions that may be smart for individuals and firms—and indeed essential to return the economy to a normal state—nevertheless magnify the distress of the economy as a whole."

So how much progress have we made in returning the economy to that "normal state"? None at all. You see, policy makers have been basing their actions on a false view of what debt is all about, and their attempts to reduce the problem have actually made it worse.

First, the facts: Last week, the McKinsey Global Institute issued a report titled "Debt and (Not Much) Deleveraging," which found, basically, that no nation has reduced its ratio of total debt to G.D.P. Household debt is down in some countries, especially in the United States. But it's up in others, and even where there has been significant private deleveraging, government debt has risen by more than private debt has fallen.

You might think our failure to reduce debt ratios shows that we aren't trying hard enough—that families and governments haven't been making a serious effort to tighten their belts, and that what the world needs is, yes, more austerity. But we have, in fact, had unprecedented austerity. As the International Monetary Fund has pointed out, real government spending excluding interest has fallen across wealthy nations—there have been deep cuts by the troubled debtors of southern Europe, but there have also been cuts in countries, like Germany and the United States, that can borrow at some of the lowest interest rates in history.

All this austerity has, however, only made things worse—and predictably so, because demands that everyone tighten their belts were based on a misunderstanding of the role debt plays in the economy.

You can see that misunderstanding at work every time someone rails against deficits with slogans like "Stop stealing from our kids." It sounds right, if you don't think about it: families who run up debts make themselves poorer, so isn't that true when we look at overall national debt?

No, it isn't. An indebted family owes money to other people; the world economy as a whole owes money to itself. And while it's true that countries can borrow from other countries, America has actually been borrowing less from abroad since 2008 than it did before, and Europe is a net lender to the rest of the world.

Because debt is money we owe to ourselves, it does not directly make the economy poorer (and paying it off doesn't make us richer). True, debt can pose a threat to financial stability—but the situation is not improved if efforts to reduce debt end up pushing the economy into deflation and depression.

Which brings us to current events, for there is a direct connection between the overall failure to deleverage and the emerging political crisis in Europe.

European leaders completely bought into the notion that the economic crisis was brought on by too much spending, by nations living beyond their means. The way forward, Chancellor Angela Merkel of Germany insisted, was a return to frugality. Europe, she declared, should emulate the famously thrifty Swabian housewife.

This was a prescription for slow-motion disaster. European debtors did, in fact, need to tighten their belts—but the austerity they were actually forced to impose was incredibly savage. Meanwhile, Germany and other core economies—which needed to spend more, to offset belt-tightening in the periphery—also tried to spend less. The result was to create an environment in which reducing debt ratios was impossible: real growth slowed to a crawl, inflation fell to almost nothing, and outright deflation has taken hold in the worst-hit nations.

Suffering voters put up with this policy disaster for a remarkably long time, believing in the promises of the elite that they would soon see their sacrifices rewarded. But as the pain went on and on, with no visible progress, radicalization was inevitable. Anyone surprised by the left's victory in Greece, or the surge of anti-establishment forces in Spain, hasn't been paying attention.

Nobody knows what happens next. Bookmakers are still giving better than even odds that Greece will stay in the euro. But if it doesn't, I don't believe the damage would stop there—a Greek exit is all too likely to threaten the whole currency project. And if the euro does fail, here's what should be written on its tombstone: "Died of a bad analogy."

CORRECTION: Feb. 19, 2015

Paul Krugman's column on Monday incorrectly described bookmakers' odds that Greece will exit the eurozone. The odds were worse than even, not better than even.

5

Crisis Management

THE TRIUMPH OF MACROECONOMICS

THE 2008 CRISIS BASICALLY TOOK EVERYONE BY SURPRISE. IT'S TRUE that some people, myself included, saw trouble brewing—but not on such a scale. It's also true that a few people did indeed predict a severe crisis, but by and large these were people who also predicted multiple other crises that didn't happen.

Yet while the crisis came as a shock, a significant fraction of the economics profession—not everyone, as we'll see in the next section, but quite a few people nonetheless—were intellectually prepared for the post-crisis environment. You see, we had a framework, a model, of how things work in a deeply depressed economy. This framework was initially hammered out during the Great Depression, then updated and refined during the Asian crisis of the 1990s and the long Japanese stagnation.

I explain this framework in "IS-LMentary," which is one of the wonkiest essays in this book, complete with a couple of slightly abstruse diagrams. Sorry about that, and you can skip it if you want. But I thought it was important to give some sense of the kind of logic that lay underneath what some of us were saying in the years immediately following the crisis. Even as it is, it's a stripped-down, simplified version of the story; but that, it turned out, was pretty much all you needed to make sense of the world after 2008.

For what this basic macroeconomic framework says is that everything changes when an economy is deeply depressed—specifically, when it's depressed enough by, say, the aftermath of a financial crisis, that even cutting interest rates all the way to zero isn't enough of a stimulus to restore full employment.

You see, in normal times, or at least what used to be normal times, the job of fighting recessions is mainly left in the hands of the Federal Reserve and its counterparts abroad—the European Central Bank, the Bank of England, the Bank of Japan, and so on. These "central banks" have the right and power to "print money" (not literally, but close enough) and use this newly created money to buy government bonds. This in turn gives them effective control over the interest rate on short-term lending—the overnight loans that banks make to each other, the one-month and three-month debt governments use to finance short-term operations, and so on. And central banks can usually fend off a recession by printing more money, driving those interest rates down, which in turn leads to more private borrowing and spending.

When something really bad happens, however, central banks can cut rates all the way to zero—and it's still not enough. And when that happens, as I said, all the rules change. As the first column in this section says, "virtue becomes vice, caution is risky, and prudence is folly." Budget deficits are helpful, not harmful; they don't even drive up interest rates. Doing too little is a much bigger risk than doing too much. And doing what seem like responsible things—holding government spending down in the face of big deficits, refraining from printing what looks like an awful lot of money—end up being ways to make the depression worse.

These were not propositions easy to sell to non-economists—to politicians, business leaders, and influential media figures. The economists in the incoming Obama administration understood this framework very well, as did Ben Bernanke, chairman of the Fed. And both the Obama administration and the Fed acted on this understanding, in the form of the Obama "stimulus" and the Fed's aggressive expansion of its asset holdings. But the stimulus was, almost literally, a half measure—it was obvious from the beginning that it was too small to do the job.

I laid all this out in "Stimulus Arithmetic," which concluded with a political warning:

"I see the following scenario: a weak stimulus plan, perhaps even weaker than what we're talking about now, is crafted to win those extra GOP votes. The plan limits the rise in unemployment, but things are still pretty bad, with the rate peaking at something like 9 percent and coming down only slowly. And then Mitch McConnell says 'See, government spending doesn't work.'

"Let's hope I've got this wrong."

Unfortunately, I didn't get it wrong; that's exactly what happened. And worse was to come; as we'll see, by 2010 most influential people turned their backs on the advice they were getting from people like, well, me.

But macroeconomics as a tool of analysis was very much vindicated. Events after 2008 spectacularly confirmed the predictions of the depression-economics framework. Massive budget deficits didn't drive up interest rates, money-printing on an enormous scale wasn't inflationary, and governments that tried to be prudent by cutting spending suffered much worse slumps as a result.

In other words, experience after 2008 was an intellectual triumph for macroeconomic analysis. It was, to be sure, a bittersweet triumph, because politicians, given good advice, were at first half-hearted about accepting it, then turned their backs on it entirely. But as I hope the columns in this section show, when it came to analysis, we really did get the big things right.

DEPRESSION ECONOMICS RETURNS

November 14, 2008

The economic news, in case you haven't noticed, keeps getting worse. Bad as it is, however, I don't expect another Great Depression. In fact, we probably won't see the unemployment rate match its post-Depression peak of 10.7 percent, reached in 1982 (although I wish I was sure about that).

We are already, however, well into the realm of what I call depression economics. By that I mean a state of affairs like that of the 1930s in which the usual tools of economic policy—above all, the Federal Reserve's ability to pump up the economy by cutting interest rates—have lost all traction. When depression economics prevails, the usual rules of economic policy no longer apply: virtue becomes vice, caution is risky, and prudence is folly.

To see what I'm talking about, consider the implications of the latest piece of terrible economic news: Thursday's report on new claims for unemployment insurance, which have now passed the half-million mark. Bad as this report was, viewed in isolation it might not seem catastrophic. After all, it was in the same ballpark as numbers reached during the 2001 recession and the 1990–1991 recession, both of which ended up being relatively mild by historical standards (although in each case it took a long time before the job market recovered).

But on both of these earlier occasions the standard policy response to a weak economy—a cut in the federal funds rate, the interest rate most directly affected by Fed policy—was still available. Today, it isn't: the effective federal funds rate (as opposed to the official target, which for technical reasons has become meaningless) has averaged less than 0.3 percent in recent days. Basically, there's nothing left to cut.

And with no possibility of further interest rate cuts, there's nothing to stop the economy's downward momentum. Rising unemployment will lead to further cuts in consumer spending, which Best Buy warned this week has already suffered a "seismic" decline. Weak consumer spending will lead to cutbacks in business investment plans. And the weakening economy will lead to more job cuts, provoking a further cycle of contraction.

To pull us out of this downward spiral, the federal government will have to provide economic stimulus in the form of higher spending and greater aid to those in distress—and the stimulus plan won't come soon enough or be strong enough unless politicians and economic officials are able to transcend several conventional prejudices.

One of these prejudices is the fear of red ink. In normal times, it's good to worry about the budget deficit—and fiscal responsibility is a virtue we'll need to relearn as soon as this crisis is past. When depression economics prevails, however, this virtue becomes a vice. F.D.R.'s premature attempt to balance the budget in 1937 almost destroyed the New Deal.

Another prejudice is the belief that policy should move cautiously. In normal times, this makes sense: you shouldn't make big changes in policy until it's clear they're needed. Under current conditions, however, caution is risky, because big changes for the worse are already happening, and any delay in acting raises the chance of a deeper economic disaster. The policy response should be as well-crafted as possible, but time is of the essence.

Finally, in normal times modesty and prudence in policy goals are good things. Under current conditions, however, it's much better to err on the side of doing too much than on the side of doing too little. The risk, if the stimulus plan turns out to be more than needed, is that the economy might overheat, leading to inflation—but the Federal Reserve can always head off that threat by raising interest rates. On the other hand, if the stimulus plan is too small there's nothing the Fed can do to make up for the shortfall. So when depression economics prevails, prudence is folly.

What does all this say about economic policy in the near future? The Obama administration will almost certainly take office in the face of an economy looking even worse than it does now. Indeed, Goldman Sachs predicts that the unemployment rate, currently at 6.5 percent, will reach 8.5 percent by the end of next year.

All indications are that the new administration will offer a major stimulus package. My own back-of-the-envelope calculations say that the package should be huge, on the order of $600 billion.

So the question becomes, will the Obama people dare to propose something on that scale?

Let's hope that the answer to that question is yes, that the new administration will indeed be that daring. For we're now in a situation where it would be very dangerous to give in to conventional notions of prudence.

IS-LMENTARY

New York Times *Blog*

October 9, 2011

A number of readers, both at this blog and other places, have been asking for an explanation of what IS-LM is all about. Fair enough— this blogosphere conversation has been an exchange among insiders, and probably a bit baffling to normal human beings (which is why I have been labeling my posts "wonkish").

[Update: IS-LM stands for investment-savings, liquidity-money—which will make a lot of sense if you keep reading.]

So, the first thing you need to know is that there are multiple correct ways of explaining IS-LM. That's because it's a model of several interacting markets, and you can enter from multiple directions, any one of which is a valid starting point.

My favorite of these approaches is to think of IS-LM as a way to reconcile two seemingly incompatible views about what determines interest rates. One view says that the interest rate is determined by the supply of and demand for savings—the "loanable funds" approach. The other says that the interest rate is determined by the trade-off between bonds, which pay interest, and money, which doesn't, but which you can use for transactions and therefore has special value due to its liquidity—the "liquidity preference" approach. (Yes, some money-like things pay interest, but normally not as much as less liquid assets.)

How can both views be true? Because we are at minimum talking about *two* variables, not one—G.D.P. as well as the interest rate. And the adjustment of G.D.P. is what makes both loanable funds and liquidity preference hold at the same time.

Start with the loanable funds side. Suppose that desired savings and desired investment spending are currently equal, and that something causes the interest rate to fall. Must it rise back to its original level? Not necessarily. An excess of desired investment over desired savings can lead to economic expansion, which drives up income. And since some of the rise in income will be saved—and assuming that investment demand doesn't rise by as much—a sufficiently large rise in G.D.P. can restore equality between desired savings and desired investment at the new interest rate.

That means that loanable funds doesn't determine the interest rate per se; it determines a set of possible combinations of the interest rate and G.D.P., with lower rates corresponding to higher G.D.P. And that's the IS curve.

Meanwhile, people deciding how to allocate their wealth are making trade-offs between money and bonds. There's a downward-sloping demand for money—the higher the interest rate, the more people will skimp on liquidity in favor of higher returns. Suppose temporarily that the Fed holds the money supply fixed; in that case the interest rate must be such as to match that demand to the quantity of money. And the Fed can move the interest rate by changing the money supply: increase the supply of money and the interest rate must fall to induce people to hold a larger quantity.

Here too, however, G.D.P. must be taken into account: a higher level of G.D.P. will mean more transactions, and hence higher demand for money, other things equal. So higher G.D.P. will mean that the interest rate needed to match supply and demand for money must rise. This means that like loanable funds, liquidity preference doesn't determine the interest rate per se; it defines a set of possible combinations of the interest rate and G.D.P.—the LM curve.

And that's IS-LM:

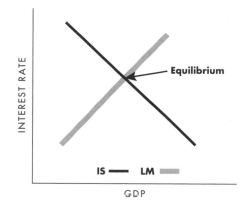

The point where the curves cross determines both G.D.P. and the interest rate, and at that point both loanable funds and liquidity preference are valid.

What use is this framework? First of all, it helps you avoid fallacies like the notion that because savings must equal investment, government spending cannot lead to a rise in total spending—which right away puts us above the level of argument that famous Chicago professors somehow find convincing. And it also gets you past confusions like the notion that government deficits, by driving up interest rates, can actually cause the economy to contract.

Most spectacularly, IS-LM turns out to be very useful for thinking about extreme conditions like the present, in which private demand has fallen so far that the economy remains depressed even at a zero interest rate. In that case the picture looks like this:

Why is the LM curve flat at zero? Because if the interest rate fell below

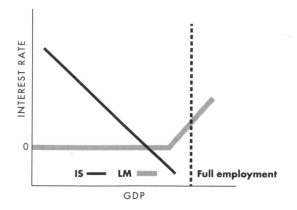

zero, people would just hold cash instead of bonds. At the margin, then, money is just being held as a store of value, and changes in the money supply have no effect. This is, of course, the liquidity trap.

And IS-LM makes some predictions about what happens in the liquidity trap. Budget deficits shift IS to the right; in the liquidity trap that has no effect on the interest rate. Increases in the money supply do nothing at all.

That's why in early 2009, when *The Wall Street Journal*, the Austrians, and the other usual suspects were screaming about soaring rates and runaway inflation, those who understood IS-LM were predicting that interest rates would stay low and that even a tripling of the monetary base would not be inflationary. Events since then have, as I see it, been a huge vindication for the IS-LM types—despite some headline inflation driven by commodity prices—and a huge failure for the soaring-rates-and-inflation crowd.

Yes, IS-LM simplifies things a lot, and can't be taken as the final word. But it has done what good economic models are supposed to do: make sense of what we see, and make highly useful predictions about what would happen in unusual circumstances. Economists who understand IS-LM have done vastly better in tracking our current crisis than people who don't.

STIMULUS ARITHMETIC (WONKISH BUT IMPORTANT)

New York Times *Blog*

January 6, 2009

Bit by bit we're getting information on the Obama stimulus plan, enough to start making back-of-the-envelope estimates of impact. The bottom line is this: we're probably looking at a plan that will shave less than 2 percentage points off the average unemployment rate for the next two years, and possibly quite a lot less. This raises real concerns about whether the incoming administration is lowballing its plans in an attempt to get bipartisan consensus.

In the extended entry, a look at my calculations.

The starting point for this discussion is Okun's Law, the relationship between changes in real G.D.P. and changes in the unemployment rate. Estimates of the Okun's Law coefficient range from 2 to 3. I'll use 2, which is an optimistic estimate for current purposes: it says that you have to raise real G.D.P. by 2 percent from what it would otherwise have been to reduce the unemployment rate 1 percentage point from what it would otherwise have been. Since G.D.P. is roughly $15 trillion, this means that you have to raise G.D.P. by $300 billion per year to reduce unemployment by 1 percentage point.

Now, what we're hearing about the Obama plan is that it calls for $775 billion over two years, with $300 billion in tax cuts and the rest in spending. Call that $150 billion per year in tax cuts, $240 billion each year in spending.

How much do tax cuts and spending raise G.D.P.? The widely cited estimates of Mark Zandi of economy.com indicate a multiplier of around 1.5 for spending, with widely varying estimates for tax cuts. Payroll tax cuts, which make up about half the Obama proposal, are pretty good, with a multiplier of 1.29; business tax cuts, which make up the rest, are much less effective.

In particular, letting businesses get refunds on past taxes based on current losses, which is reportedly a key feature of the plan, looks an awful lot like a lump-sum transfer with no incentive effects.

Let's be generous and assume that the overall multiplier on tax cuts is 1. Then the per-year effect of the plan on G.D.P. is $150 \times 1 + 240 \times 1.5 = \$510$ billion. Since it takes \$300 billion to reduce the unemployment rate by 1 percentage point, this is shaving 1.7 points off what unemployment would otherwise have been.

Finally, compare this with the economic outlook. "Full employment" clearly means an unemployment rate near 5—the CBO says 5.2 for the NAIRU [non-accelerating-inflation rate of unemployment], which seems high to me. Unemployment is currently about 7 percent, and heading much higher; Obama himself says that absent stimulus it could go into double digits. Suppose that we're looking at an economy that, absent stimulus, would have an average unemployment rate of 9 percent over the next two years; this plan would cut that to 7.3 percent, which would be a help but could easily be spun by critics as a failure.

And that gets us to politics. This really does look like a plan that falls well short of what advocates of strong stimulus were hoping for—and it seems as if that was done in order to win Republican votes. Yet even if the plan gets the hoped-for eighty votes in the Senate, which seems doubtful, responsibility for the plan's perceived failure, if it's spun that way, will be placed on Democrats.

I see the following scenario: a weak stimulus plan, perhaps even weaker than what we're talking about now, is crafted to win those extra G.O.P. votes. The plan limits the rise in unemployment, but things are still pretty bad, with the rate peaking at something like 9 percent and coming down only slowly. And then Mitch McConnell says "See, government spending doesn't work."

Let's hope I've got this wrong.

THE OBAMA GAP

January 8, 2009

"I don't believe it's too late to change course, but it will be if we don't take dramatic action as soon as possible. If nothing is done, this recession could linger for years."

So declared President-elect Barack Obama on Thursday, explaining why the nation needs an extremely aggressive government response to the economic downturn. He's right. This is the most dangerous economic crisis since the Great Depression, and it could all too easily turn into a prolonged slump.

But Mr. Obama's prescription doesn't live up to his diagnosis. The economic plan he's offering isn't as strong as his language about the economic threat. In fact, it falls well short of what's needed.

Bear in mind just how big the U.S. economy is. Given sufficient demand for its output, America would produce more than $30 trillion worth of goods and services over the next two years. But with both consumer spending and business investment plunging, a huge gap is opening up between what the American economy can produce and what it's able to sell.

And the Obama plan is nowhere near big enough to fill this "output gap."

Earlier this week, the Congressional Budget Office came out with its latest analysis of the budget and economic outlook. The budget office says that in the absence of a stimulus plan, the unemployment rate would rise above 9 percent by early 2010, and stay high for years to come.

Grim as this projection is, by the way, it's actually optimistic compared with some independent forecasts. Mr. Obama himself has been saying that without a stimulus plan, the unemployment rate could go into double digits.

Even the CBO says, however, that "economic output over the next two years will average 6.8 percent below its potential." This translates into $2.1 trillion of lost production. "Our economy could fall $1 trillion short of its full capacity," declared Mr. Obama on Thursday. Well, he was actually understating things.

To close a gap of more than $2 trillion—possibly a lot more, if the budget office projections turn out to be too optimistic—Mr. Obama offers a $775 billion plan. And that's not enough.

Now, fiscal stimulus can sometimes have a "multiplier" effect: in addition to the direct effects of, say, investment in infrastructure on demand, there can be a further indirect effect as higher incomes lead to higher consumer spending. Standard estimates suggest that a dollar of public spending raises G.D.P. by around $1.50.

But only about 60 percent of the Obama plan consists of public spending. The rest consists of tax cuts—and many economists are skeptical about how much these tax cuts, especially the tax breaks for business, will actually do to boost spending. (A number of Senate Democrats apparently share these doubts.) Howard Gleckman of the nonpartisan Tax Policy Center summed it up in the title of a recent blog posting: "Lots of buck, not much bang."

The bottom line is that the Obama plan is unlikely to close more than half of the looming output gap, and could easily end up doing less than a third of the job.

Why isn't Mr. Obama trying to do more?

Is the plan being limited by fear of debt? There are dangers associated with large-scale government borrowing—and this week's CBO report projected a $1.2 trillion deficit for this year. But it would be even more dangerous to fall short in rescuing the economy. The president-elect spoke eloquently and accurately on Thursday about the consequences of failing to act—there's a real risk that we'll slide into a prolonged, Japanese-style deflationary trap—but the consequences of failing to act adequately aren't much better.

Is the plan being limited by a lack of spending opportunities? There are only a limited number of "shovel-ready" public investment projects—that is, projects that can be started quickly enough to help the economy in the near term. But there are other forms of public spending, especially on health care, that could do good while aiding the economy in its hour of need.

Or is the plan being limited by political caution? Press reports last month indicated that Obama aides were anxious to keep the final price tag on the plan below the politically sensitive trillion-dollar mark. There also have been suggestions that the plan's inclusion of large business tax cuts, which add to its cost but will do little for the economy, is an attempt to win Republican votes in Congress.

Whatever the explanation, the Obama plan just doesn't look adequate to the economy's need. To be sure, a third of a loaf is better than none. But right now we seem to be facing two major economic gaps: the gap between the economy's potential and its likely performance, and the gap between Mr. Obama's stern economic rhetoric and his somewhat disappointing economic plan.

THE STIMULUS TRAGEDY

February 20, 2014

Five years have passed since President Obama signed the American Recovery and Reinvestment Act—the "stimulus"—into law. With the passage of time, it has become clear that the act did a vast amount of good. It helped end the economy's plunge; it created or saved millions of jobs; it left behind an important legacy of public and private investment.

It was also a political disaster. And the consequences of that political disaster—the perception that stimulus failed—have haunted economic policy ever since.

Let's start with the good the stimulus did.

The case for stimulus was that we were suffering from a huge shortfall in overall spending, and that the hit to the economy from the financial crisis and the bursting of the housing bubble was so severe that the Federal Reserve, which normally fights recessions by cutting short-term interest rates, couldn't overcome this slump on its own. The idea, then, was to provide a temporary boost both by having the government directly spend more and by using tax cuts and public aid to boost family incomes, inducing more private spending.

Opponents of stimulus argued vociferously that deficit spending would send interest rates skyrocketing, "crowding out" private spending. Proponents responded, however, that crowding out—a real issue when the economy is near full employment—wouldn't happen in a deeply depressed economy, awash in excess capacity and excess savings. And stimulus supporters were right: far from soaring, interest rates fell to historic lows.

What about positive evidence for the benefits of stimulus? That's trickier, because it's hard to disentangle the effects of the Recovery Act from all the other things that were going on at the time. Nonetheless, most careful studies have found evidence of strong positive effects on employment and output.

Even more important, I'd argue, is the huge natural experiment Europe has provided on the effects of sharp changes in government spending. You see, some but not all members of the euro area, the group of countries sharing Europe's common currency, were forced into imposing draconian fiscal austerity, that is, negative stimulus. If stimulus opponents had been right about the way the world works, these austerity programs wouldn't have had severe adverse economic effects, because cuts in government spending would have been offset by rising private spending. In fact, austerity led to nasty, in some cases catastrophic, declines in output and employment. And private spending in countries imposing harsh austerity ended up falling instead of rising, amplifying the direct effects of government cutbacks.

All the evidence, then, points to substantial positive short-run effects from the Obama stimulus. And there were surely long-term benefits, too: big investments in everything from green energy to electronic medical records.

So why does everyone—or, to be more accurate, everyone except those who have seriously studied the issue—believe that the stimulus was a failure? Because the U.S. economy continued to perform poorly—not disastrously, but poorly—after the stimulus went into effect.

There's no mystery about why: America was coping with the legacy of a giant housing bubble. Even now, housing has only partly recovered, while consumers are still held back by the huge debts they ran up during the bubble years. And the stimulus was both too small and too short-lived to overcome that dire legacy.

This is not, by the way, a case of making excuses after the fact. Regular readers know that I was more or less tearing my hair out in early 2009, warning that the Recovery Act was inadequate—and that by falling short, the act would end up discrediting the very idea of stimulus. And so it proved.

There's a long-running debate over whether the Obama administration could have gotten more. The administration compounded the damage with excessively optimistic forecasts, based on the false premise that the economy would quickly bounce back once confidence in the financial system was restored.

But that's all water under the bridge. The important point is that U.S. fiscal policy went completely in the wrong direction after 2010. With the stimulus perceived as a failure, job creation almost disappeared from inside-the-Beltway discourse, replaced with obsessive concern over budget deficits. Government spending, which had been temporarily boosted both by the Recovery Act and by safety-net programs like food stamps and unemployment benefits, began falling, with public investment hit worst. And this anti-stimulus has destroyed millions of jobs.

In other words, the overall narrative of the stimulus is tragic. A policy initiative that was good but not good enough ended up being seen as a failure, and set the stage for an immensely destructive wrong turn.

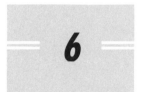

The Crisis in Economics

THE COST OF BAD IDEAS

THERE ARE MANY JOKES ABOUT THE INABILITY OF ECONOMISTS TO agree on anything. Most of those jokes are unfair—if anything, my sense is that herd behavior, accepting ideas that are considered sensible because everyone else accepts them, is usually a bigger problem than discord. But it is true that macroeconomics, the subfield that studies recession, recoveries, inflation, and other economywide events, is a sharply divided field.

As I explained in the essay that began the last section, one brand of macroeconomics—the brand that ultimately descends from the writings of John Maynard Keynes in the 1930s—actually had a very good run in the years that followed the global financial crisis. But there was another brand, with very different ideas; and the discord between these schools of thought became very noisy and, I'd argue, destructive within a few months after the fall of Lehman Brothers.

Within the profession, these schools are often referred to as "saltwater" and "freshwater," because it so happens that the more or less Keynesian economists tend to be at coastal U.S. universities while the anti-Keynesians are inland. The article "How Did Economists Get It So Wrong?" goes through the divergence between these schools at some length. So let me just say a few words here.

The story here begins with the Great Depression, a cataclysmic economic event that had many intellectuals declaring capitalism a failed system. But some economists, led by John Maynard Keynes, argued that the failure had much shallower causes than, say, Marxists insisted—that they were fairly narrow and had what amounted to technocratic solutions. "We have magneto [alternator] trouble," he insisted, not a defunct engine.

He also declared that his analysis was "moderately conservative" in its implications. Slumps could be fought with appropriate government policies: low interest rates for relatively mild recessions, deficit spending for deeper downturns. And given these policies, much of the rest of the economy could be left up to markets. Indeed, this position—call it free-market Keynesianism—became more or less the standard view of U.S. economists, especially after the publication of Paul Samuelson's groundbreaking textbook in 1948.

Conservatives, however, weren't happy with this formulation. They viewed Keynesian economics as the thin end of the wedge: Once you accepted a government role in fighting recessions, you might adopt a more expansive view of government in general. During the forties and fifties they fought a rear-guard action, trying to prevent the teaching of Keynesian economics in universities.

Eventually, however, they found a more sophisticated champion. Milton Friedman accepted the Keynesian view that the Great Depression was a problem of inadequate demand. He argued, however, that it could have been prevented with an even narrower, more technocratic policy than Keynes recommended: if the Federal Reserve, which controls the nation's money supply, would simply commit itself to keeping that money supply growing at a slow, steady rate, major slumps wouldn't happen.

Friedman also argued that while policy could prevent episodes of very high unemployment, it couldn't keep unemployment persistently low—that this would lead to accelerating inflation. The stagflation of the 1970s was widely seen as vindication of his claim.

But even this wasn't enough for free-market economists. They argued—correctly, on logical grounds—that if people were perfectly rational, even Friedmanite economics wouldn't work: changes in the money supply should have no effect on employment even in the short run, and in particular that attempts to reduce inflation should not, as even Friedman asserted, require a temporary rise in the unemployment rate.

Awkwardly, however, the facts refused to cooperate with this analysis. As I point out in "That Eighties Show," the big disinflation of the early 1980s in fact brought along with it a very severe recession—the worst since the 1930s, not matched until the 2008 crisis.

And then a funny thing happened. Half the macroeconomics profession—the saltwater half—took this as evidence that while Keynes needed updating, there was still a lot of useful insight there. The other half said, in effect, if the facts don't fit our theory, we need to reinterpret the facts, engaging in whatever intellectual contortions it takes to preserve the free-market faith.

Do such intellectual disputes matter? Freshwater economics has had remarkably little direct policy influence. As I explain in "Bad Faith, Pathos, and G.O.P. Economics," political conservatives prefer to get their advice from outright hacks rather than real researchers of any stripe. But the fresh-water side did muddle the message. At a time when policymakers needed clarity about what needed to be done, what they heard was cacophony.

Oh, and there's one final article here about so-called Modern Monetary Theory. This is an odd doctrine, which is mostly just a special case of IS-LM (described in the previous section), with a few new confusions. But its pro-ponents don't know that; they think they've come up with profound, radical insights. And a few progressive politicians have been half-convinced; I try to unconvince them.

THE MYTHICAL SEVENTIES

New York Times *Blog*

May 19, 2013

Matt O'Brien is probably right to suggest that Michael Kinsley's problems—and those of quite a few other people, some of whom have real influence on policy—is that they're still living in the 1970s. I do, however, resent that thing about 60-year-old men . . .

But it's actually even worse than Matt says. For the 1970s such people remember as a cautionary tale bears little resemblance to the 1970s that actually happened.

In elite mythology, the origins of the crisis of the seventies, like the supposed origins of our current crisis, lay in excess: too much debt, too much coddling of those slovenly proles via a strong welfare state. The suffering of 1979–1982 was necessary payback.

None of that is remotely true.

There was no deficit problem: government debt was low and stable or falling as a share of G.D.P. during the seventies. Rising welfare rolls may have been a big political problem, but a runaway welfare state more broadly just wasn't an issue—hey, these days right-wingers complaining about a nation of takers tend to use the low-dependency seventies as a baseline.

What we did have was a wage-price spiral: workers demanding large wage increases (those were the days when workers actually could make demands) because they expected lots of inflation, firms raising prices because of rising costs, all exacerbated by big oil shocks. It was mainly a case of self-fulfilling expectations, and the problem was to break the cycle.

So why did we need a terrible recession? Not to pay for our past sins, but simply as a way to cool the action. Someone—I'm pretty sure it was

Martin Baily—described the inflation problem as being like what happens when everyone at a football game stands up to see the action better, and the result is that everyone is uncomfortable but nobody actually gets a better view. And the recession was, in effect, stopping the game until everyone was seated again.

The difference, of course, was that this timeout destroyed millions of jobs and wasted trillions of dollars.

Was there a better way? Ideally, we should have been able to get all the relevant parties in a room and say, look, this inflation has to stop; you workers, reduce your wage demands, you businesses, cancel your price increases, and for our part, we agree to stop printing money so the whole thing is over. That way, you'd get price stability without the recession. And in some small, cohesive countries that is more or less what happened. (Check out the Israeli stabilization of 1985.)

But America wasn't like that, and the decision was made to do it the hard, brutal way. This was not a policy triumph! It was, in a way, a confession of despair.

It worked on the inflation front, although some of the other myths about all that are just as false as the myths about the 1970s. No, America didn't return to vigorous productivity growth—that didn't happen until the mid 1990s. Sixty-year-old men should remember that a decade after the Volcker disinflation we were still very much in a national funk; remember the old joke that the Cold War was over, and Japan won?

So it would be bad enough if we were basing policy today on lessons from the seventies. It's even worse that we're basing policy today on a mythical seventies that never was.

THAT EIGHTIES SHOW

New York Times *Blog*

May 19, 2014

I've been giving various talks and fireside chats here in Oxford, and one thing I keep coming back to is the pivotal role of the 1980s in the development of economic thought.

This isn't what you usually hear—the seventies have taken on mythical status, and are constantly invoked by inflation worriers, while the eighties get mentioned, if at all, as somehow proving the truth of supply-side economics. But what really happened in the early eighties was a decisive refutation of Lucasian macroeconomics—albeit a refutation met in many places with denial.

For those wondering what I'm talking about: in the 1970s rational-expectations macroeconomists, led above all by Chicago's Robert Lucas, made an extremely influential case against any kind of activist policy. The key proposition in that case was an assertion, based on Lucas-type models, that only unanticipated changes in monetary policy had real effects. As soon as people understood that, say, the central bank had targeted a lower rate of inflation, prices and wages would adjust, without the need for sustained high unemployment.

What actually happened in the eighties, however, was that central banks—most famously the Fed, but also the Thatcherite Bank of England and others—drastically tightened monetary policy to bring inflation down. And inflation did indeed come down—eventually. But along the way there were deep recessions and soaring unemployment, which went on much longer than you could justify with any plausible story about the monetary shock being unanticipated.

This was very much a vindication of more or less Keynesian views about the economy, and the eighties were in fact marked by the New Keynesian comeback. But many economists had already dug themselves in too deep, denouncing Keynesian economics as nonsense, declaring it dead. Unable to backtrack, they went even deeper, insisting despite all appearances that monetary policy had no real effects whatsoever, that it was all technological shocks.

But leaving that half of the macroeconomics profession aside, for the rest of us the eighties were just as important as the seventies in setting attitudes toward policy. If you like, the seventies showed the limits of policy, but the eighties showed that there were limits to those limits—that monetary policy (and fiscal policy, under some conditions) remained powerful as a tool to stabilize the economy. And that insight has stood the test of time.

HOW DID ECONOMISTS GET IT SO WRONG?

New York Times *Magazine*

September 2, 2009

I. MISTAKING BEAUTY FOR TRUTH

It's hard to believe now, but not long ago economists were congratulating themselves over the success of their field. Those successes—or so they believed—were both theoretical and practical, leading to a golden era for the profession. On the theoretical side, they thought that they had resolved their internal disputes. Thus, in a 2008 paper titled "The State of Macro" (that is, macroeconomics, the study of big-picture issues like recessions), Olivier Blanchard of M.I.T., now the chief economist at the International Monetary Fund, declared that "the state of macro is good." The battles of yesteryear, he said, were over, and there had been a "broad convergence of vision." And in the real world, economists believed they had things under control: the "central problem of depression-prevention has been solved," declared Robert Lucas of the University of Chicago in his 2003 presidential address to the American Economic Association. In 2004, Ben Bernanke, a former Princeton professor who is now the chairman of the Federal Reserve Board, celebrated the Great Moderation in economic performance over the previous two decades, which he attributed in part to improved economic policymaking.

Last year, everything came apart.

Few economists saw our current crisis coming, but this predictive failure was the least of the field's problems. More important was the profession's blindness to the very possibility of catastrophic failures in a market economy. During the golden years, financial economists came to believe that markets were inherently stable—indeed, that stocks and other assets were always priced just right. There was nothing in the prevailing models suggesting the possibility of the kind of collapse that happened last year. Meanwhile, macroeconomists were divided in their views. But the main division was between those who insisted that free-market economies never go astray and those who believed that economies may stray now and then but that any major deviations from the path of prosperity could and would be corrected by the all-powerful Fed. Neither side was prepared to cope with an economy that went off the rails despite the Fed's best efforts.

And in the wake of the crisis, the fault lines in the economics profession have yawned wider than ever. Lucas says the Obama administration's stimulus plans are "schlock economics," and his Chicago colleague John Cochrane says they're based on discredited "fairy tales." In response, Brad DeLong of the University of California, Berkeley, writes of the "intellectual collapse" of the Chicago School, and I myself have written that comments from Chicago economists are the product of a Dark Age of macroeconomics in which hard-won knowledge has been forgotten.

What happened to the economics profession? And where does it go from here?

As I see it, the economics profession went astray because economists, as a group, mistook beauty, clad in impressive-looking mathematics, for truth. Until the Great Depression, most economists clung to a vision of capitalism as a perfect or nearly perfect system. That vision wasn't sustainable in the face of mass unemployment, but as memories of the Depression faded, economists fell back in love with the old, idealized vision of an economy in which rational individuals interact in perfect markets, this time gussied up with fancy equations. The renewed romance with the idealized market was, to be sure, partly a response to shifting political winds, partly a response to financial incentives. But while sabbaticals at the Hoover Institution and job opportunities on Wall Street are nothing to sneeze at, the central cause of the profession's failure was the desire for an all-encompassing, intellectually elegant approach that also gave economists a chance to show off their mathematical prowess.

Unfortunately, this romanticized and sanitized vision of the economy led most economists to ignore all the things that can go wrong. They turned a blind eye to the limitations of human rationality that often lead to bubbles and busts; to the problems of institutions that run amok; to the imperfections of markets—especially financial markets—that can cause the economy's operating system to undergo sudden, unpredictable crashes; and to the dangers created when regulators don't believe in regulation.

It's much harder to say where the economics profession goes from here. But what's almost certain is that economists will have to learn to live with messiness. That is, they will have to acknowledge the importance of irrational and often unpredictable behavior, face up to the often idiosyncratic imperfections of markets, and accept that an elegant economic "theory of everything" is a long way off. In practical terms, this will translate into more cautious policy advice—and a reduced willingness to dismantle economic safeguards in the faith that markets will solve all problems.

II. FROM SMITH TO KEYNES AND BACK

The birth of economics as a discipline is usually credited to Adam Smith, who published *The Wealth of Nations* in 1776. Over the next 160 years an extensive body of economic theory was developed, whose central message was: Trust the market. Yes, economists admitted that there were cases in which markets might fail, of which the most important was the case of "externalities"—costs that people impose on others without paying the price, like traffic congestion or pollution. But the basic presumption of "neoclassical" economics (named after the late-19th-century theorists who elaborated on the concepts of their "classical" predecessors) was that we should have faith in the market system.

This faith was, however, shattered by the Great Depression. Actually, even in the face of total collapse some economists insisted that whatever happens in a market economy must be right: "Depressions are not simply evils," declared Joseph Schumpeter in 1934—1934! They are, he added, "forms of something which has to be done." But many, and eventually most, economists turned to the insights of John Maynard Keynes for both an explanation of what had happened and a solution to future depressions.

Keynes did not, despite what you may have heard, want the government to run the economy. He described his analysis in his 1936 masterwork, *The*

General Theory of Employment, Interest and Money, as "moderately conservative in its implications." He wanted to fix capitalism, not replace it. But he did challenge the notion that free-market economies can function without a minder, expressing particular contempt for financial markets, which he viewed as being dominated by short-term speculation with little regard for fundamentals. And he called for active government intervention—printing more money and, if necessary, spending heavily on public works—to fight unemployment during slumps.

It's important to understand that Keynes did much more than make bold assertions. *The General Theory* is a work of profound, deep analysis— analysis that persuaded the best young economists of the day. Yet the story of economics over the past half century is, to a large degree, the story of a retreat from Keynesianism and a return to neoclassicism. The neoclassical revival was initially led by Milton Friedman of the University of Chicago, who asserted as early as 1953 that neoclassical economics works well enough as a description of the way the economy actually functions to be "both extremely fruitful and deserving of much confidence." But what about depressions?

Friedman's counterattack against Keynes began with the doctrine known as monetarism. Monetarists didn't disagree in principle with the idea that a market economy needs deliberate stabilization. "We are all Keynesians now," Friedman once said, although he later claimed he was quoted out of context. Monetarists asserted, however, that a very limited, circumscribed form of government intervention—namely, instructing central banks to keep the nation's money supply, the sum of cash in circulation and bank deposits, growing on a steady path—is all that's required to prevent depressions. Famously, Friedman and his collaborator, Anna Schwartz, argued that if the Federal Reserve had done its job properly, the Great Depression would not have happened. Later, Friedman made a compelling case against any deliberate effort by government to push unemployment below its "natural" level (currently thought to be about 4.8 percent in the United States): excessively expansionary policies, he predicted, would lead to a combination of inflation and high unemployment—a prediction that was borne out by the stagflation of the 1970s, which greatly advanced the credibility of the anti-Keynesian movement.

Eventually, however, the anti-Keynesian counterrevolution went far beyond Friedman's position, which came to seem relatively moderate compared with what his successors were saying. Among financial economists, Keynes's disparaging vision of financial markets as a "casino" was replaced by "efficient market" theory, which asserted that financial markets always get asset prices right given the available information. Meanwhile, many macroeconomists completely rejected Keynes's framework for understanding economic slumps. Some returned to the view of Schumpeter and other apologists for the Great Depression, viewing recessions as a good thing, part of the economy's adjustment to change. And even those not willing to go that far argued that any attempt to fight an economic slump would do more harm than good.

Not all macroeconomists were willing to go down this road: many became self-described New Keynesians, who continued to believe in an active role for the government. Yet even they mostly accepted the notion that investors and consumers are rational and that markets generally get it right.

Of course, there were exceptions to these trends: a few economists challenged the assumption of rational behavior, questioned the belief that financial markets can be trusted, and pointed to the long history of financial crises that had devastating economic consequences. But they were swimming against the tide, unable to make much headway against a pervasive and, in retrospect, foolish complacency.

III. PANGLOSSIAN FINANCE

In the 1930s, financial markets, for obvious reasons, didn't get much respect. Keynes compared them to "those newspaper competitions in which the competitors have to pick out the six prettiest faces from a hundred photographs, the prize being awarded to the competitor whose choice most nearly corresponds to the average preferences of the competitors as a whole; so that each competitor has to pick, not those faces which he himself finds prettiest, but those that he thinks likeliest to catch the fancy of the other competitors."

And Keynes considered it a very bad idea to let such markets, in which speculators spent their time chasing one another's tails, dictate important business decisions: "When the capital development of a country becomes a by-product of the activities of a casino, the job is likely to be ill-done."

By 1970 or so, however, the study of financial markets seemed to have been taken over by Voltaire's Dr. Pangloss, who insisted that we live in the best of all possible worlds. Discussion of investor irrationality, of bubbles, of destructive speculation had virtually disappeared from academic discourse. The field was dominated by the "efficient-market hypothesis," promulgated by Eugene Fama of the University of Chicago, which claims that financial markets price assets precisely at their intrinsic worth given all publicly available information. (The price of a company's stock, for example, always accurately reflects the company's value given the information available on the company's earnings, its business prospects, and so on.) And by the 1980s, finance economists, notably Michael Jensen of the Harvard Business School, were arguing that because financial markets always get prices right, the best thing corporate chieftains can do, not just for themselves but for the sake of the economy, is to maximize their stock prices. In other words, finance economists believed that we should put the capital development of the nation in the hands of what Keynes had called a "casino."

It's hard to argue that this transformation in the profession was driven by events. True, the memory of 1929 was gradually receding, but there continued to be bull markets, with widespread tales of speculative excess, followed by bear markets. In 1973–1974, for example, stocks lost 48 percent of their value. And the 1987 stock crash, in which the Dow plunged nearly 23 percent in a day for no clear reason, should have raised at least a few doubts about market rationality.

These events, however, which Keynes would have considered evidence of the unreliability of markets, did little to blunt the force of a beautiful idea. The theoretical model that finance economists developed by assuming that every investor rationally balances risk against reward—the so-called Capital Asset Pricing Model, or CAPM (pronounced cap-em)—is wonderfully elegant. And if you accept its premises it's also extremely useful. CAPM not only tells you how to choose your portfolio—even more important from the financial industry's point of view, it tells you how to put a price on financial derivatives, claims on claims. The elegance and apparent usefulness of the new theory led to a string of Nobel prizes for its creators, and many of the theory's adepts also received more mundane rewards: armed with their new models and formidable math skills—the more arcane uses of CAPM

require physicist-level computations—mild-mannered business-school professors could and did become Wall Street rocket scientists, earning Wall
Street paychecks.

To be fair, finance theorists didn't accept the efficient-market hypothesis
merely because it was elegant, convenient, and lucrative. They also produced
a great deal of statistical evidence, which at first seemed strongly support-
ive. But this evidence was of an oddly limited form. Finance economists
rarely asked the seemingly obvious (though not easily answered) question
of whether asset prices made sense given real-world fundamentals like earnings. Instead, they asked only whether asset prices made sense given other
asset prices. Larry Summers, now the top economic adviser in the Obama
administration, once mocked finance professors with a parable about
"ketchup economists" who "have shown that two-quart bottles of ketchup
invariably sell for exactly twice as much as one-quart bottles of ketchup," and
conclude from this that the ketchup market is perfectly efficient.

But neither this mockery nor more polite critiques from economists like
Robert Shiller of Yale had much effect. Finance theorists continued to believe
that their models were essentially right, and so did many people making
real-world decisions. Not least among these was Alan Greenspan, who was
then the Fed chairman and a long-time supporter of financial deregulation
whose rejection of calls to rein in subprime lending or address the ever-
inflating housing bubble rested in large part on the belief that modern financial economics had everything under control. There was a telling moment in
2005, at a conference held to honor Greenspan's tenure at the Fed. One brave
attendee, Raghuram Rajan (of the University of Chicago, surprisingly), presented a paper warning that the financial system was taking on potentially
dangerous levels of risk. He was mocked by almost all present—including,
by the way, Larry Summers, who dismissed his warnings as "misguided."

By October of last year, however, Greenspan was admitting that he was
in a state of "shocked disbelief," because "the whole intellectual edifice"
had "collapsed." Since this collapse of the intellectual edifice was also a collapse of real-world markets, the result was a severe recession—the worst, by
many measures, since the Great Depression. What should policymakers do?
Unfortunately, macroeconomics, which should have been providing clear

guidance about how to address the slumping economy, was in its own state of disarray.

IV. THE TROUBLE WITH MACRO

"We have involved ourselves in a colossal muddle, having blundered in the control of a delicate machine, the working of which we do not understand. The result is that our possibilities of wealth may run to waste for a time—perhaps for a long time." So wrote John Maynard Keynes in an essay titled "The Great Slump of 1930," in which he tried to explain the catastrophe then overtaking the world. And the world's possibilities of wealth did indeed run to waste for a long time; it took World War II to bring the Great Depression to a definitive end.

Why was Keynes's diagnosis of the Great Depression as a "colossal muddle" so compelling at first? And why did economics, circa 1975, divide into opposing camps over the value of Keynes's views?

I like to explain the essence of Keynesian economics with a true story that also serves as a parable, a small-scale version of the messes that can afflict entire economies. Consider the travails of the Capitol Hill Baby-Sitting Co-op.

This co-op, whose problems were recounted in a 1977 article in *The Journal of Money, Credit and Banking*, was an association of about 150 young couples who agreed to help one another by baby-sitting for one another's children when parents wanted a night out. To ensure that every couple did its fair share of baby-sitting, the co-op introduced a form of scrip: coupons made out of heavy pieces of paper, each entitling the bearer to one half-hour of sitting time. Initially, members received twenty coupons on joining and were required to return the same amount on departing the group.

Unfortunately, it turned out that the co-op's members, on average, wanted to hold a reserve of more than twenty coupons, perhaps in case they should want to go out several times in a row. As a result, relatively few people wanted to spend their scrip and go out, while many wanted to baby-sit so they could add to their hoard. But since baby-sitting opportunities arise only when someone goes out for the night, this meant that baby-sitting jobs were hard to find, which made members of the co-op even more reluctant to go out, making baby-sitting jobs even scarcer . . .

In short, the co-op fell into a recession.

O.K., what do you think of this story? Don't dismiss it as silly and trivial: economists have used small-scale examples to shed light on big questions ever since Adam Smith saw the roots of economic progress in a pin factory, and they're right to do so. The question is whether this particular example, in which a recession is a problem of inadequate demand—there isn't enough demand for baby-sitting to provide jobs for everyone who wants one—gets at the essence of what happens in a recession.

Forty years ago most economists would have agreed with this interpretation. But since then macroeconomics has divided into two great factions: "saltwater" economists (mainly in coastal U.S. universities), who have a more or less Keynesian vision of what recessions are all about; and "freshwater" economists (mainly at inland schools), who consider that vision nonsense.

Freshwater economists are, essentially, neoclassical purists. They believe that all worthwhile economic analysis starts from the premise that people are rational and markets work, a premise violated by the story of the baby-sitting co-op. As they see it, a general lack of sufficient demand isn't possible, because prices always move to match supply with demand. If people want more baby-sitting coupons, the value of those coupons will rise, so that they're worth, say, forty minutes of baby-sitting rather than half an hour—or, equivalently, the cost of an hour's baby-sitting would fall from two coupons to 1.5. And that would solve the problem: the purchasing power of the coupons in circulation would have risen, so that people would feel no need to hoard more, and there would be no recession.

But don't recessions look like periods in which there just isn't enough demand to employ everyone willing to work? Appearances can be deceiving, say the freshwater theorists. Sound economics, in their view, says that overall failures of demand can't happen—and that means that they don't. Keynesian economics has been "proved false," Cochrane, of the University of Chicago, says.

Yet recessions do happen. Why? In the 1970s the leading freshwater macroeconomist, the Nobel laureate Robert Lucas, argued that recessions were caused by temporary confusion: workers and companies had trouble distinguishing overall changes in the level of prices because of inflation or deflation from changes in their own particular business situation. And Lucas warned that any attempt to fight the business cycle would be counterproductive: activist policies, he argued, would just add to the confusion.

By the 1980s, however, even this severely limited acceptance of the idea that recessions are bad things had been rejected by many freshwater economists. Instead, the new leaders of the movement, especially Edward Prescott, who was then at the University of Minnesota (you can see where the freshwater moniker comes from), argued that price fluctuations and changes in demand actually had nothing to do with the business cycle. Rather, the business cycle reflects fluctuations in the rate of technological progress, which are amplified by the rational response of workers, who voluntarily work more when the environment is favorable and less when it's unfavorable. Unemployment is a deliberate decision by workers to take time off.

Put baldly like that, this theory sounds foolish—was the Great Depression really the Great Vacation? And to be honest, I think it really is silly. But the basic premise of Prescott's "real business cycle" theory was embedded in ingeniously constructed mathematical models, which were mapped onto real data using sophisticated statistical techniques, and the theory came to dominate the teaching of macroeconomics in many university departments. In 2004, reflecting the theory's influence, Prescott shared a Nobel with Finn Kydland of Carnegie Mellon University.

Meanwhile, saltwater economists balked. Where the freshwater economists were purists, saltwater economists were pragmatists. While economists like N. Gregory Mankiw at Harvard, Olivier Blanchard at M.I.T., and David Romer at the University of California, Berkeley, acknowledged that it was hard to reconcile a Keynesian demand-side view of recessions with neoclassical theory, they found the evidence that recessions are, in fact, demand-driven too compelling to reject. So they were willing to deviate from the assumption of perfect markets or perfect rationality, or both, adding enough imperfections to accommodate a more or less Keynesian view of recessions. And in the saltwater view, active policy to fight recessions remained desirable.

But the self-described New Keynesian economists weren't immune to the charms of rational individuals and perfect markets. They tried to keep their deviations from neoclassical orthodoxy as limited as possible. This meant that there was no room in the prevailing models for such things as bubbles and banking-system collapse. The fact that such things continued to happen in the real world—there was a terrible financial and macroeconomic crisis in much of Asia in 1997–1998 and a depression-level slump in Argentina in 2002—wasn't reflected in the mainstream of New Keynesian thinking.

Even so, you might have thought that the differing worldviews of freshwater and saltwater economists would have put them constantly at loggerheads over economic policy. Somewhat surprisingly, however, between around 1985 and 2007 the disputes between freshwater and saltwater economists were mainly about theory, not action. The reason, I believe, is that New Keynesians, unlike the original Keynesians, didn't think fiscal policy—changes in government spending or taxes—was needed to fight recessions. They believed that monetary policy, administered by the technocrats at the Fed, could provide whatever remedies the economy needed. At a ninetieth birthday celebration for Milton Friedman, Ben Bernanke, formerly a more or less New Keynesian professor at Princeton, and by then a member of the Fed's governing board, declared of the Great Depression: "You're right. We did it. We're very sorry. But thanks to you, it won't happen again." The clear message was that all you need to avoid depressions is a smarter Fed.

And as long as macroeconomic policy was left in the hands of the maestro Greenspan, without Keynesian-type stimulus programs, freshwater economists found little to complain about. (They didn't believe that monetary policy did any good, but they didn't believe it did any harm, either.)

It would take a crisis to reveal both how little common ground there was and how Panglossian even New Keynesian economics had become.

V. NOBODY COULD HAVE PREDICTED . . .

In recent, rueful economics discussions, an all-purpose punch line has become "Nobody could have predicted . . ." It's what you say with regard to disasters that could have been predicted, should have been predicted, and actually were predicted by a few economists who were scoffed at for their pains.

Take, for example, the precipitous rise and fall of housing prices. Some economists, notably Robert Shiller, did identify the bubble and warn of painful consequences if it were to burst. Yet key policymakers failed to see the obvious. In 2004, Alan Greenspan dismissed talk of a housing bubble: "a national severe price distortion," he declared, was "most unlikely." Home-price increases, Ben Bernanke said in 2005, "largely reflect strong economic fundamentals."

How did they miss the bubble? To be fair, interest rates were unusually low, possibly explaining part of the price rise. It may be that Greenspan and Bernanke also wanted to celebrate the Fed's success in pulling the economy out of the 2001 recession; conceding that much of that success rested on the creation of a monstrous bubble would have placed a damper on the festivities.

But there was something else going on: a general belief that bubbles just don't happen. What's striking, when you reread Greenspan's assurances, is that they weren't based on evidence—they were based on the a priori assertion that there simply can't be a bubble in housing. And the finance theorists were even more adamant on this point. In a 2007 interview, Eugene Fama, the father of the efficient-market hypothesis, declared that "the word 'bubble' drives me nuts," and went on to explain why we can trust the housing market: "Housing markets are less liquid, but people are very careful when they buy houses. It's typically the biggest investment they're going to make, so they look around very carefully and they compare prices. The bidding process is very detailed."

Indeed, home buyers generally do carefully compare prices—that is, they compare the price of their potential purchase with the prices of other houses. But this says nothing about whether the overall price of houses is justified. It's ketchup economics, again: because a two-quart bottle of ketchup costs twice as much as a one-quart bottle, finance theorists declare that the price of ketchup must be right.

In short, the belief in efficient financial markets blinded many if not most economists to the emergence of the biggest financial bubble in history. And efficient-market theory also played a significant role in inflating that bubble in the first place.

Now that the undiagnosed bubble has burst, the true riskiness of supposedly safe assets has been revealed and the financial system has demonstrated its fragility. U.S. households have seen $13 trillion in wealth evaporate. More than six million jobs have been lost, and the unemployment rate appears headed for its highest level since 1940. So what guidance does modern economics have to offer in our current predicament? And should we trust it?

VI. THE STIMULUS SQUABBLE

Between 1985 and 2007 a false peace settled over the field of macroeconomics. There hadn't been any real convergence of views between the saltwater and freshwater factions. But these were the years of the Great Moderation— an extended period during which inflation was subdued and recessions were relatively mild. Saltwater economists believed that the Federal Reserve had everything under control. Freshwater economists didn't think the Fed's actions were actually beneficial, but they were willing to let matters lie.

But the crisis ended the phony peace. Suddenly the narrow, technocratic policies both sides were willing to accept were no longer sufficient—and the need for a broader policy response brought the old conflicts out into the open, fiercer than ever.

Why weren't those narrow, technocratic policies sufficient? The answer, in a word, is zero.

During a normal recession, the Fed responds by buying Treasury bills— short-term government debt—from banks. This drives interest rates on government debt down; investors seeking a higher rate of return move into other assets, driving other interest rates down as well; and normally these lower interest rates eventually lead to an economic bounceback. The Fed dealt with the recession that began in 1990 by driving short-term interest rates from 9 percent down to 3 percent. It dealt with the recession that began in 2001 by driving rates from 6.5 percent to 1 percent. And it tried to deal with the current recession by driving rates down from 5.25 percent to zero.

But zero, it turned out, isn't low enough to end this recession. And the Fed can't push rates below zero, since at near-zero rates investors simply hoard cash rather than lending it out. So by late 2008, with interest rates basically at what macroeconomists call the "zero lower bound" even as the recession continued to deepen, conventional monetary policy had lost all traction.

Now what? This is the second time America has been up against the zero lower bound, the previous occasion being the Great Depression. And it was precisely the observation that there's a lower bound to interest rates that led Keynes to advocate higher government spending: when monetary policy is ineffective and the private sector can't be persuaded to spend more, the public sector must take its place in supporting the economy. Fiscal stimulus is the Keynesian answer to the kind of depression-type economic situation we're currently in.

Such Keynesian thinking underlies the Obama administration's economic policies—and the freshwater economists are furious. For twenty-five or so years they tolerated the Fed's efforts to manage the economy, but a full-blown Keynesian resurgence was something entirely different. Back in 1980, Lucas, of the University of Chicago, wrote that Keynesian economics was so ludicrous that "at research seminars, people don't take Keynesian theorizing seriously anymore; the audience starts to whisper and giggle to one another." Admitting that Keynes was largely right, after all, would be too humiliating a comedown.

And so Chicago's Cochrane, outraged at the idea that government spending could mitigate the latest recession, declared: "It's not part of what anybody has taught graduate students since the 1960s. They [Keynesian ideas] are fairy tales that have been proved false. It is very comforting in times of stress to go back to the fairy tales we heard as children, but it doesn't make them less false." (It's a mark of how deep the division between saltwater and freshwater runs that Cochrane doesn't believe that "anybody" teaches ideas that are, in fact, taught in places like Princeton, M.I.T., and Harvard.)

Meanwhile, saltwater economists, who had comforted themselves with the belief that the great divide in macroeconomics was narrowing, were shocked to realize that freshwater economists hadn't been listening at all. Freshwater economists who inveighed against the stimulus didn't sound like scholars who had weighed Keynesian arguments and found them wanting. Rather, they sounded like people who had no idea what Keynesian economics was about, who were resurrecting pre-1930 fallacies in the belief that they were saying something new and profound.

And it wasn't just Keynes whose ideas seemed to have been forgotten. As Brad DeLong of the University of California, Berkeley, has pointed out in his laments about the Chicago School's "intellectual collapse," the school's current stance amounts to a wholesale rejection of Milton Friedman's ideas, as well. Friedman believed that Fed policy rather than changes in government spending should be used to stabilize the economy, but he never asserted that an increase in government spending cannot, under any circumstances, increase employment. In fact, rereading Friedman's 1970 summary of his ideas, "A Theoretical Framework for Monetary Analysis," what's striking is how Keynesian it seems.

And Friedman certainly never bought into the idea that mass unemployment represents a voluntary reduction in work effort or the idea that recessions are actually good for the economy. Yet the current generation of freshwater economists has been making both arguments. Thus Chicago's Casey Mulligan suggests that unemployment is so high because many workers are choosing not to take jobs: "Employees face financial incentives that encourage them not to work . . . decreased employment is explained more by reductions in the supply of labor (the willingness of people to work) and less by the demand for labor (the number of workers that employers need to hire)." Mulligan has suggested, in particular, that workers are choosing to remain unemployed because that improves their odds of receiving mortgage relief. And Cochrane declares that high unemployment is actually good: "We should have a recession. People who spend their lives pounding nails in Nevada need something else to do."

Personally, I think this is crazy. Why should it take mass unemployment across the whole nation to get carpenters to move out of Nevada? Can anyone seriously claim that we've lost 6.7 million jobs because fewer Americans want to work? But it was inevitable that freshwater economists would find themselves trapped in this cul-de-sac: if you start from the assumption that people are perfectly rational and markets are perfectly efficient, you have to conclude that unemployment is voluntary and recessions are desirable.

Yet if the crisis has pushed freshwater economists into absurdity, it has also created a lot of soul-searching among saltwater economists. Their framework, unlike that of the Chicago School, both allows for the possibility of involuntary unemployment and considers it a bad thing. But the New Keynesian models that have come to dominate teaching and research assume that people are perfectly rational and financial markets are perfectly efficient. To get anything like the current slump into their models, New Keynesians are forced to introduce some kind of fudge factor that for reasons unspecified temporarily depresses private spending. (I've done exactly that in some of my own work.) And if the analysis of where we are now rests on this fudge factor, how much confidence can we have in the models' predictions about where we are going?

The state of macro, in short, is not good. So where does the profession go from here?

VII. FLAWS AND FRICTIONS

Economics, as a field, got in trouble because economists were seduced by the vision of a perfect, frictionless market system. If the profession is to redeem itself, it will have to reconcile itself to a less alluring vision—that of a market economy that has many virtues but that is also shot through with flaws and frictions. The good news is that we don't have to start from scratch. Even during the heyday of perfect-market economics, there was a lot of work done on the ways in which the real economy deviated from the theoretical ideal. What's probably going to happen now—in fact, it's already happening—is that flaws-and-frictions economics will move from the periphery of economic analysis to its center.

There's already a fairly well-developed example of the kind of economics I have in mind: the school of thought known as behavioral finance. Practitioners of this approach emphasize two things. First, many real-world investors bear little resemblance to the cool calculators of efficient-market theory: they're all too subject to herd behavior, to bouts of irrational exuberance and unwarranted panic. Second, even those who try to base their decisions on cool calculation often find that they can't, that problems of trust, credibility, and limited collateral force them to run with the herd.

On the first point: even during the heyday of the efficient-market hypothesis, it seemed obvious that many real-world investors aren't as rational as the prevailing models assumed. Larry Summers once began a paper on finance by declaring: "THERE ARE IDIOTS. Look around." But what kind of idiots (the preferred term in the academic literature, actually, is "noise traders") are we talking about? Behavioral finance, drawing on the broader movement known as behavioral economics, tries to answer that question by relating the apparent irrationality of investors to known biases in human cognition, like the tendency to care more about small losses than small gains or the tendency to extrapolate too readily from small samples (e.g., assuming that because home prices rose in the past few years, they'll keep on rising).

Until the crisis, efficient-market advocates like Eugene Fama dismissed the evidence produced on behalf of behavioral finance as a collection of "curiosity items" of no real importance. That's a much harder position to maintain now that the collapse of a vast bubble—a bubble correctly diagnosed by behavioral economists like Robert Shiller of Yale, who related it to past episodes of "irrational exuberance"—has brought the world economy to its knees.

On the second point: suppose that there are, indeed, idiots. How much do they matter? Not much, argued Milton Friedman in an influential 1953 paper: smart investors will make money by buying when the idiots sell and selling when they buy and will stabilize markets in the process. But the second strand of behavioral finance says that Friedman was wrong, that financial markets are sometimes highly unstable, and right now that view seems hard to reject.

Probably the most influential paper in this vein was a 1997 publication by Andrei Shleifer of Harvard and Robert Vishny of Chicago, which amounted to a formalization of the old line that "the market can stay irrational longer than you can stay solvent." As they pointed out, arbitrageurs— the people who are supposed to buy low and sell high—need capital to do their jobs. And a severe plunge in asset prices, even if it makes no sense in terms of fundamentals, tends to deplete that capital. As a result, the smart money is forced out of the market, and prices may go into a downward spiral.

The spread of the current financial crisis seemed almost like an object lesson in the perils of financial instability. And the general ideas underlying models of financial instability have proved highly relevant to economic policy: a focus on the depleted capital of financial institutions helped guide policy actions taken after the fall of Lehman, and it looks (cross your fingers) as if these actions successfully headed off an even bigger financial collapse.

Meanwhile, what about macroeconomics? Recent events have pretty decisively refuted the idea that recessions are an optimal response to fluctuations in the rate of technological progress; a more or less Keynesian view is the only plausible game in town. Yet standard New Keynesian models left no room for a crisis like the one we're having, because those models generally accepted the efficient-market view of the financial sector.

There were some exceptions. One line of work, pioneered by none other than Ben Bernanke working with Mark Gertler of New York University, emphasized the way the lack of sufficient collateral can hinder the ability of businesses to raise funds and pursue investment opportunities. A related line of work, largely established by my Princeton colleague Nobuhiro Kiyotaki and John Moore of the London School of Economics, argued that prices of assets such as real estate can suffer self-reinforcing plunges that in turn depress the economy as a whole. But until now the impact of dysfunctional finance hasn't been at the core even of Keynesian economics. Clearly, that has to change.

VIII. RE-EMBRACING KEYNES

So here's what I think economists have to do. First, they have to face up to the inconvenient reality that financial markets fall far short of perfection, that they are subject to extraordinary delusions and the madness of crowds. Second, they have to admit—and this will be very hard for the people who giggled and whispered over Keynes—that Keynesian economics remains the best framework we have for making sense of recessions and depressions. Third, they'll have to do their best to incorporate the realities of finance into macroeconomics.

Many economists will find these changes deeply disturbing. It will be a long time, if ever, before the new, more realistic approaches to finance and macroeconomics offer the same kind of clarity, completeness, and sheer beauty that characterizes the full neoclassical approach. To some economists that will be a reason to cling to neoclassicism, despite its utter failure to make sense of the greatest economic crisis in three generations. This seems, however, like a good time to recall the words of H. L. Mencken: "There is always an easy solution to every human problem—neat, plausible and wrong."

When it comes to the all-too-human problem of recessions and depressions, economists need to abandon the neat but wrong solution of assuming that everyone is rational and markets work perfectly. The vision that emerges as the profession rethinks its foundations may not be all that clear; it certainly won't be neat; but we can hope that it will have the virtue of being at least partly right.

BAD FAITH, PATHOS, AND G.O.P ECONOMICS

December 27, 2018

A s 2018 draws to an end, we're seeing many articles about the state of the economy. What I'd like to do, however, is talk about something different—the state of economics, at least as it relates to the political situation. And that state is not good: the bad faith that dominates conservative politics at every level is infecting right-leaning economists, too.

This is sad, but it's also pathetic. For even as once-respected economists abase themselves in the face of Trumpism, the G.O.P. is making it ever clearer that their services aren't wanted, that only hacks need apply.

What you need to know when talking about economics and politics is that there are three kinds of economist in modern America: liberal professional economists, conservative professional economists and professional conservative economists.

By "liberal professional economists" I mean researchers who try to understand the economy as best they can, but who, being human, also have political preferences, which in their case puts them on the left side of the U.S. political spectrum, although usually only modestly left of center. Conservative professional economists are their counterparts on the center right.

Professional conservative economists are something quite different. They're people who even center-right professionals consider charlatans and cranks; they make a living by pretending to do actual economics—often incompetently—but are actually just propagandists. And no, there isn't really a corresponding category on the other side, in part because the billionaires who finance such propaganda are much more likely to be on the right than on the left.

But let me leave the pure hacks on one side for a moment, and talk about the people who at least used to seem to be trying to do real economics.

Do economists' political preferences shape their research? They surely affect the choice of subject: Liberals are more likely to be interested in rising inequality or the economics of climate change than conservatives. And human nature being what it is, some of them—O.K., of us—occasionally engage in motivated reasoning, reaching conclusions that cater to their politics.

I used to believe, however, that such lapses were the exception, not the rule, and the liberal economists I know try hard to avoid falling into that trap, and apologize when they do.

But do conservative economists do the same? Increasingly, the answer seems to be no, at least for those who play a prominent role in public discourse.

Even during the Obama years, it was striking how many well-known Republican-leaning economists followed the party line on economic policy, even when that party line was in conflict with the nonpolitical professional consensus.

Thus, when a Democrat was in the White House, G.O.P. politicians opposed anything that might mitigate the costs of the 2008 financial crisis and its aftermath; so did many economists. Most famously, in 2010 a who's who of Republican economists denounced the efforts of the Federal Reserve to fight unemployment, warning that they risked "currency debasement and inflation."

Were these economists arguing in good faith? Even at the time, there were good reasons to suspect otherwise. For one thing, those terrible, irresponsible Fed actions were pretty much exactly what Milton Friedman prescribed for depressed economies. For another, some of those Fed critics engaged in Donald Trump–like conspiracy theorizing, accusing the Fed of printing money, not to help the economy, but to "bail out fiscal policy," i.e., to help Barack Obama.

It was also telling that none of the economists who warned, wrongly, about looming inflation were willing to admit their error after the fact.

But the real test came after 2016. A complete cynic might have expected economists who denounced budget deficits and easy money under a Democrat to suddenly reverse position under a Republican president.

And that total cynic would have been exactly right. After years of hysteria about the evils of debt, establishment Republican economists enthusiastically endorsed a budget-busting tax cut. After denouncing easy-money policies when unemployment was sky-high, some echoed Trump's demands for low interest rates with unemployment under 4 percent—and the rest remained conspicuously silent.

What explains this epidemic of bad faith? Some of it is clearly ambition on the part of conservative economists still hoping for high-profile appointments. Some of it, I suspect, may be just the desire to stay on the inside with powerful people.

But there's something pathetic about this professional self-abasement, because the rewards center-right economists long for haven't come, and never will.

It's not just that Trump has assembled an administration of the worst and the dimmest. The truth is that the modern G.O.P. doesn't want to hear from serious economists, whatever their politics. It prefers charlatans and cranks, who are its kind of people.

So what we've learned about economics these past two years is that many conservative economists were, in fact, willing to compromise their professional ethics for political ends—and that they sold their integrity for nothing.

WHAT'S WRONG WITH FUNCTIONAL FINANCE?
(WONKISH)

February 12, 2019

The doctrine behind MMT was smart but not completely right

Well, it looks as if policy debates over the next couple of years will be at least somewhat affected by the doctrine of Modern Monetary Theory, which some progressives appear to believe means that they don't need to worry about how to pay for their initiatives. That's actually wrong even if you set aside concerns about MMT analysis. But first it seems to me that I need to set out what's right and what's wrong about MMT.

Unfortunately, that's a very hard argument to have—modern MMTers are messianic in their claims to have proved even conventional Keynesianism wrong, tend to be unclear about what exactly their differences with conventional views are, and also have a strong habit of dismissing out of hand any attempt to make sense of what they're saying. The good news is that MMT seems to be pretty much the same thing as Abba Lerner's "functional finance" doctrine from 1943. And Lerner was admirably clear, making it easy to see both the important virtues of and the problems with his argument.

So what I want to do in this note is explain why I'm not a full believer in Lerner's functional finance; I think this critique applies to MMT as well, although if past debates are any indication, I will promptly be told that I don't understand, am a corrupt tool of the oligarchy, or something.

O.K., Lerner: His argument was that countries that (a) rely on fiat money they control and (b) don't borrow in someone else's currency don't face any debt constraints, because they can always print money to service their debt. What they face, instead, is an inflation constraint: too much fiscal stimulus will cause an overheating economy. So their budget policies should be entirely focused on getting the level of aggregate demand right: the budget deficit should be big enough to produce full employment, but not so big as to produce inflationary overheating.

This is a smart take, and at the time he wrote—coming off the 1930s, with a reasonable expectation that the economy would lapse back into chronic weakness once the war was over—was a much better guide to policy than conventional fiscal thinking. And it also looks pretty good in today's world, where we once again had a long period of depressed demand despite zero interest rates and still look pretty fragile. Indeed, it looks vastly better than the "Eek! We're turning into Greece!" panic that dominated policy discussion for much of the 2010s.

So what are the problems? First, Lerner really neglected the trade-off between monetary and fiscal policy. Second, while he did address the potential problem of snowballing debt, his response didn't fully address the limitations, both technical and political, on tax hikes and/or spending cuts. Introducing these limitations makes debt potentially more of a problem than he acknowledges.

From a modern perspective, "functional finance" is really cavalier in its discussion of monetary policy. Lerner says that the interest rate should be set at the level that produces "the most desirable level of investment," and that fiscal policy should then be chosen to achieve full employment given that interest rate. What is the optimal interest rate? He doesn't say—maybe because through the thirties the zero lower bound made that point moot.

Anyway, what actually happens at least much of the time—although, crucially, not when we're at the zero lower bound—is more or less the opposite: political trade-offs determine taxes and spending, and monetary policy adjusts the interest rate to achieve full employment without inflation. Under those conditions budget deficits do crowd out private spending, because tax cuts or spending increases will lead to higher interest rates. And this means that there is no uniquely determined correct level of deficit spending; it's a choice that depends on how you value the trade-off.

What about debt? A lot depends on whether the interest rate is higher or lower than the economy's sustainable growth rate. If $r<g$, which is true now and has mostly been true in the past, the level of debt really isn't too much of an issue. But if $r>g$ you do have the possibility of a debt snowball: the higher the ratio of debt to G.D.P. the faster, other things equal, that ratio will grow. And debt can't go to infinity—it can't exceed total wealth, and in fact as debt gets ever higher people will demand ever-increasing returns to hold it. So at some point the government would be forced to run large enough primary (non-interest) surpluses to limit debt growth.

Now, Lerner basically acknowledges this point. But he assumes that the government always can and will run these surpluses as needed. He dismisses any concern about the incentive effects of high tax rates; certainly Very Serious People grossly exaggerate these effects, but they're not completely imaginary. And he says nothing at all about the political difficulty of achieving the required surpluses, yet such difficulties seem likely to be central if debt gets to very high levels.

A numerical example may help make the point. Imagine that one way or another we get up to debt equal to 300 percent of G.D.P., and that $r-g = .015$—the interest rate is 1.5 percentage points above the growth rate. Then stabilizing the ratio of debt to G.D.P. would require a primary surplus equal to 4.5 percent of G.D.P.

That's not impossible: Britain ran surpluses that big for several decades after Waterloo. But it's a lot to ask of a modern polity. Are we going to slash Medicare and Social Security? Are we going to impose a value-added tax, not to finance new programs, but simply to service the debt? It's possible, but you do have to wonder whether the temptation to engage in some form of financial repression/debt restructuring/inflation would prevail. And more to the point, investors would wonder about that, pushing $r-g$ even higher.

The bottom line is that while functional finance has a lot going for it, it's not the kind of axiomatically true doctrine that Lerner—and, I think, modern MMTers—imagined it to be. Deficits and debt can matter, and not just because of the effects of deficit spending on aggregate demand.

That said, I don't think these objections are all that central to the budget issues facing progressives in the near future. You don't have to be a deficit scold or debt-worrier to believe that really big progressive programs will require major new revenue sources.

Austerity

VERY SERIOUS PEOPLE

I PICKED UP THE PHRASE "VERY SERIOUS PEOPLE" FROM DUNCAN BLACK, who blogs under the name Atrios. He used it, I think, to refer to all the influential people who were quite sure that invading Iraq was a good idea, because that's what all the influential people were saying—and because it sounded like a tough-minded stance that was, well, serious. But Iraq was hardly the only example of the phenomenon.

I began using the phrase a lot around a year after the fall of Lehman Brothers. For the first year of the global financial crisis, economic policy in major economies generally moved in the right direction, although inadequately so. But in late 2009 I watched in amazement and horror as more and more public figures began deemphasizing the problem of mass unemployment and obsessing instead about the dangers of budget deficits.

It was true that deficits soared as the world descended into economic crisis. This was natural: revenues plunge when the economy crashes, while some kinds of spending, like unemployment benefits, rise automatically. The rise in deficits was also a good thing. When almost everyone in the world is trying to spend less than their income, the result is a vicious contraction—because my spending is your income, and your spending is my income. What you need to limit the damage is for somebody to be willing to spend more than their income. And governments were playing that crucial role.

Indeed, the fact that governments are a much bigger share of the economy than they were in 1930, and that their deficits therefore grew a lot more in the face of a global slump, is probably the biggest reason the Great Recession didn't turn into a full replay of the Great Depression. Moreover, budget deficits weren't causing any visible economic problems. Interest rates remained low, suggesting both that investors weren't worried about debt and that government borrowing wasn't "crowding out" private investment.

But worrying about budget deficits and calling for sacrifice to reduce them—sacrifice by other people, of course—sounds serious and hard-headed. Also, Greece had a genuine budget crisis at the end of 2009, giving deficit scare-mongers a useful example, even though the Greek situation didn't look at all like the situation facing the U.S., Britain, or most other advanced economies.

And so the Very Serious People collectively decided that it was time to pivot from fighting unemployment to fiscal austerity, mainly spending cuts. This turn to austerity had very nasty consequences: it delayed recovery in the U.S. and Britain, and sent much of Europe back into recession, as well as inflicting a lot of direct hardship via those spending cuts. In turn, these economic consequences helped pave the way for later political disasters, both Brexit and Trump.

So where were the economists in all this? Unfortunately, there will almost always be some economist somewhere, maybe even an economist who has done solid work in the past, who will tell Very Serious People what they want to hear. And what these economists say gets amplified out of all proportion to the amount of evidence or professional backing for their assertions.

In this case, one paper, by the economists Alberto Alesina and Silvia Ardagna, claimed to find evidence that cutting government spending inspired so much private-sector confidence that overall spending would actually rise. In "Myths of Austerity," I mocked this as belief in the "confidence fairy." Indeed, a closer look at the evidence, and then the experience of austerity in practice, showed that the doctrine of "expansionary austerity" was all wrong. But key policymakers seized on the doctrine.

Meanwhile, Carmen Reinhart and Ken Rogoff—who had done fine work in the past—came out with a paper that was, well, sloppy, asserting that terrible things happen to economies when debt crosses a magic threshold of 90 percent of G.D.P. This work also fell apart on examination, but only after it had served as an excuse for destructive policies in much of Europe.

Finally, by around 2013 or so the Very Serious People found something new to worry about. Instead of seeing persistent high unemployment as a problem of too little spending—in fact, largely the result of the austerity policies they had all agreed were the responsible thing to do—they decided that the reason Americans couldn't find work was that they didn't have the needed skills. For a while there everybody who was anyone just knew that the "skills gap" meant that unemployment was never going to get back down to pre-crisis levels.

Strange to say, as I write this the unemployment rate is below 4 percent, and the skills gap is nowhere to be seen.

MYTHS OF AUSTERITY

July 1, 2010

When I was young and naïve, I believed that important people took positions based on careful consideration of the options. Now I know better. Much of what Serious People believe rests on prejudices, not analysis. And these prejudices are subject to fads and fashions.

Which brings me to the subject of today's column. For the last few months, I and others have watched, with amazement and horror, the emergence of a consensus in policy circles in favor of immediate fiscal austerity. That is, somehow it has become conventional wisdom that now is the time to slash spending, despite the fact that the world's major economies remain deeply depressed.

This conventional wisdom isn't based on either evidence or careful analysis. Instead, it rests on what we might charitably call sheer speculation, and less charitably call figments of the policy elite's imagination—specifically, on belief in what I've come to think of as the invisible bond vigilante and the confidence fairy.

Bond vigilantes are investors who pull the plug on governments they perceive as unable or unwilling to pay their debts. Now there's no question that countries can suffer crises of confidence (see Greece, debt of). But what the advocates of austerity claim is that (a) the bond vigilantes are about to attack America, and (b) spending anything more on stimulus will set them off.

What reason do we have to believe that any of this is true? Yes, America has long-run budget problems, but what we do on stimulus over the next couple of years has almost no bearing on our ability to deal with these long-run problems. As Douglas Elmendorf, the director of the Congressional Budget Office, recently put it, "There is no intrinsic contradiction between providing additional fiscal stimulus today, while the unemployment rate is high and many factories and offices are underused, and imposing fiscal restraint several years from now, when output and employment will probably be close to their potential."

Nonetheless, every few months we're told that the bond vigilantes have arrived, and we must impose austerity now now now to appease them. Three months ago, a slight uptick in long-term interest rates was greeted with near hysteria: "Debt Fears Send Rates Up," was the headline at *The Wall Street Journal*, although there was no actual evidence of such fears, and Alan Greenspan pronounced the rise a "canary in the mine."

Since then, long-term rates have plunged again. Far from fleeing U.S. government debt, investors evidently see it as their safest bet in a stumbling economy. Yet the advocates of austerity still assure us that bond vigilantes will attack any day now if we don't slash spending immediately.

But don't worry: spending cuts may hurt, but the confidence fairy will take away the pain. "The idea that austerity measures could trigger stagnation is incorrect," declared Jean-Claude Trichet, the president of the European Central Bank, in a recent interview. Why? Because "confidence-inspiring policies will foster and not hamper economic recovery."

What's the evidence for the belief that fiscal contraction is actually expansionary, because it improves confidence? (By the way, this is precisely the doctrine expounded by Herbert Hoover in 1932.) Well, there have been historical cases of spending cuts and tax increases followed by economic growth. But as far as I can tell, every one of those examples proves, on closer examination, to be a case in which the negative effects of austerity were offset by other factors, factors not likely to be relevant today. For example, Ireland's era of austerity-with-growth in the 1980s depended on a drastic move from trade deficit to trade surplus, which isn't a strategy everyone can pursue at the same time.

And current examples of austerity are anything but encouraging. Ireland has been a good soldier in this crisis, grimly implementing savage spending cuts. Its reward has been a Depression-level slump—and financial markets continue to treat it as a serious default risk. Other good soldiers, like Latvia and Estonia, have done even worse—and all three nations have, believe it or not, had worse slumps in output and employment than Iceland, which was forced by the sheer scale of its financial crisis to adopt less orthodox policies.

So the next time you hear serious-sounding people explaining the need for fiscal austerity, try to parse their argument. Almost surely, you'll discover that what sounds like hardheaded realism actually rests on a foundation of fantasy, on the belief that invisible vigilantes will punish us if we're bad and the confidence fairy will reward us if we're good. And real-world policy—policy that will blight the lives of millions of working families—is being built on that foundation.

THE EXCEL DEPRESSION

April 18, 2013

In this age of information, math errors can lead to disaster. NASA's Mars Orbiter crashed because engineers forgot to convert to metric measurements; JPMorgan Chase's "London Whale" venture went bad in part because modelers divided by a sum instead of an average. So, did an Excel coding error destroy the economies of the Western world?

The story so far: at the beginning of 2010, two Harvard economists, Carmen Reinhart and Kenneth Rogoff, circulated a paper, "Growth in a Time of Debt," that purported to identify a critical "threshold," a tipping point, for government indebtedness. Once debt exceeds 90 percent of gross domestic product, they claimed, economic growth drops off sharply.

Ms. Reinhart and Mr. Rogoff had credibility thanks to a widely admired earlier book on the history of financial crises, and their timing was impeccable. The paper came out just after Greece went into crisis and played right into the desire of many officials to "pivot" from stimulus to austerity. As a result, the paper instantly became famous; it was, and is, surely the most influential economic analysis of recent years.

In fact, Reinhart-Rogoff quickly achieved almost sacred status among self-proclaimed guardians of fiscal responsibility; their tipping-point claim was treated not as a disputed hypothesis but as unquestioned fact. For example, a *Washington Post* editorial earlier this year warned against any relaxation on the deficit front, because we are "dangerously near the 90 percent mark that economists regard as a threat to sustainable economic growth." Notice the phrasing: "economists," not "some economists," let alone "some economists, vigorously disputed by other economists with equally good credentials," which was the reality.

For the truth is that Reinhart-Rogoff faced substantial criticism from the start, and the controversy grew over time. As soon as the paper was released, many economists pointed out that a negative correlation between debt and economic performance need not mean that high debt causes low growth. It could just as easily be the other way around, with poor economic performance leading to high debt. Indeed, that's obviously the case for Japan, which went deep into debt only after its growth collapsed in the early 1990s.

Over time, another problem emerged: other researchers, using seemingly comparable data on debt and growth, couldn't replicate the Reinhart-Rogoff results. They typically found some correlation between high debt and slow growth—but nothing that looked like a tipping point at 90 percent or, indeed, any particular level of debt.

Finally, Ms. Reinhart and Mr. Rogoff allowed researchers at the University of Massachusetts to look at their original spreadsheet—and the mystery of the irreproducible results was solved. First, they omitted some data; second, they used unusual and highly questionable statistical procedures; and finally, yes, they made an Excel coding error. Correct these oddities and errors, and you get what other researchers have found: some correlation between high debt and slow growth, with no indication of which is causing which, but no sign at all of that 90 percent "threshold."

In response, Ms. Reinhart and Mr. Rogoff have acknowledged the coding error, defended their other decisions, and claimed that they never asserted that debt necessarily causes slow growth. That's a bit disingenuous because they repeatedly insinuated that proposition even if they avoided saying it outright. But, in any case, what really matters isn't what they meant to say, it's how their work was read: austerity enthusiasts trumpeted that supposed 90 percent tipping point as a proven fact and a reason to slash government spending even in the face of mass unemployment.

So the Reinhart-Rogoff fiasco needs to be seen in the broader context of austerity mania: the obviously intense desire of policymakers, politicians, and pundits across the Western world to turn their backs on the unemployed and instead use the economic crisis as an excuse to slash social programs.

What the Reinhart-Rogoff affair shows is the extent to which austerity has been sold on false pretenses. For three years, the turn to austerity has been presented not as a choice but as a necessity. Economic research, austerity advocates insisted, showed that terrible things happen once debt exceeds 90 percent of G.D.P. But "economic research" showed no such thing; a couple of economists made that assertion, while many others disagreed. Policymakers abandoned the unemployed and turned to austerity because they wanted to, not because they had to.

So will toppling Reinhart-Rogoff from its pedestal change anything? I'd like to think so. But I predict that the usual suspects will just find another dubious piece of economic analysis to canonize, and the depression will go on and on.

JOBS AND SKILLS AND ZOMBIES

March 30, 2014

A few months ago, Jamie Dimon, the chief executive of JPMorgan Chase, and Marlene Seltzer, the chief executive of Jobs for the Future, published an article in Politico titled "Closing the Skills Gap." They began portentously: "Today, nearly 11 million Americans are unemployed. Yet, at the same time, 4 million jobs sit unfilled"—supposedly demonstrating "the gulf between the skills job seekers currently have and the skills employers need."

Actually, in an ever-changing economy there are always some positions unfilled even while some workers are unemployed, and the current ratio of vacancies to unemployed workers is far below normal. Meanwhile, multiple careful studies have found no support for claims that inadequate worker skills explain high unemployment.

But the belief that America suffers from a severe "skills gap" is one of those things that everyone important knows must be true, because everyone they know says it's true. It's a prime example of a zombie idea—an idea that should have been killed by evidence, but refuses to die.

And it does a lot of harm. Before we get there, however, what do we actually know about skills and jobs?

Think about what we would expect to find if there really were a skills shortage. Above all, we should see workers with the right skills doing well, while only those without those skills are doing badly. We don't.

Yes, workers with a lot of formal education have lower unemployment than those with less, but that's always true, in good times and bad. The crucial point is that unemployment remains much higher among workers at all education levels than it was before the financial crisis. The same is true across occupations: workers in every major category are doing worse than they were in 2007.

Some employers do complain that they're finding it hard to find workers with the skills they need. But show us the money: if employers are really crying out for certain skills, they should be willing to offer higher wages to attract workers with those skills. In reality, however, it's very hard to find groups of workers getting big wage increases, and the cases you can find don't fit the conventional wisdom at all. It's good, for example, that workers who know how to operate a sewing machine are seeing significant raises in wages, but I very much doubt that these are the skills people who make a lot of noise about the alleged gap have in mind.

And it's not just the evidence on unemployment and wages that refutes the skills-gap story. Careful surveys of employers—like those recently conducted by researchers at both M.I.T. and the Boston Consulting Group— similarly find, as the consulting group declared, that "worries of a skills gap crisis are overblown."

The one piece of evidence you might cite in favor of the skills-gap story is the sharp rise in long-term unemployment, which could be evidence that many workers don't have what employers want. But it isn't. At this point, we know a lot about the long-term unemployed, and they're pretty much indistinguishable in skills from laid-off workers who quickly find new jobs. So what's their problem? It's the very fact of being out of work, which makes employers unwilling even to look at their qualifications.

So how does the myth of a skills shortage not only persist, but remain part of what "everyone knows"? Well, there was a nice illustration of the process last fall, when some news media reported that 92 percent of top executives said that there was, indeed, a skills gap. The basis for this claim? A telephone survey in which executives were asked, "Which of the following do you feel best describes the 'gap' in the U.S. workforce skills gap?" followed by a list of alternatives. Given the loaded question, it's actually amazing that 8 percent of the respondents were willing to declare that there was no gap.

The point is that influential people move in circles in which repeating the skills-gap story—or, better yet, writing about skill gaps in media outlets like Politico—is a badge of seriousness, an assertion of tribal identity. And the zombie shambles on.

Unfortunately, the skills myth—like the myth of a looming debt crisis—is having dire effects on real-world policy. Instead of focusing on the way disastrously wrongheaded fiscal policy and inadequate action by the Federal Reserve have crippled the economy and demanding action, important people piously wring their hands about the failings of American workers.

Moreover, by blaming workers for their own plight, the skills myth shifts attention away from the spectacle of soaring profits and bonuses even as employment and wages stagnate. Of course, that may be another reason corporate executives like the myth so much.

So we need to kill this zombie, if we can, and stop making excuses for an economy that punishes workers.

STRUCTURAL HUMBUG

New York Times *Blog*

August 3, 2013

O.K., this is really depressing. The *PBS Newshour* isn't always a good place to get the best analysis, but it's a terrific place to take the pulse of Washington conventional wisdom—and as Dean Baker notes, that conventional wisdom has clearly swung to the view that our high unemployment is "structural," not something that could be solved simply by boosting demand.

And the question is, where the heck is that coming from?

As Dean also says, the professional consensus has very much moved the other way; you hear a lot less about structural factors from economists actually studying the data than you did a few years ago. Nor is there even much of a partisan divide; solid Republicans like Eddie Lazear say things like this:

> The recession of 2007–2009 witnessed high rates of unemployment that have been slow to recede. This has led many to conclude that structural changes have occurred in the labor market and that the economy will not return to the low rates of unemployment that prevailed in the recent past. Is this true? The question is important because central banks may be able to reduce unemployment that is cyclic in nature, but not that which is structural. An analysis of labor market data suggests that there are no structural changes that can explain movements in unemployment rates over recent years. Neither industrial nor demographic shifts nor a mismatch of skills

with job vacancies is behind the increased rates of unemployment. Although mismatch increased during the recession, it retreated at the same rate. The patterns observed are consistent with unemployment being caused by cyclic phenomena that are more pronounced during the current recession than in prior recessions.

Indeed: one strong indicator that the problem *isn't* structural is that as the economy has (partially) recovered, the recovery has tended to be fastest in precisely the same regions and occupations that were initially hit hardest. Goldman Sachs looks at unemployment in the "sand states" that had the biggest housing bubbles versus the rest of the country; they saw a much bigger rise in unemployment than other states, but have also seen a much more rapid decline since 2010.

So the states that took the biggest hit have recovered faster than the rest of the country, which is what you'd expect if it was all cycle, not structural change.

I've done a quick and dirty take on unemployment by occupation, looking at changes in unemployment rates from the 2007 business cycle peak to the unemployment peak in 2009–2010, and then the subsequent decline; it looks like this:

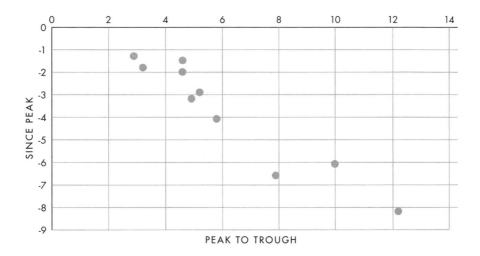

UNEMPLOYMENT CHANGES BY OCCUPATION. *Source: U.S. Bureau of Labor Statistics.*

It's the same as the geographical story: the occupations that took the biggest hit have had the strongest recoveries.

In short, the data strongly point toward a cyclical, not a structural story—and there is broad agreement, for once, among economists on this point. Yet somehow, it's clear, Beltway groupthink has arrived at the opposite conclusion—so much so that the actual economic consensus on this issue wasn't even represented on the *Newshour*.

As I said, this is really, really depressing.

8

The Euro

A BRIDGE TOO FAR

THE RECOVERY OF EUROPE AFTER WORLD WAR II IS ONE OF THE HAPPI-
est, most encouraging stories in human history. What the nations of Western
Europe built, literally out of the rubble of a terrible war, wasn't just prosperity and peace but the most decent societies in human history. And yes, I'm
including America in that comparison: I love my country, I still think we
offer a sense of personal possibility nobody else has managed to match, but
we do a far worse job of taking care of those in need than almost anyplace
north of the Mediterranean and west of the old Iron Curtain.

Underlying a lot of what went right in Europe was what people sometimes call the "European project." The idea behind this project was to end
the continent's ghastly history of war by drawing its nations together, not
with a dramatic act of political union, but with ever-closer economic links
and the common institutions that manage these links.

First, in 1952, came the Coal and Steel Community, which integrated
French and German heavy industry in a way that would, it was hoped, make
future wars almost impossible. Then, in 1959, came the Common Market,
which eliminated all tariffs between its members—and also required them
to act together on trade policy toward other countries, because you couldn't
have France and Germany charging different tariffs on, say, Canadian wheat.
Then came things like harmonization of regulations, free movement of people, joint development aid to lagging regions, and along the way a change in
name to the European Union.

Not everything about this process was wonderful. The Brussels-based
bureaucracy that manages pan-European affairs is even more detached from
ordinary people's lives, even more insular in its outlook, than most national
civil services. I used to joke that when talking with Eurocrats you needed
subtitles, even if they were speaking fluent English, to understand what they

were really saying: an extended, elliptical discourse about "widening versus deepening" actually translated into "We should never have let the Greeks in."

Nor did national rivalries disappear. Sometime around 1990 there was a joke memo circulating, supposedly from the European Commission, about adopting a common European language. As a practical matter, declared the memo, this would have to be English, but with a few improvements. For example, since you never know whether to use the soft or hard pronunciation of "c," the hard "c" would be replaced with "k," in order korrekt pronunciation to ensure. And further komprehensibility to enhance, people all verbs at the end of each sentence put should. And so on. By the end, the memo was pretty much written in German.

Still, the European project was, overall, a huge success story, not just improving the lives of hundreds of millions but showing how terrible legacies from the past could be overcome by people of good will.

And then came the euro.

As a political symbol, a single European money seemed like a natural next step in the European project. Europe had become a place of peace, open borders, free movement of people, shared standards on everything from the design of traffic signs to consumer safety requirements. Why not make doing business even easier, further enhance the sense of shared identity, by adopting a common currency?

Unfortunately, monetary economics is about more than political symbolism. Sharing a currency with your neighbors does indeed have some significant advantages—I wouldn't want to have to exchange New York dollars for New Jersey dollars every time I crossed the Hudson. But it also has serious disadvantages.

Economists had long been aware that when a country locks itself into a shared money with its neighbors, it reduces its ability to deal with "asymmetric shocks"—an ugly but useful piece of jargon. Suppose that you are, say, Finland, with an economy built around two big exports: cell phones made by Ericsson and wood pulp used to produce paper. Then along comes technological change that batters Ericsson's market share and also reduces office use of paper. What do you do?

Well, you need new exports; but to get there you have to give businesses some incentive to do new things, typically by reducing wages and prices relative to those of other countries. If you have your own currency, that's usually easy: wages are normally set in that currency, so just letting the currency drop on world markets produces an immediate improvement in competitiveness. In fact, that's what happened in Finland in the early 1990s, when the fall of the Soviet Union and a local banking crisis combined to produce a nasty economic slump.

But when things got problematic for Finland after 2008, the country no longer had its own currency. Neither did, for example, Spain, discussed in the first article in this section. So their only way out was a long, painful slog of reducing wages in the face of high unemployment.

The idea that there is a difficult economic trade-off between the convenience of a shared currency and its disadvantages when trouble hits has another ugly but useful name, the theory of "optimum currency areas." When proposals for creating the euro were first floated, many U.S.-based economists invoked that theory and argued that given the realities on the ground the euro was a bad idea. But the Europeans were too enamored of their vision—too romantic, I would say—to listen.

The treaty that set Europe on the road to the euro was signed in 1992, in the Dutch city of Maastricht. I remember joking that they had picked the wrong Dutch city; they should have chosen Arnhem, site of the famous military disaster portrayed in the film *A Bridge Too Far*. Unfortunately, the travails of the euro have confirmed those worries, with some new problems—like the problems of having a unified currency without a shared safety net for banks—also emerging.

Most of the stories of political and economic trouble told in this book are about bad things done by basically bad people. The euro is a bit different: in this case the road to hell was indeed paved with good intentions. Unfortunately it led to hell all the same.

THE SPANISH PRISONER

November 28, 2010

T he best thing about the Irish right now is that there are so few of them. By itself, Ireland can't do all that much damage to Europe's prospects. The same can be said of Greece and of Portugal, which is widely regarded as the next potential domino.

But then there's Spain. The others are tapas; Spain is the main course.

What's striking about Spain, from an American perspective, is how much its economic story resembles our own. Like America, Spain experienced a huge property bubble, accompanied by a huge rise in private-sector debt. Like America, Spain fell into recession when that bubble burst, and has experienced a surge in unemployment. And like America, Spain has seen its budget deficit balloon thanks to plunging revenues and recession-related costs.

But unlike America, Spain is on the edge of a debt crisis. The U.S. government is having no trouble financing its deficit, with interest rates on long-term federal debt under 3 percent. Spain, by contrast, has seen its borrowing cost shoot up in recent weeks, reflecting growing fears of a possible future default.

Why is Spain in so much trouble? In a word, it's the euro.

Spain was among the most enthusiastic adopters of the euro back in 1999, when the currency was introduced. And for a while things seemed to go swimmingly: European funds poured into Spain, powering private-sector spending, and the Spanish economy experienced rapid growth.

Through the good years, by the way, the Spanish government appeared to be a model of both fiscal and financial responsibility: unlike Greece, it ran budget surpluses, and unlike Ireland, it tried hard (though with only partial success) to regulate its banks. At the end of 2007 Spain's public debt, as a share of the economy, was only about half as high as Germany's, and even now its banks are in nowhere near as bad shape as Ireland's.

But problems were developing under the surface. During the boom, prices and wages rose more rapidly in Spain than in the rest of Europe, helping to feed a large trade deficit. And when the bubble burst, Spanish industry was left with costs that made it uncompetitive with other nations.

Now what? If Spain still had its own currency, like the United States—or like Britain, which shares some of the same characteristics—it could have let that currency fall, making its industry competitive again. But with Spain on the euro, that option isn't available. Instead, Spain must achieve "internal devaluation": it must cut wages and prices until its costs are back in line with its neighbors'.

And internal devaluation is an ugly affair. For one thing, it's slow: it normally takes years of high unemployment to push wages down. Beyond that, falling wages mean falling incomes, while debt stays the same. So internal devaluation worsens the private sector's debt problems.

What all this means for Spain is very poor economic prospects over the next few years. America's recovery has been disappointing, especially in terms of jobs—but at least we've seen some growth, with real G.D.P. more or less back to its pre-crisis peak, and we can reasonably expect future growth to help bring our deficit under control. Spain, on the other hand, hasn't recovered at all. And the lack of recovery translates into fears about Spain's fiscal future.

Should Spain try to break out of this trap by leaving the euro, and reestablishing its own currency? Will it? The answer to both questions is, probably not. Spain would be better off now if it had never adopted the euro—but trying to leave would create a huge banking crisis, as depositors raced to move their money elsewhere. Unless there's a catastrophic bank crisis anyway—which seems plausible for Greece and increasingly possible in Ireland, but unlikely though not impossible for Spain—it's hard to see any Spanish government taking the risk of "de-euroizing."

So Spain is in effect a prisoner of the euro, leaving it with no good options.

The good news about America is that we aren't in that kind of trap: we still have our own currency, with all the flexibility that implies. By the way, so does Britain, whose deficits and debt are comparable to Spain's, but which investors don't see as a default risk.

The bad news about America is that a powerful political faction is trying to shackle the Federal Reserve, in effect removing the one big advantage we have over the suffering Spaniards. Republican attacks on the Fed—demands that it stop trying to promote economic recovery and focus instead on keeping the dollar strong and fighting the imaginary risks of inflation—amount to a demand that we voluntarily put ourselves in the Spanish prison.

Let's hope that the Fed doesn't listen. Things in America are bad, but they could be much worse. And if the hard-money faction gets its way, they will be.

CRASH OF THE BUMBLEBEE

July 29, 2012

Last week Mario Draghi, the president of the European Central Bank, declared that his institution "is ready to do whatever it takes to preserve the euro"—and markets celebrated. In particular, interest rates on Spanish bonds fell sharply, and stock markets soared everywhere.

But will the euro really be saved? That remains very much in doubt.

First of all, Europe's single currency is a deeply flawed construction. And Mr. Draghi, to his credit, actually acknowledged that. "The euro is like a bumblebee," he declared. "This is a mystery of nature because it shouldn't fly but instead it does. So the euro was a bumblebee that flew very well for several years." But now it has stopped flying. What can be done? The answer, he suggested, is "to graduate to a real bee."

Never mind the dubious biology, we get the point. In the long run, the euro will be workable only if the European Union becomes much more like a unified country.

Consider, for example, the comparison between Spain and Florida. Both had huge housing bubbles followed by dramatic crashes. But Spain is in crisis in a way Florida isn't. Why? Because when the slump hit, Florida could count on Washington to keep paying for Social Security and Medicare, to guarantee the solvency of its banks, to provide emergency aid to its unemployed, and more. Spain had no such safety net, and in the long run, that has to be fixed.

But the creation of a United States of Europe won't happen soon, if ever, while the crisis of the euro is now. So what can be done to save the currency?

Well, why was the bumblebee able to fly for a while? Why did the euro seem to work for its first eight or so years? Because the structure's flaws were papered over by a boom in southern Europe. The creation of the euro convinced investors that it was safe to lend to countries like Greece and Spain that had previously been considered risky, so money poured into these countries—mainly, by the way, to finance private rather than public borrowing, with Greece the exception.

And for a while everyone was happy. In southern Europe, huge housing bubbles led to a surge in construction employment, even as manufacturing became increasingly uncompetitive. Meanwhile, the German economy, which had been languishing, perked up thanks to rapidly rising exports to those bubble economies in the south. The euro, it seemed, was working.

Then the bubbles burst. The construction jobs vanished, and unemployment in the south soared; it's now well above 20 percent in both Spain and Greece. At the same time, revenues plunged; for the most part, big budget deficits are a result, not a cause, of the crisis. Nonetheless, investors took flight, driving up borrowing costs. In an attempt to soothe the financial markets, the afflicted countries imposed harsh austerity measures that deepened their slumps. And the euro as a whole is looking dangerously shaky.

What could turn this dangerous situation around? The answer is fairly clear: policymakers would have to (a) do something to bring southern Europe's borrowing costs down and (b) give Europe's debtors the same kind of opportunity to export their way out of trouble that Germany received during the good years—that is, create a boom in Germany that mirrors the boom in southern Europe between 1999 and 2007. (And yes, that would mean a temporary rise in German inflation.) The trouble is that Europe's policymakers seem reluctant to do (a) and completely unwilling to do (b).

In his remarks, Mr. Draghi—who I suspect understands all of this— basically floated the idea of having the central bank buy lots of southern European bonds to bring those borrowing costs down. But over the next two days German officials appeared to throw cold water on that idea. In principle, Mr. Draghi could just overrule German objections, but would he really be willing to do that?

And bond purchases are the easy part. The euro can't be saved unless Germany is also willing to accept substantially higher inflation over the next few years—and so far I have seen no sign that German officials are even willing to discuss this issue, let alone accept what's necessary. Instead, they're still insisting, despite failure after failure—remember when Ireland was supposedly on the road to rapid recovery?—that everything will be fine if debtors just stick to their austerity programs.

So could the euro be saved? Yes, probably. Should it be saved? Yes, even though its creation now looks like a huge mistake. For failure of the euro wouldn't just cause economic disruption; it would be a giant blow to the wider European project, which has brought peace and democracy to a continent with a tragic history.

But will it actually be saved? Despite Mr. Draghi's show of determination, that is, as I said, very much in doubt.

EUROPE'S IMPOSSIBLE DREAM

July 20, 2015

There's a bit of a lull in the news from Europe, but the underlying situation is as terrible as ever. Greece is experiencing a slump worse than the Great Depression, and nothing happening now offers hope of recovery. Spain has been hailed as a success story, because its economy is finally growing—but it still has 22 percent unemployment. And there is an arc of stagnation across the continent's top: Finland is experiencing a depression comparable to that in southern Europe, and Denmark and the Netherlands are also doing very badly.

How did things go so wrong? The answer is that this is what happens when self-indulgent politicians ignore arithmetic and the lessons of history. And no, I'm not talking about leftists in Greece or elsewhere; I'm talking about ultra-respectable men in Berlin, Paris, and Brussels, who have spent a quarter-century trying to run Europe on the basis of fantasy economics.

To someone who didn't know much economics, or chose to ignore awkward questions, establishing a unified European currency sounded like a great idea. It would make doing business across national borders easier, while serving as a powerful symbol of unity. Who could have foreseen the huge problems the euro would eventually cause?

Actually, lots of people. In January 2010 two European economists published an article titled "It Can't Happen, It's a Bad Idea, It Won't Last," mocking American economists who had warned that the euro would cause big problems. As it turned out, the article was an accidental classic: at the very moment it was being written, all those dire warnings were in the process of being vindicated. And the article's intended hall of shame—the long list of economists it cites for wrongheaded pessimism—has instead become a sort of honor roll, a who's who of those who got it more or less right.

The only big mistake of the euroskeptics was underestimating just how much damage the single currency would do.

The point is that it wasn't at all hard to see, right from the beginning, that currency union without political union was a very dubious project. So why did Europe go ahead with it?

Mainly, I'd say, because the idea of the euro sounded so good. That is, it sounded forward-looking, European-minded, exactly the kind of thing that appeals to the kind of people who give speeches at Davos. Such people didn't want nerdy economists telling them that their glamorous vision was a bad idea.

Indeed, within Europe's elite it quickly became very hard to raise objections to the currency project. I remember the atmosphere of the early 1990s very well: anyone who questioned the desirability of the euro was effectively shut out of the discussion. Furthermore, if you were an American expressing doubts you were invariably accused of ulterior motives—of being hostile to Europe, or wanting to preserve the dollar's "exorbitant privilege."

And the euro came. For a decade after its introduction a huge financial bubble masked its underlying problems. But now, as I said, all of the skeptics' fears have been vindicated.

Furthermore, the story doesn't end there. When the predicted and predictable strains on the euro began, Europe's policy response was to impose draconian austerity on debtor nations—and to deny the simple logic and historical evidence indicating that such policies would inflict terrible economic damage while failing to achieve the promised debt reduction.

It's astonishing even now how blithely top European officials dismissed warnings that slashing government spending and raising taxes would cause deep recessions, how they insisted that all would be well because fiscal discipline would inspire confidence. (It didn't.) The truth is that trying to deal with large debts through austerity alone—in particular, while simultaneously pursuing a hard-money policy—has never worked. It didn't work for Britain after World War I, despite immense sacrifices; why would anyone expect it to work for Greece?

What should Europe do now? There are no good answers—but the reason there are no good answers is because the euro has turned into a Roach Motel, a trap that's hard to escape. If Greece still had its own currency, the case for devaluing that currency, improving Greek competitiveness and ending deflation, would be overwhelming.

The fact that Greece no longer has a currency, that it would have to create one from scratch, vastly raises the stakes. My guess is that euro exit will still prove necessary. And in any case it will be essential to write down much of Greece's debt.

But we're not having a clear discussion of these options, because European discourse is still dominated by ideas the continent's elite would like to be true, but aren't. And Europe is paying a terrible price for this monstrous self-indulgence.

WHAT'S THE MATTER WITH EUROPE?

May 21, 2018

I f you had to identify a place and time where the humanitarian dream—
the vision of a society offering decent lives to all its members—came closest to realization, that place and time would surely be Western Europe
in the six decades after World War II. It was one of history's miracles: a continent ravaged by dictatorship, genocide, and war transformed itself into a
model of democracy and broadly shared prosperity.

Indeed, by the early years of this century Europeans were in many ways
better off than Americans. Unlike us, they had guaranteed health care, which
went along with higher life expectancy; they had much lower rates of poverty; they were actually more likely than we were to be gainfully employed
during their prime working years.

But now Europe is in big trouble. So, of course, are we. In particular,
while democracy is under siege on both sides of the Atlantic, the collapse of
freedom, if it comes, will probably happen here first. But it's worth taking
a break from our own Trumpian nightmare to look at Europe's woes, some
but not all of which parallel ours.

Many of Europe's problems come from the disastrous decision, a generation ago, to adopt a single currency. The creation of the euro led to a temporary wave of euphoria, with vast amounts of money flowing into nations
like Spain and Greece; then the bubble burst. And while countries like Iceland that retained their own money were able to quickly regain competitiveness by devaluing their currencies, eurozone nations were forced into a
protracted depression, with extremely high unemployment, as they strug-
gled to get their costs down.

This depression was made worse by an elite consensus, in the teeth of the evidence, that the root of Europe's troubles was not misaligned costs but fiscal profligacy, and that the solution was draconian austerity that made the depression even worse.

Some of the victims of the euro crisis, like Spain, have finally managed to claw their way back to competitiveness. Others, however, haven't. Greece remains a disaster area—and Italy, one of the three big economies remaining in the European Union, has now suffered two lost decades: G.D.P. per capita is no higher now than it was in 2000.

So it isn't really surprising that when Italy held elections in March, the big winners were anti–European Union parties—the populist Five Star Movement and the far-right League. In fact, the surprise is that it didn't happen sooner.

Those parties are now set to form a government. While the policies of that government aren't completely clear, they'll surely involve a break with the rest of Europe on multiple fronts: a reversal of fiscal austerity that may well end with exit from the euro, along with a crackdown on immigrants and refugees.

Nobody knows how this will end, but developments elsewhere in Europe offer some scary precedents. Hungary has effectively become a one-party autocracy, ruled by an ethnonationalist ideology. Poland seems well down the same path.

So what went wrong with the "European project"—the long march toward peace, democracy, and prosperity, underpinned by ever-closer economic and political integration? As I said, the giant mistake of the euro played a big role. But Poland, which never joined the euro, sailed through the economic crisis pretty much unscathed; yet democracy there is collapsing all the same.

I would suggest, however, that there's a deeper story here. There have always been dark forces in Europe (as there are here). When the Berlin Wall fell, a political scientist I know joked, "Now that Eastern Europe is free from the alien ideology of Communism, it can return to its true path: fascism." We both knew he had a point.

What kept these dark forces in check was the prestige of a European elite committed to democratic values. But that prestige was squandered through mismanagement—and the damage was compounded by unwillingness to face up to what was happening. Hungary's government has turned its back on everything Europe stands for—but it's still getting large-scale aid from Brussels.

And here, it seems to me, is where we see parallels with developments in America.

True, we didn't suffer a euro-style disaster. (Yes, we have a continentwide currency, but we have the federalized fiscal and banking institutions that make such a currency workable.) But the bad judgment of our "centrist" elites has rivaled that of their European counterparts. Remember that in 2010–2011, with America still suffering from mass unemployment, most of the Very Serious People in Washington were obsessed with . . . entitlement reform.

Meanwhile our centrists, along with much of the news media, spent years in denial about the radicalization of the G.O.P., engaging in almost pathological false equivalence. And now America finds itself governed by a party with as little respect for democratic norms or rule of law as Hungary's Fidesz.

The point is that what's wrong with Europe is, in a deep sense, the same thing that's wrong with America. And in both cases, the path to redemption will be very, very hard

9

Fiscal Phonies

THE GULLIBILITY OF THE DEFICIT SCOLDS

"TV STARS HAVE THE EMMYS, ATHLETES HAVE THE ESPYS, NOW BUDGET wonks have a major award to call their own." So began a gushing article published in January 2011 by the Center for a Responsible Federal Budget, describing a ceremony that granted "Fiscy Awards" to several political figures.

CRFB was one of a bevy of "fiscal responsibility" organizations that had high profiles in Washington circa 2010. The proliferation of such organizations was in part a kind of illusion, since many of them were financed by the same people, especially billionaire Pete Peterson. But their influence was real; CRFB wasn't wrong in describing the event as "star-studded," at least in the political version of starhood.

But there were a couple of funny things about the Fiscy event. One was that it came at a time when U.S. unemployment was still above 9 percent—more than 14 million Americans without jobs, of whom more than 6 million had been out of work for six months or more. Meanwhile, there was a good case to be made that the budget deficit was falling too fast. Most of the provisions of the American Recovery and Reinvestment Act—the "Obama stimulus"—expired at the end of 2010, and the rapid fading out of stimulus was one reason unemployment remained high throughout 2011.

So why was there a ceremony honoring men supposedly working to bring down deficits, but none to honor people trying to create jobs?

But even putting all of that aside, one of the three Fiscy awards went to Representative Paul Ryan, who would later become Speaker of the House. And even if you accepted the notion that being a deficit hawk was a good thing in January 2011, Ryan wasn't actually a deficit hawk; he was simply a phony. His supposed plan to reduce deficits—the plan that got him the award—was transparently fraudulent. It depended among other things on assuming that the government would be able to raise an additional trillion dollars in revenue by closing loopholes—but Ryan refused to specify which loopholes.

Sure enough, when he got the chance in 2017, Ryan rammed through a tax cut that will add around $2 trillion to the national debt without closing any loopholes whatsoever.

I could have told the people granting those awards that Ryan was a phony. In fact, I did, months before, in the first article in this section, "The Flimflam Man." Nonetheless, Ryan continued to produce plans, or rather "plans," in which the flimflam just kept getting more blatant—and a lot of Washington continued to treat him with great respect.

But the gullibility that led to the elevation of Ryan was itself part of a broader phenomenon. People who made a big deal about the deficit—I'm pretty sure I stole the term "deficit scolds" from someone, but I don't know who—proved, again and again, to be suckers for people whose actual interests had nothing to do with government debt and everything to do with a right-wing political agenda. As I wrote in "The Hijacked Commission," "a process meant to deal with real problems [was] hijacked on behalf of an ideological agenda." How much of this was naïveté, how much the true motives of the deficit scolds, is an interesting question.

And what was it all about, anyway? In 2019 Olivier Blanchard, one of the most influential (and relatively apolitical) economists of our era, made a big splash with a paper arguing, with a lot of evidence, that the whole issue of debt had been greatly overrated. I'd been saying similar things for years; but Blanchard truly drove the point home. And it was a point that became very relevant after Democrats won big in the 2018 midterms, and began thinking about how—but more crucially, whether, to pay for the agenda they themselves would pursue if they recaptured the White House in 2020.

THE FLIMFLAM MAN

August 5, 2010

One depressing aspect of American politics is the susceptibility of the political and media establishment to charlatans. You might have thought, given past experience, that DC insiders would be on their guard against conservatives with grandiose plans. But no: as long as someone on the right claims to have bold new proposals, he's hailed as an innovative thinker. And nobody checks his arithmetic.

Which brings me to the innovative thinker du jour: Representative Paul Ryan of Wisconsin.

Mr. Ryan has become the Republican Party's poster child for new ideas thanks to his "Roadmap for America's Future," a plan for a major overhaul of federal spending and taxes. News media coverage has been overwhelmingly favorable; on Monday, *The Washington Post* put a glowing profile of Mr. Ryan on its front page, portraying him as the G.O.P.'s fiscal conscience. He's often described with phrases like "intellectually audacious."

But it's the audacity of dopes. Mr. Ryan isn't offering fresh food for thought; he's serving up leftovers from the 1990s, drenched in flimflam sauce.

Mr. Ryan's plan calls for steep cuts in both spending and taxes. He'd have you believe that the combined effect would be much lower budget deficits, and, according to that *Washington Post* report, he speaks about deficits "in apocalyptic terms." And the *Post* also tells us that his plan would, indeed, sharply reduce the flow of red ink: "The Congressional Budget Office has estimated that Rep. Paul Ryan's plan would cut the budget deficit in half by 2020."

But the budget office has done no such thing. At Mr. Ryan's request, it produced an estimate of the budget effects of his proposed spending cuts—period. It didn't address the revenue losses from his tax cuts.

The nonpartisan Tax Policy Center has, however, stepped into the breach. Its numbers indicate that the Ryan plan would reduce revenue by almost $4 trillion over the next decade. If you add these revenue losses to the numbers the *Post* cites, you get a much larger deficit in 2020, roughly $1.3 trillion.

And that's about the same as the budget office's estimate of the 2020 deficit under the Obama administration's plans. That is, Mr. Ryan may speak about the deficit in apocalyptic terms, but even if you believe that his proposed spending cuts are feasible—which you shouldn't—the Roadmap wouldn't reduce the deficit. All it would do is cut benefits for the middle class while slashing taxes on the rich.

And I do mean slash. The Tax Policy Center finds that the Ryan plan would cut taxes on the richest 1 percent of the population in half, giving them 117 percent of the plan's total tax cuts. That's not a misprint. Even as it slashed taxes at the top, the plan would raise taxes for 95 percent of the population.

Finally, let's talk about those spending cuts. In its first decade, most of the alleged savings in the Ryan plan come from assuming zero dollar growth in domestic discretionary spending, which includes everything from energy policy to education to the court system. This would amount to a 25 percent cut once you adjust for inflation and population growth. How would such a severe cut be achieved? What specific programs would be slashed? Mr. Ryan doesn't say.

After 2020, the main alleged saving would come from sharp cuts in Medicare, achieved by dismantling Medicare as we know it, and instead giving seniors vouchers and telling them to buy their own insurance. Does this sound familiar? It should. It's the same plan Newt Gingrich tried to sell in 1995.

And we already know, from experience with the Medicare Advantage program, that a voucher system would have higher, not lower, costs than our current system. The only way the Ryan plan could save money would be by making those vouchers too small to pay for adequate coverage. Wealthy older Americans would be able to supplement their vouchers, and get the care they need; everyone else would be out in the cold.

In practice, that probably wouldn't happen: older Americans would be outraged—and they vote. But this means that the supposed budget savings from the Ryan plan are a sham.

So why have so many in Washington, especially in the news media, been taken in by this flimflam? It's not just inability to do the math, although that's part of it. There's also the unwillingness of self-styled centrists to face up to the realities of the modern Republican Party; they want to pretend, in the teeth of overwhelming evidence, that there are still people in the G.O.P. making sense. And last but not least, there's deference to power—the G.O.P. is a resurgent political force, so one mustn't point out that its intellectual heroes have no clothes.

But they don't. The Ryan plan is a fraud that makes no useful contribution to the debate over America's fiscal future.

THE HIJACKED COMMISSION

November 11, 2010

Count me among those who always believed that President Obama made a big mistake when he created the National Commission on Fiscal Responsibility and Reform—a supposedly bipartisan panel charged with coming up with solutions to the nation's long-run fiscal problems. It seemed obvious, as soon as the commission's membership was announced, that "bipartisanship" would mean what it so often does in Washington: a compromise between the center-right and the hard-right.

My misgivings increased as we got a better feel for the views of the commission's co-chairmen. It soon became clear that Erskine Bowles, the Democratic co-chairman, had a very Republican-sounding small-government agenda. Meanwhile, Alan Simpson, the Republican co-chairman, revealed the kind of honest broker he is by sending an abusive email to the executive director of the National Older Women's League in which he described Social Security as being "like a milk cow with 310 million tits."

We've known for a long time, then, that nothing good would come from the commission. But on Wednesday, when the co-chairmen released a PowerPoint outlining their proposal, it was even worse than the cynics expected.

Start with the declaration of "Our Guiding Principles and Values." Among them is, "Cap revenue at or below 21% of G.D.P." This is a guiding principle? And why is a commission charged with finding every possible route to a balanced budget setting an upper (but not lower) limit on revenue?

Matters become clearer once you reach the section on tax reform. The goals of reform, as Mr. Bowles and Mr. Simpson see them, are presented in the form of seven bullet points. "Lower Rates" is the first point; "Reduce the Deficit" is the seventh.

So how, exactly, did a deficit-cutting commission become a commission whose first priority is cutting tax rates, with deficit reduction literally at the bottom of the list?

Actually, though, what the co-chairmen are proposing is a mixture of tax cuts and tax increases—tax cuts for the wealthy, tax increases for the middle class. They suggest eliminating tax breaks that, whatever you think of them, matter a lot to middle-class Americans—the deductibility of health benefits and mortgage interest—and using much of the revenue gained thereby, not to reduce the deficit, but to allow sharp reductions in both the top marginal tax rate and in the corporate tax rate.

It will take time to crunch the numbers here, but this proposal clearly represents a major transfer of income upward, from the middle class to a small minority of wealthy Americans. And what does any of this have to do with deficit reduction?

Let's turn next to Social Security. There were rumors beforehand that the commission would recommend a rise in the retirement age, and sure enough, that's what Mr. Bowles and Mr. Simpson do. They want the age at which Social Security becomes available to rise along with average life expectancy. Is that reasonable?

The answer is no, for a number of reasons—including the point that working until you're 69, which may sound doable for people with desk jobs, is a lot harder for the many Americans who still do physical labor.

But beyond that, the proposal seemingly ignores a crucial point: while average life expectancy is indeed rising, it's doing so mainly for high earners, precisely the people who need Social Security least. Life expectancy in the bottom half of the income distribution has barely inched up over the past three decades. So the Bowles-Simpson proposal is basically saying that janitors should be forced to work longer because these days corporate lawyers live to a ripe old age.

Still, can't we say that for all its flaws, the Bowles-Simpson proposal is a serious effort to tackle the nation's long-run fiscal problem? No, we can't.

It's true that the PowerPoint contains nice-looking charts showing deficits falling and debt levels stabilizing. But it becomes clear, once you spend a little time trying to figure out what's going on, that the main driver of those pretty charts is the assumption that the rate of growth in health care costs will slow dramatically. And how is this to be achieved? By "establishing a process to regularly evaluate cost growth" and taking "additional steps as needed." What does that mean? I have no idea.

It's no mystery what has happened on the deficit commission: as so often happens in modern Washington, a process meant to deal with real problems has been hijacked on behalf of an ideological agenda. Under the guise of facing our fiscal problems, Mr. Bowles and Mr. Simpson are trying to smuggle in the same old, same old—tax cuts for the rich and erosion of the social safety net.

Can anything be salvaged from this wreck? I doubt it. The deficit commission should be told to fold its tents and go away.

WHAT'S IN THE RYAN PLAN?

New York Times *Blog*

August 16, 2012

A number of commenters have asked for a summary of what's actually in the Ryan plan. So this is a utility post.

The first thing you should know is that there are a couple of vintages of the plan, with some changes in detail, but not in general thrust. As it happens, the best nonpartisan analysis, in my judgment, is the CBO report on the first vintage; as I said, details change, but the general idea remains the same.

So, what's in the plan? You need to distinguish between the first decade, before the phasing out of Medicare as we know it begins, and after.

THE FIRST DECADE

In the first decade, the big things are (1) conversion of Medicaid into a block grant program, with much lower funding than projected under current law and (2) sharp cuts in top tax rates and corporate taxes.

Is this a deficit-reduction program? Not on the face of it: it's basically a trade-off of reduced aid to the poor for reduced taxes on the rich, with the net effect of the specific proposals being to increase, not reduce, the deficit. Yet Ryan claims a big deficit reduction, via two big "magic asterisks." First, he insists that the tax cuts won't reduce revenue, because they'll be offset with unspecified "base-broadening." Here's the CBO explanation: "The path for revenues as a percentage of G.D.P. was specified by Chairman Ryan's staff. The path rises steadily from about 15 percent of G.D.P. in 2010 to 19 percent in 2028 and remains at that level thereafter. There were no specifications of particular revenue provisions that would generate that path."

Howard Gleckman of the Tax Policy Center calls these unspecified sources of revenue "mystery meat," and strongly suggests that nothing like this would actually happen.

Second, there are large assumed cuts in discretionary spending relative to current policy—again, CBO: "That combination of other mandatory and discretionary spending was specified to decline from 12 percent of G.D.P. in 2010 to about 6 percent in 2021 and then move in line with the G.D.P. price deflator beginning in 2022, which would generate a further decline relative to G.D.P. No proposals were specified that would generate that path."

So, whenever you hear people talking about Ryan's deficit reductions, bear in mind that over the first decade all of the alleged deficit reduction comes from revenue and spending numbers that are simply asserted, not the result of any policies actually described in the "plan."

AFTER THE FIRST DECADE

After the first decade, Medicare is gradually transformed into a voucher scheme, with the value of the vouchers lagging well behind projected health care costs. Even so, however, much of the supposed deficit reduction comes not from Medicare but from further cuts in discretionary spending relative to G.D.P., with the number eventually falling to 3.5 percent of G.D.P. There is, once again, no specification of how this is to be accomplished; bear in mind that this number includes defense, which is currently around 4 percent of G.D.P.

IS THIS A PLAN?

Ryan basically proposes three big things: slashing Medicaid, cutting taxes on corporations and high-income people, and replacing Medicare with a drastically less well funded voucher system. These concrete proposals would, taken together, actually increase the deficit for the first decade and beyond.

All the claims of major deficit reduction therefore rest on the magic asterisks. In that sense, this isn't even a plan, it's just a set of assertions.

MELTING SNOWBALLS AND THE WINTER OF DEBT

January 9, 2019

D o you remember the winter of debt?

In late 2010 and early 2011, the U.S. economy had barely begun to recover from the 2008 financial crisis. Around 9 percent of the labor force was still unemployed; long-term unemployment was especially severe, with more than 6 million Americans having been out of work for six months or more. You might have expected the continuing employment crisis to be the focus of most economic policy discussion.

But no: Washington was obsessed with debt. The Simpson-Bowles report was the talk of the town. Paul Ryan's impassioned (and, of course, hypocritical) denunciations of federal debt won him media adulation and awards. And between the capital's debt obsession, the Republican takeover of the House, and a hard right turn in state governments, America was about to embark on a period of cutbacks in government spending unprecedented in the face of high unemployment.

Some of us protested bitterly against this policy turn, arguing that a period of mass unemployment was no time for fiscal austerity. And we were mostly right. Why only "mostly"? Because it's becoming increasingly doubtful whether there's any right time for fiscal austerity. The obsession with debt is looking foolish even at full employment.

That's the message I take from Olivier Blanchard's presidential address to the American Economic Association. To be fair, Blanchard—one of the world's leading macroeconomists, formerly the extremely influential chief economist of the IMF—was cautious in his pronouncements, and certainly didn't go all MMT and say that debt never matters. But his analysis nonetheless makes the Fix the Debt fixation (yes, they're still out there) look even worse than before.

Blanchard starts with the commonplace observation that interest rates on government debt are quite low, which in itself means that worries about debt are overblown. But he makes a more specific point: the average interest rate on debt is less than the economy's growth rate ("r<g"). Moreover, this isn't a temporary aberration: interest rates less than growth are actually the norm, broken only for a relatively short stretch in the 1980s.

Why does this matter? There are actually two separate but related implications of low interest rates. First, fears of a runaway spiral of rising debt are based on a myth. Second, raising private investment shouldn't be a huge priority.

On the first point: diatribes about debt often come with ominous warnings that debt may snowball over time. That is, high debt will mean high interest payments, which drive up deficits, leading to even more debt, which leads to even higher interest rates, and so on.

But what matters for government solvency isn't the absolute level of debt but its level relative to the tax base, which in turn basically corresponds to the size of the economy. And the dollar value of G.D.P. normally grows over time, due to both growth and inflation. Other things equal, this gradually melts the snowball: even if debt is rising in dollar terms, it will shrink as a percentage of G.D.P. if deficits aren't too large.

The classic example is what happened to U.S. debt from World War II. When and how did we pay it off? The answer is that we never did. Yet as Figure 1 shows, despite rising dollar debt, by 1970 growth and inflation had reduced the debt to an easily handled share of G.D.P.

And if interest rates are less than G.D.P. growth, this effect means that debt tends to melt away of its own accord: a high debt level means higher interest payments, but it also means more melting, and the latter effect predominates. A self-reinforcing debt spiral just doesn't happen.

Blanchard's second point is subtler but still important. In general, debt scolds warn not just about threats to government solvency but about growth. The claim is that high public debt feeds current consumption at the expense of investment for the future. And high debt does indeed prob-

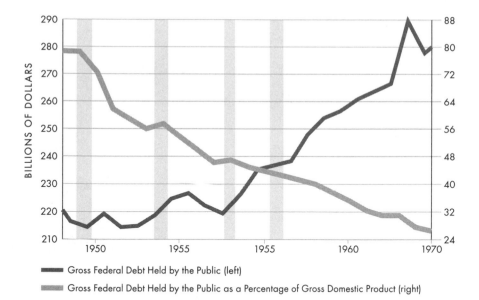

Gross Federal Debt Held by the Public (left)

Gross Federal Debt Held by the Public as a Percentage of Gross Domestic Product (right)

FIGURE 1. *Source: U.S. Bureau of Economic Analysis, Council of Economic Advisers.*

ably have that effect when the economy is near full employment (although in 2010–2011 more deficit spending would have led to more, not less, private investment).

But how important is it to suppress consumption to free up resources for investment? What Blanchard points out is that low interest rates are an indication that the private sector sees fairly low returns on investment, so that diverting more resources to private investment won't make that much difference to growth. True, the rate of return on investment is surely higher than the interest rate on safe assets like U.S. Treasuries. But Blanchard makes the case that it's not as much higher as many seem to think.

Does this mean that we should eat, drink, be merry, and forget about the future? No—but private investment isn't the big issue, since it probably doesn't have a very high rate of return. Blanchard doesn't say this, but what we should probably be worrying about instead is public investment in infrastructure, which has been neglected and suffers from obvious deficiencies.

Yet the debt obsession led to less, not more, public investment. Figure 2 shows public construction spending as a percentage of G.D.P. It rose briefly

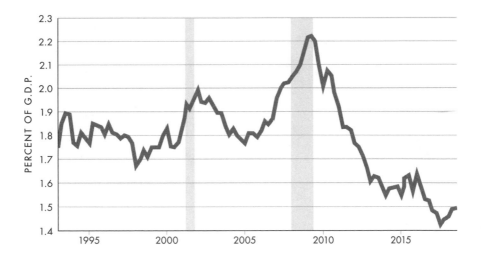

FIGURE 2. PUBLIC CONSTRUCTION SPENDING. *Source: U.S. Bureau of Economic Analysis, U.S. Bureau of the Census.*

during the Obama stimulus (partly because G.D.P. was down), then plunged to historically low levels, where it has stayed. For all the talk about taking care of future generations, debt scolds have almost surely hurt, not helped, our future prospects.

Notice, by the way, that I haven't even talked about business-cycle-related reasons to stop obsessing over debt. An environment of persistently low interest rates raises concerns about secular stagnation—a tendency to suffer repeated intractable slumps, because the Fed doesn't have enough ammunition to fight them. And such slumps may reduce long-term growth as well: the experience since 2008 suggests a high degree of hysteresis, in which seemingly short-run downturns end up reducing long-run economic potential.

But even without these concerns, debt looks like a hugely overblown issue, and the way debt displaced unemployment at the heart of public debate in 2010–2011 just keeps looking worse.

DEMOCRATS, DEBT, AND DOUBLE STANDARDS

February 11, 2019

Much of Donald Trump's State of the Union address was devoted to describing the menaces he claims face America—mainly the menace of scary brown people, but also the menace of socialism. And there has been a lot of discussion in the news media of what he said on those topics.

There has, however, been little coverage of one of the most revealing aspects of the SOTU: what Trump said about the menace of America's historically large government debt.

But wait, you may object—he didn't say anything about debt. Indeed he didn't—not one word. But that's what was so revealing.

After all, Republicans spent the entire Obama administration inveighing constantly about the dangers of debt, warning that America faced a looming crisis unless deficits were drastically reduced. Now that they're in power, however—and with the deficit surging thanks to a huge tax cut for corporations and the rich—they've totally dropped the subject.

According to ABC News, Mick Mulvaney, Trump's acting chief of staff, explained to G.O.P. members of Congress why debt wouldn't get a single mention in the SOTU: "Nobody cares."

And you know, he's kind of right. It's not just Republicans who suddenly seemed to stop caring about debt. For years deficit scolds dominated discourse inside the Beltway; much of the news media treated the urgency of fiscal austerity as an unquestioned fact, abandoning the usual rules of reportorial neutrality and plunging into outright advocacy. Yet since Trump's election those voices have become oddly muted.

What we've just seen confirmed, then, is what some of us were trying to tell you from the beginning: all that wailing about debt was hypocritical.

Republicans never actually cared about debt; they just pretended to be deficit hawks as a way to hamstring President Barack Obama's agenda. And many centrists have turned out to have a double standard, reserving passionate concern about debt for times when Democrats hold power.

But while the about-face on debt has, as I said, been deeply revealing, there are still two big questions. First, how much *should* we care about debt? Second, will a double standard continue to prevail? That is, will the deficit scolds suddenly get vocal again if and when Democrats regain power?

On the first question: One surprising thing about the debt obsession that peaked around 2011 is that it never had much basis in economic analysis. On the contrary, everything we know about fiscal policy says that it's a mistake to focus on deficit reduction when unemployment is high and interest rates are low, as they were when the fiscal scolds were at their loudest.

The case for worrying about debt is stronger now, given low unemployment. But interest rates are still very low by historical standards—less than 1 percent after adjusting for inflation. This is so low that we needn't fear that debt will snowball, with interest payments blowing up the deficit. It also suggests that we're suffering from chronic weakness in private investment demand (which, by the way, the 2017 tax cut doesn't seem to have boosted at all).

So in the past few months a number of prominent economists—including the former chief economist of the International Monetary Fund and top economists from the Obama administration—have published analyses saying that even now, with unemployment quite low, debt is much less of a problem than previously thought.

It's still a bad idea to run up debt for no good reason—say, to provide tax breaks that corporations just use to buy back their own stock, which is, of course, what the G.O.P. did. But borrowing at ultra-low interest rates to pay for investments in the future—infrastructure, of course, but also things like nutrition and health care for the young, who are the workers of tomorrow— is very defensible.

Which brings us to the question of double standards.

You don't have to agree with everything in proposals for a "Green New

Deal" to acknowledge that it's very much an investment program, not a mere giveaway. So it has been very dismaying to see how much commentary on these proposals either demands an immediate, detailed explanation of how Democrats would pay for their ideas, or dismisses the whole thing as impractical. Was there the same pushback against Republican tax cuts? No.

Look, we've seen this over and over again—three times since 1980. Republicans rail against budget deficits when they're out of power, then drop all their concerns and send the deficit soaring once they are in a position to cut taxes. Then when it's the Democrats' turn, they're expected to clean up the Republicans' red ink rather than address their own priorities. Enough already.

I'm not saying that Democrats should completely ignore the fiscal implications of their actions. Really big spending plans, especially if they don't clearly involve investment—for example, a major expansion of federal health spending—will have to be paid for with new taxes. But if and when Democrats are in a position to make policy, they should be ambitious, and not let the deficit scolds scare them into thinking small.

ON PAYING FOR A PROGRESSIVE AGENDA

February 19, 2019

Whoever gets the Democratic nomination, she or he will run in part on proposals to increase government spending. And you know what that will mean: there will be demands that the candidate explain how all this will be paid for. Many of those demands will be made in bad faith, from people who never ask the same questions about tax cuts. But there are some real questions about the fiscal side of a progressive agenda.

Well, I have some thoughts about that, inspired in part by looking at Elizabeth Warren's proposals on both the tax and spending side. By the way, I don't know whether Warren will or even should get the nomination. But she's a major intellectual figure, and is pushing her party toward serious policy discussion in a way that will have huge influence whatever her personal trajectory.

In particular, Warren's latest proposal on child care—and the instant pushback from the usual suspects—has me thinking that we could use a rough typology of spending proposals, classified by how they might be paid for. Specifically, let me suggest that there are three broad categories of progressive expenditure: investment, benefits enhancement, and major system overhaul, which need to be thought about differently from a fiscal point of view.

So, first off, investment—typically spending on infrastructure or research, but there may be some room at the margin for including spending on things like childhood development in the same category. The defining characteristic here is that it's spending that will enhance society's future productivity. How should we pay for that kind of outlay?

The answer is, we shouldn't. Think of all the people who say that the government should be run like a business. Actually it shouldn't, but the two kinds of institution do have this in common: if you can raise funds cheaply and apply them to high-return projects, you should go ahead and borrow. And federal borrowing costs are very low—less than 1 percent, adjusted for inflation—while we are desperately in need of public investment, i.e., it has a high social return. So we should just do it, without looking for pay-fors.

Much of what seems to be in the Green New Deal falls into that category. To the extent that it's a public investment program, demands that its supporters show how they'll pay for it show more about the critics' bad economics than about the GND's logic.

My second category is a bit harder to define, but what I'm thinking of are initiatives that either expand an existing public program or use subsidies to create incentives for expanding some kind of socially desirable private activity—in each case involving sums that are significant but not huge, say a fraction of a percent of G.D.P.

The Affordable Care Act falls into that category. It expanded Medicaid while using a combination of regulation and subsidies to make private insurance more available to families above the new Medicaid line. Warren's childcare proposal, which reportedly will come in at around one-third of a percent of G.D.P., also fits. So would a "Medicare for All" proposal that involves allowing people to buy in to government insurance, rather than offering that insurance free of charge.

It's harder to justify borrowing for this kind of initiative than borrowing for investment. True, with interest rates low and demand weak it makes some sense to run persistent deficits, but there are surely enough investment needs to use up that allowance. So you want some kind of pay-for. But the sums are small enough that the revenue involved could be raised by fairly narrow-gauge taxes—in particular, taxes that hit only high-income Americans.

That is, in fact, how Obamacare was financed: the revenue component came almost entirely from taxes on high incomes (there were some small items like the tax on tanning parlors). And Warren has in fact proposed additional taxes on the wealthy—her proposed tax on fortunes over $50 million would yield something like four times the cost of her child care proposal.

So benefit enhancement can, I'd argue, be paid for with taxes on high incomes and large fortunes. It doesn't have to impose on the middle class.

Finally, my third category is major system overhaul, of which the archetype would be replacing employer-based private health insurance with a tax-financed public program—the purist version of Medicare for All. A really major expansion of Social Security might fall into that category too, although smaller enhancements might not.

Proposals in this category are literally an order of magnitude more expensive than benefit enhancements: private health insurance currently amounts to 6 percent of G.D.P. To implement these proposals, then, we'd need a lot more revenue, which would have to come from things like payroll taxes and/or a value-added tax that hit the middle class.

You can argue that most middle-class families would be better off in the end, that the extra benefits would more than compensate for the higher taxes. And you'd probably be right. But this would be a much heavier political lift. You don't have to be a neoliberal tool to wonder whether major system overhaul should be part of the Democratic platform right now, even if it's something many progressives aspire to.

My main point now, however, is that when people ridicule progressive proposals as silly and unaffordable, they're basically revealing their own biases and ignorance. Investment can and should be debt-financed; benefit enhancements can be largely paid for with high-end taxes. Howard Schultz won't like it, but that's his problem.

10

Tax Cuts

THE ULTIMATE ZOMBIE

RONALD REAGAN PASSED A BIG TAX CUT IN AUGUST 1981. AS IT HAPPENS, the U.S. economy was just entering a recession—the second phase of what many consider the "double-dip recession" of 1979–1982, which sent unemployment to its highest level since the Great Depression. By late 1982, however, the economy began to recover, experiencing two years of very rapid growth before settling back to a more normal pace.

As you may have noticed, 1981 was a long time ago. IBM had just introduced its first desktop PC, one in which all commands had to be typed in. Smartphones were decades away. Social attitudes were almost unrecognizable by modern standards; for example, only a third of American whites thought interracial marriages were acceptable.

Yet to this day conservatives hold up those two years of growth as proof of the magical power of tax cuts for rich people.

As it happens, they're wrong even about what happened in 1982–1984. The recession of the early 1980s was more or less a deliberate creation of the Federal Reserve, which drastically raised interest rates in an attempt to squeeze down a high rate of inflation. In 1982 the Fed relented, sending interest rates sharply down, and it was this monetary easing, not the Reagan tax cut, that mostly explained the 1982–1984 boom.

But even aside from that misinterpretation, why does the right keep harping on such an old incident to justify its favorite policy? Why doesn't it say something about more recent successes?

Because there haven't been any.

The doctrine that low taxes on the wealthy are the secret of prosperity has been tested again and again since the 1980s. It was tested in 1993, when Bill Clinton raised taxes, and conservatives predicted disaster; instead, he presided over a huge economic expansion. It was tested under George W.

Bush, who cut taxes again, and whose supporters promised a boom; what he actually got was lackluster growth followed by financial collapse. It was tested in 2013, when Barack Obama allowed some of the Bush tax cuts to expire, while raising some other taxes to pay for Obamacare; the economy just kept chugging along.

It was, finally, tested by Donald Trump, who passed a big tax cut in 2017 amid promises of another economic miracle; even as late as early 2019, the Trump tax cut was looking like a big fizzle.

There were also tests at the state level. In 2011 California and Kansas moved in opposite directions. California raised taxes, amid cries from the right that it was committing "economic suicide," while Kansas cut taxes, promising an economic surge. As it turned out, California did fine, while Kansas ended up with a budget crisis, and a vote by Republican legislators to reverse many of the tax cuts.

In short, few economic doctrines have been as thoroughly tested, and thoroughly refuted, as the claim that low taxes on the rich accomplish great things for everyone. Yet the doctrine persists. In fact, it has tightened its grip on the Republican Party, to the point where almost nobody in the party dares to express skepticism.

I originally saw the term "zombie ideas" in an article about, of all things, Canadian health care, where it referred to false claims like the assertion that vast numbers of Canadians were constantly crossing into the United States in pursuit of medical treatment. As the article pointed out, this claim had been refuted many times, and should have been killed as an argument against Canada's health system. Instead, however, it just kept shambling along, eating people's brains.

Well, belief in the magic of tax cuts for the rich is the ultimate zombie. And the truth is that it's not hard to see why it has proved impossible to kill. After all, think about who benefits from the persistence of the belief that low taxes on the rich are a great thing. All it takes are a few billionaires willing to spend a small fraction of their wealth supporting politicians, think tanks— or actually "think" tanks—and partisan media willing to spread the tax-cut virus. That's easily enough to keep the zombies lurching along.

Some of the articles in this section represent efforts to shoot those zombies in the head, yet again. After all, one must keep trying.

But here's the thing: the public has never bought into the tax-cut message. Polls consistently show that voters want the rich to pay more, not less, in taxes. And especially since the 2018 midterms some Democrats have been emboldened, once again willing to propose taxes on high incomes and extreme wealth to pay for social priorities. In the final part of this section, I talk about some of those ideas.

THE TWINKIE MANIFESTO

November 18, 2012

The Twinkie, it turns out, was introduced way back in 1930. In our memories, however, the iconic snack will forever be identified with the 1950s, when Hostess popularized the brand by sponsoring *The Howdy Doody Show*. And the demise of Hostess has unleashed a wave of baby boomer nostalgia for a seemingly more innocent time.

Needless to say, it wasn't really innocent. But the fifties—the Twinkie Era—do offer lessons that remain relevant in the 21st century. Above all, the success of the postwar American economy demonstrates that, contrary to today's conservative orthodoxy, you can have prosperity without demeaning workers and coddling the rich.

Consider the question of tax rates on the wealthy. The modern American right, and much of the alleged center, is obsessed with the notion that low tax rates at the top are essential to growth. Remember that Erskine Bowles and Alan Simpson, charged with producing a plan to curb deficits, nonetheless somehow ended up listing "lower tax rates" as a "guiding principle."

Yet in the 1950s incomes in the top bracket faced a marginal tax rate of 91, that's right, 91 percent, while taxes on corporate profits were twice as large, relative to national income, as in recent years. The best estimates suggest that circa 1960 the top 0.01 percent of Americans paid an effective federal tax rate of more than 70 percent, twice what they pay today.

Nor were high taxes the only burden wealthy businessmen had to bear. They also faced a labor force with a degree of bargaining power hard to imagine today. In 1955 roughly a third of American workers were union members. In the biggest companies, management and labor bargained as equals, so much so that it was common to talk about corporations serving an array of "stakeholders" as opposed to merely serving stockholders.

Squeezed between high taxes and empowered workers, executives were relatively impoverished by the standards of either earlier or later generations. In 1955 *Fortune* magazine published an essay, "How Top Executives Live," which emphasized how modest their lifestyles had become compared with days of yore. The vast mansions, armies of servants, and huge yachts of the 1920s were no more; by 1955 the typical executive, *Fortune* claimed, lived in a smallish suburban house, relied on part-time help, and skippered his own relatively small boat.

The data confirm *Fortune's* impressions. Between the 1920s and the 1950s real incomes for the richest Americans fell sharply, not just compared with the middle class but in absolute terms. According to estimates by the economists Thomas Piketty and Emmanuel Saez, in 1955 the real incomes of the top 0.01 percent of Americans were less than half what they had been in the late 1920s, and their share of total income was down by three-quarters.

Today, of course, the mansions, armies of servants, and yachts are back, bigger than ever—and any hint of policies that might crimp plutocrats' style is met with cries of "socialism." Indeed, the whole Romney campaign was based on the premise that President Obama's threat to modestly raise taxes on top incomes, plus his temerity in suggesting that some bankers had behaved badly, were crippling the economy. Surely, then, the far less plutocrat-friendly environment of the 1950s must have been an economic disaster, right?

Actually, some people thought so at the time. Paul Ryan and many other modern conservatives are devotees of Ayn Rand. Well, the collapsing, moocher-infested nation she portrayed in *Atlas Shrugged*, published in 1957, was basically Dwight Eisenhower's America.

Strange to say, however, the oppressed executives *Fortune* portrayed in 1955 didn't go Galt and deprive the nation of their talents. On the contrary, if *Fortune* is to be believed, they were working harder than ever. And the high-tax, strong-union decades after World War II were in fact marked by spectacular, widely shared economic growth: nothing before or since has matched the doubling of median family income between 1947 and 1973.

Which brings us back to the nostalgia thing.

There are, let's face it, some people in our political life who pine for the days when minorities and women knew their place, gays stayed firmly in the closet, and congressmen asked, "Are you now or have you ever been?" The rest of us, however, are very glad those days are gone. We are, morally, a much better nation than we were. Oh, and the food has improved a lot, too.

Along the way, however, we've forgotten something important—namely, that economic justice and economic growth aren't incompatible. America in the 1950s made the rich pay their fair share; it gave workers the power to bargain for decent wages and benefits; yet contrary to right-wing propaganda then and now, it prospered. And we can do that again.

THE BIGGEST TAX SCAM IN HISTORY

November 27, 2017

Donald Trump likes to declare that every good thing that happens while he's in office—job growth, rising stock prices, whatever—is the biggest, greatest, best ever. Then the fact-checkers weigh in and quickly determine that the claim is false.

But what's happening in the Senate right now really does deserve Trumpian superlatives. The bill Republican leaders are trying to ram through this week without hearings, without time for even a basic analysis of its likely economic impact, is the biggest tax scam in history. It's such a big scam that it's not even clear who's being scammed—middle-class taxpayers, people who care about budget deficits, or both.

One thing is clear, however: one way or another, the bill would hurt most Americans. The only big winners would be the wealthy—especially those who mainly collect income from their assets rather than working for a living—plus tax lawyers and accountants who would have a field day exploiting the many loopholes the legislation creates.

The core of the bill is a huge redistribution of income from lower- and middle-income families to corporations and business owners. Corporate tax rates go down sharply, while ordinary families are nickel-and-dimed by a series of tax changes, no one of which is that big a deal in itself, but which add up to significant tax increases on almost two-thirds of middle-class taxpayers.

Meanwhile, the bill would partially repeal Obamacare, in a way that would sharply reduce aid to lower-income families and raise the cost of insurance for many in the middle class.

You might wonder how such a thing could possibly pass the Senate. But that's where the scamming comes in.

While the underlying structure of the bill involves raising taxes on the middle class, the bill also includes a number of temporary tax breaks that would, at first, offset these tax increases. As a result, in the first few years most middle-class families would see modest tax cuts.

But the operative word here is "temporary." All of these tax breaks either dwindle over time or are scheduled to expire at some point; by 2027 the bill is, as I said, a tax increase on the middle class used to pay for tax cuts that mainly benefit the wealthy.

Why would anyone write a bill full of provisions that evaporate over time? There's no economic or policy logic behind it. Instead, it's all about trying to have it both ways, making a safe space for political double talk.

Here's how it works: If you point out that the bill hugely favors the wealthy at the expense of ordinary families, Republicans will point to the next few years, when the class-war nature of the plan is obscured by those temporary tax breaks—and claim that whatever the language of the law says, those tax breaks will actually be made permanent by later Congresses.

But if you point out that the bill is fiscally irresponsible, they'll say that it "only" raises the deficit by $1.5 trillion over the next decade and doesn't raise deficits at all after that—because, you see, those tax breaks will expire by 2027, so the tax hikes will raise a lot of revenue. By the way, the claim that middle-class taxes will rise is crucial to passing the bill: only bills that don't raise deficits after ten years can bypass the filibuster and be enacted by a simple Senate majority.

The point, of course, is that these claims can't both be true. Either this bill is a big tax hike on the middle class, or it's a huge budget-buster. Which is it? Nobody really knows; probably even the people who wrote this monstrosity don't know. But someone is being scammed, bigly.

Oh, and ignore claims that tax cuts for corporations would jump-start the economy and pay for themselves. Of the forty-two ideologically diverse economists surveyed by the University of Chicago on the impact of Republican tax plans, only one agreed that they would lead to substantial economic growth, while none disagreed with the proposition that they would substantially increase U.S. debt.

So it's a giant scam. And while the exact nature of the scam may be unclear, ordinary American families would end up being the victims either way.

For suppose those temporary tax breaks did end up becoming permanent, so that the budget deficit soared on a long-term basis. Then what? You know the answer: Republicans would suddenly revert to the pretense that they're deficit hawks, and demand "entitlement reform"—that is, cuts in Medicare, Medicaid, and Social Security, programs that ordinary families depend on. In fact, they're already talking about those cuts—they've started the switch even before getting the suckers to take the bait.

So will they manage to pull off this giant con job? The reason they're rushing this to the Senate floor without a single hearing, without a full assessment from Congress's own official scorekeepers, is their hope that they can pass the thing before people figure out what they're up to.

And the question is whether there are enough Republican senators with principles, who believe that policies should not be sold with lies, to stop this bum's rush.

THE TRUMP TAX SCAM, PHASE 2

October 18, 2018

When the Trump tax cut was on the verge of being enacted, I called it "the biggest tax scam in history," and made a prediction: deficits would soar, and when they did, Republicans would once again pretend to care about debt and demand cuts in Medicare, Medicaid, and Social Security.

Sure enough, the deficit is soaring. And this week Mitch McConnell, the Senate majority leader, after declaring the surge in red ink "very disturbing," called for, you guessed it, cuts in "Medicare, Social Security and Medicaid." He also suggested that Republicans might repeal the Affordable Care Act—taking away health care from tens of millions—if they do well in the midterm elections.

Any political analyst who didn't see this coming should find a different profession. After all, "starve the beast"—cut taxes on the rich, then use the resulting deficits as an excuse to hack away at the safety net—has been G.O.P. strategy for decades.

Oh, and anyone asking why Republicans believed claims that the tax cut would pay for itself is being naïve. Whatever they may have said, they never actually believed that the tax cut would be deficit-neutral; they pushed for a tax cut because it was what wealthy donors wanted, and because their posturing as deficit hawks was always fraudulent. They didn't really buy into economic nonsense; it would be more accurate to say that economic nonsense bought them.

That said, even I have been surprised by a couple of things about the G.O.P.'s budget bait-and-switch. One is the timing: I would have expected

McConnell to hold his tongue until after the midterms. The other is the lying: I knew Donald Trump and his allies would be dishonest, but I didn't expect the lies to be as baldfaced as they are.

What are they lying about? For starters, about the causes of a sharply higher deficit, which they claim is the result of higher spending, not lost revenue. Mick Mulvaney, Trump's budget director, even tried to claim that the deficit is up because of the costs of hurricane relief.

The flimsy justification for such claims is that in dollar terms, federal revenue over the past year is slightly up from the previous year, while spending is about 3 percent higher.

But that's a junk argument, and everyone knows it. Both revenue and spending normally grow every year thanks to inflation, population growth, and other factors. Revenue during Barack Obama's second term grew more than 7 percent a year. The sources of the deficit surge are measured by how much we've deviated from that normal growth, and the answer is that it's all about the tax cut.

Dishonesty about the sources of the deficit is, however, more or less a standard Republican tactic. What's new is the double talk that pervades G.O.P. positioning on the budget and, to be fair, just about every major policy issue.

What do I mean by double talk? Well, consider the fact that even as McConnell blames "entitlements" (that is, Medicare and Social Security) for deficits, and declares (falsely) that Medicare in particular is "unsustainable," Paul Ryan's super PAC has been running ads accusing *Democrats* of wanting to cut Medicare. The cynicism is breathtaking.

But then, it's no more cynical than the behavior of Republicans like Dean Heller, Josh Hawley, and even Ted Cruz who voted to repeal the Affordable Care Act, which protects Americans with pre-existing medical conditions, or supported a lawsuit trying to strip that protection out of the act, and are now running on the claim that they want to . . . protect people with pre-existing conditions.

The point is that we're now in a political campaign where one side's claimed position on every major policy issue is the opposite of its true position. Republicans have concluded that they can't win an argument on the issues, but rather than changing their policies, they're squirting out clouds of ink and hoping voters won't figure out where they really stand.

Why do they think they can get away with this? The main answer is obviously contempt for their own supporters, many of whom get their news from Fox and other propaganda outlets that slavishly follow the party line. And even in appeals to those supporters who rely on other sources, Republicans believe that they can neutralize the deep unpopularity of their actual policies by misrepresenting their positions, and win by playing to racism and fear.

But let's be clear: G.O.P. cynicism also involves a lot of contempt for the mainstream news media. Historically, media organizations have been remarkably unwilling to call out lies; the urge to play it safe with he-said-she-said reporting has very much worked to Republicans' advantage, given the reality that the modern G.O.P. lies a lot more than Democrats do. Even the most blatant falsehood tends to be reported with headlines about how "Democrats say" it's false, not that it's actually false.

Anyway, at this point Republicans are proclaiming that war is peace, freedom is slavery, ignorance is strength, and the party that keeps trying to kill Medicare is actually the program's greatest defender.

Can a campaign this dishonest actually win? We'll find out in less than three weeks.

WHY WAS TRUMP'S TAX CUT A FIZZLE?

November 15, 2018

L ast week's blue wave means that Donald Trump will go into the 2020 election with only one major legislative achievement: a big tax cut for corporations and the wealthy. Still, that tax cut was supposed to accomplish big things. Republicans thought it would give them a big electoral boost, and they predicted dramatic economic gains. What they got instead, however, was a big fizzle.

The political payoff, of course, never arrived. And the economic results have been disappointing. True, we've had two quarters of fairly fast economic growth, but such growth spurts are fairly common—there was a substantially bigger spurt in 2014, and hardly anyone noticed. And this growth was driven largely by consumer spending and, surprise, government spending, which wasn't what the tax cutters promised.

Meanwhile, there's no sign of the vast investment boom the law's backers promised. Corporations have used the tax cut's proceeds largely to buy back their own stock rather than to add jobs and expand capacity.

But why have the tax cut's impacts been so minimal? Leave aside the glitch-filled changes in individual taxes, which will keep accountants busy for years; the core of the bill was a huge cut in corporate taxes. Why hasn't this done more to increase investment?

The answer, I'd argue, is that business decisions are a lot less sensitive to financial incentives—including tax rates—than conservatives claim. And appreciating that reality doesn't just undermine the case for the Trump tax cut. It undermines Republican economic doctrine as a whole.

About business decisions: it's a dirty little secret of monetary analysis that changes in interest rates affect the economy mainly through their effect on the housing market and the international value of the dollar (which in turn affects the competitiveness of U.S. goods on world markets). Any direct effect on business investment is so small that it's hard even to see it in the data. What drives such investment is, instead, perceptions about market demand.

Why is this the case? One main reason is that business investments have relatively short working lives. If you're considering whether to take out a mortgage to buy a house that will stand for many decades, the interest rate matters a lot. But if you're thinking about taking out a loan to buy, say, a work computer that will either break down or become obsolescent in a few years, the interest rate on the loan will be a minor consideration in deciding whether to make the purchase.

And the same logic applies to tax rates: there aren't many potential business investments that will be worth doing with a 21 percent profits tax, the current rate, but weren't worth doing at 35 percent, the rate before the Trump tax cut.

Also, a substantial fraction of corporate profits really represents rewards to monopoly power, not returns on investment—and cutting taxes on monopoly profits is a pure giveaway, offering no reason to invest or hire.

Now, proponents of the tax cut, including Trump's own economists, made a big deal about how we now have a global capital market, in which money flows to wherever it gets the highest after-tax return. And they pointed to countries with low corporate taxes, like Ireland, which appear to attract lots of foreign investment.

The key word here is, however, "appear." Corporations do have a strong incentive to cook their books—I'm sorry, manage their internal pricing—in such a way that reported profits pop up in low-tax jurisdictions, and this in turn leads on paper to large overseas investments.

But there's much less to these investments than meets the eye. For example, the vast sums corporations have supposedly invested in Ireland have yielded remarkably few jobs and remarkably little income for the Irish themselves—because most of that huge investment in Ireland is nothing more than an accounting fiction.

Now you know why the money U.S. companies reported moving home after taxes were cut hasn't shown up in jobs, wages, and investment: nothing really moved. Overseas subsidiaries transferred some assets back to their parent companies, but this was just an accounting maneuver, with almost no impact on anything real.

So the basic result of lower taxes on corporations is that corporations pay less in taxes—full stop. Which brings me to the problem with conservative economic doctrine.

That doctrine is all about the supposed need to give the already privileged incentives to do nice things for the rest of us. We must, the right says, cut taxes on the wealthy to induce them to work hard, and cut taxes on corporations to induce them to invest in America.

But this doctrine keeps failing in practice. President George W. Bush's tax cuts didn't produce a boom; President Barack Obama's tax hike didn't cause a depression. Tax cuts in Kansas didn't jump-start the state's economy; tax hikes in California didn't slow growth.

And with the Trump tax cut, the doctrine has failed again. Unfortunately, it's difficult to get politicians to understand something when their campaign contributions depend on their not understanding it.

THE TRUMP TAX CUT: EVEN WORSE THAN YOU'VE HEARD

January 1, 2019

The 2017 tax cut has received pretty bad press, and rightly so. Its proponents made big promises about soaring investment and wages, and also assured everyone that it would pay for itself; none of that has happened.

Yet coverage actually hasn't been negative enough. The story you mostly read runs something like this: the tax cut has caused corporations to bring some money home, but they've used it for stock buybacks rather than to raise wages, and the boost to growth has been modest. That doesn't sound great, but it's still better than the reality: no money has, in fact, been brought home, and the tax cut has probably reduced national income. Indeed, at least 90 percent of Americans will end up poorer thanks to that cut.

Let me explain each point in turn.

First, when people say that U.S. corporations have "brought money home" they're referring to dividends overseas subsidiaries have paid to their parent corporations. These did indeed surge briefly in 2018, as the tax law made it advantageous to transfer some assets from the books of those subsidiaries to the home companies; these transactions also showed up as a reduction in the measured stake of the parents in the subsidiaries, i.e., as negative direct investment (Figure 1).

But these transactions are simply rearrangements of companies' books for tax purposes; they don't necessarily correspond to anything real. Suppose that Multinational Megacorp USA decides to have its subsidiary, Mul-

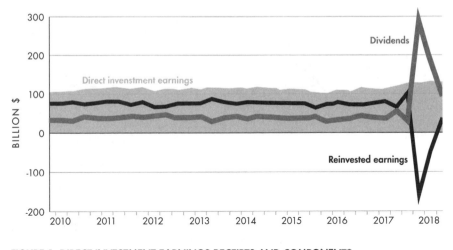

FIGURE 1. DIRECT INVESTMENT EARNINGS RECEIPTS AND COMPONENTS.
Source: U.S. Bureau of Economic Analysis.

tinational Mega Ireland, transfer some assets to the home company. This will produce the kind of simultaneous and opposite movement in dividends and direct investment you see in Figure 1. But the company's overall balance sheet—which always included the assets of MM Ireland—hasn't changed at all. No real resources have been transferred; MM USA has neither gained nor lost the ability to invest here.

If you want to know whether investable funds are really being transferred to the U.S., you need to look at the overall balance on financial account—or, what should be the same (and is more accurately measured), the inverse of the balance on current account. Figure 2 shows that balance as a share of G.D.P.—and as you can see, basically nothing has happened.

So the tax cut induced some accounting maneuvers, but did nothing to promote capital flows to America.

The tax cut did, however, have one important international effect: we're now paying more money to foreigners.

Bear in mind that the one clear, overwhelming result of the tax cut is a big break for corporations: federal tax receipts on corporate income have plunged (Figure 3).

The key point to realize is that in today's globalized corporate system, a

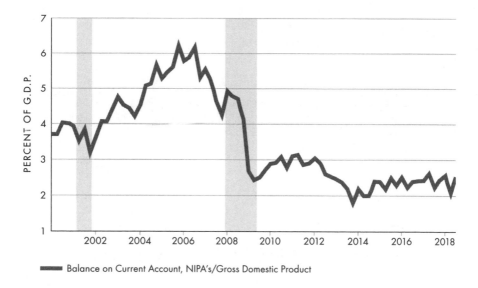

Balance on Current Account, NIPA's/Gross Domestic Product

FIGURE 2. *Source: U.S. Bureau of Economic Analysis.*

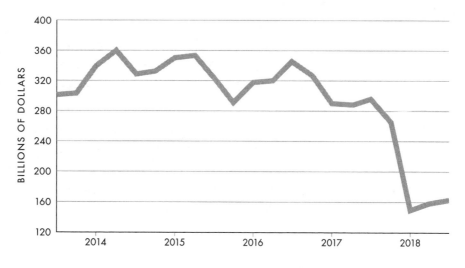

FIGURE 3. CORPORATE TAX RECEIPTS. *Source: U.S. Bureau of Economic Analysis.*

lot of any country's corporate sector, our own very much included, is actually owned by foreigners, either directly because corporations here are foreign subsidiaries, or indirectly because foreigners own American stocks. Indeed, roughly a third of U.S. corporate profits basically flow to foreign nationals—

which means that a third of the tax cut flowed abroad, rather than staying at home. This probably outweighs any positive effect on G.D.P. growth. So the tax cut probably made America poorer, not richer.

And it certainly made most Americans poorer. While two-thirds of the corporate tax cut may have gone to U.S. residents, 84 percent of stocks are held by the wealthiest 10 percent of the population. Everyone else will see hardly any benefit.

Meanwhile, since the tax cut isn't paying for itself, it will eventually have to be paid for some other way—either by raising other taxes, or by cutting spending on programs people value. The cost of these hikes or cuts will be much less concentrated on the top 10 percent than the benefit of the original tax cut. So it's a near-certainty that the vast majority of Americans will be worse off thanks to Trump's only major legislative success.

As I said, even the mainly negative reporting doesn't convey how bad a deal this whole thing is turning out to be.

THE ECONOMICS OF SOAKING THE RICH

January 5, 2019

I have no idea how well Alexandria Ocasio-Cortez will perform as a member of Congress. But her election is already serving a valuable purpose. You see, the mere thought of having a young, articulate, telegenic nonwhite woman serve is driving many on the right mad—and in their madness they're inadvertently revealing their true selves.

Some of the revelations are cultural: the hysteria over a video of AOC dancing in college says volumes, not about her, but about the hysterics. But in some ways the more important revelations are intellectual: the right's denunciation of AOC's "insane" policy ideas serves as a very good reminder of who is actually insane.

The controversy of the moment involves AOC's advocacy of a tax rate of 70–80 percent on very high incomes, which is obviously crazy, right? I mean, who thinks that makes sense? Only ignorant people like . . . um, Peter Diamond, Nobel laureate in economics and arguably the world's leading expert on public finance. (Although Republicans blocked him from an appointment to the Federal Reserve Board with claims that he was unqualified. Really.) And it's a policy nobody has ever implemented, aside from . . . the United States, for thirty-five years after World War II—including the most successful period of economic growth in our history.

To be more specific, Diamond, in work with Emmanuel Saez—one of our leading experts on inequality—estimated the optimal top tax rate to be 73 percent. Some put it higher: Christina Romer, top macroeconomist and former head of President Obama's Council of Economic Advisers, estimates it at more than 80 percent.

Where do these numbers come from? Underlying the Diamond-Saez analysis are two propositions: diminishing marginal utility and competitive markets.

Diminishing marginal utility is the common-sense notion that an extra dollar is worth a lot less in satisfaction to people with very high incomes than to those with low incomes. Give a family with an annual income of $20,000 an extra $1,000 and it will make a big difference to their lives. Give a guy who makes $1 million an extra thousand and he'll barely notice it.

What this implies for economic policy is that we shouldn't care what a policy does to the incomes of the very rich. A policy that makes the rich a bit poorer will affect only a handful of people, and will barely affect their life satisfaction, since they will still be able to buy whatever they want.

So why not tax them at 100 percent? The answer is that this would eliminate any incentive to do whatever it is they do to earn that much money, which would hurt the economy. In other words, tax policy toward the rich should have nothing to do with the interests of the rich, per se, but should only be concerned with how incentive effects change the behavior of the rich, and how this affects the rest of the population.

But here's where competitive markets come in. In a perfectly competitive economy, with no monopoly power or other distortions—which is the kind of economy conservatives want us to believe we have—everyone gets paid his or her marginal product. That is, if you get paid $1,000 an hour, it's because each extra hour you work adds $1,000 worth to the economy's output.

In that case, however, why do we care how hard the rich work? If a rich man works an extra hour, adding $1,000 to the economy, but gets paid $1,000 for his efforts, the combined income of everyone else doesn't change, does it? Ah, but it does—because he pays taxes on that extra $1,000. So the social benefit from getting high-income individuals to work a bit harder is the tax revenue generated by that extra effort—and conversely the cost of their working less is the reduction in the taxes they pay.

Or to put it a bit more succinctly, when taxing the rich, all we should care about is how much revenue we raise. The optimal tax rate on people with very high incomes is the rate that raises the maximum possible revenue.

And that's something we can estimate, given evidence on how responsive the pre-tax income of the wealthy actually is to tax rates. As I said,

Diamond and Saez put the optimal rate at 73 percent, Romer at over 80 percent—which is consistent with what AOC said.

An aside: what if we take into account the reality that markets aren't perfectly competitive, that there's a lot of monopoly power out there? The answer is that this almost surely makes the case for even higher tax rates, since high income people presumably get a lot of those monopoly rents.

So AOC, far from showing her craziness, is fully in line with serious economic research. (I hear that she's been talking to some very good economists.) Her critics, on the other hand, do indeed have crazy policy ideas—and tax policy is at the heart of the crazy.

You see, Republicans almost universally advocate low taxes on the wealthy, based on the claim that tax cuts at the top will have huge beneficial effects on the economy. This claim rests on research by . . . well, nobody. There isn't any body of serious work supporting G.O.P. tax ideas, because the evidence is overwhelmingly against those ideas.

Look at the history of top marginal income tax rates (left) versus growth

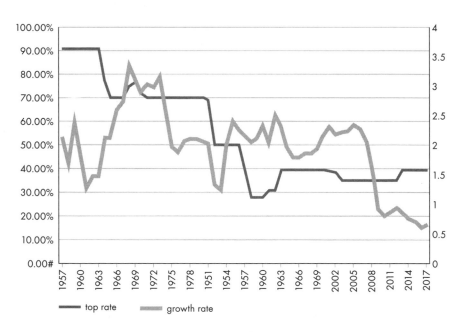

TOP TAX RATES AND GROWTH. *Source: Urban-Brookings Tax Policy Center, U.S. Bureau of Economic Analysis.*

in real G.D.P. per capita (right, measured over ten years, to smooth out short-run fluctuations):

What we see is that America used to have very high tax rates on the rich—higher even than those AOC is proposing—and did just fine. Since then tax rates have come way down, and if anything the economy has done less well.

Why do Republicans adhere to a tax theory that has no support from nonpartisan economists and is refuted by all available data? Well, ask who benefits from low taxes on the rich, and it's obvious.

And because the party's coffers demand adherence to nonsense economics, the party prefers "economists" who are obvious frauds and can't even fake their numbers effectively.

Which brings me back to AOC, and the constant effort to portray her as flaky and ignorant. Well, on the tax issue she's just saying what good economists say; and she definitely knows more economics than almost everyone in the G.O.P. caucus, not least because she doesn't "know" things that aren't true.

ELIZABETH WARREN DOES TEDDY ROOSEVELT

January 28, 2019

America invented progressive taxation. And there was a time when leading American politicians were proud to proclaim their willingness to tax the wealthy, not just to raise revenue, but to limit excessive concentration of economic power.

"It is important," said Theodore Roosevelt in 1906, "to grapple with the problems connected with the amassing of enormous fortunes"—some of them, he declared, "swollen beyond all healthy limits."

Today we are once again living in an era of extraordinary wealth concentrated in the hands of a few people, with the net worth of the wealthiest 0.1 percent of Americans almost equal to that of the bottom 90 percent combined. And this concentration of wealth is growing; as Thomas Piketty famously argued in his book *Capital in the 21st Century*, we seem to be heading toward a society dominated by vast, often inherited fortunes.

So can today's politicians rise to the challenge? Well, Elizabeth Warren has released an impressive proposal for taxing extreme wealth. And whether or not she herself becomes the Democratic nominee for president, it says good things about her party that something this smart and daring is even part of the discussion.

The Warren proposal would impose a 2 percent annual tax on an individual household's net worth in excess of $50 million, and an additional 1 percent on wealth in excess of $1 billion. The proposal was released along with an analysis by Emmanuel Saez and Gabriel Zucman of Berkeley, two of the world's leading experts on inequality.

Saez and Zucman found that this tax would affect only a small number of very wealthy people—around 75,000 households. But because these households are so wealthy, it would raise a lot of revenue, around $2.75 trillion over the next decade.

Make no mistake: this is a pretty radical plan.

I asked Saez how much it would raise the share of income (as opposed to wealth) that the economic elite pays in taxes. His estimate was that it would raise the average tax rate on the top 0.1 percent to 48 percent from 36 percent, and bring the average tax on the top 0.01 percent up to 57 percent. Those are high numbers, although they're roughly comparable to average tax rates in the 1950s.

Would such a plan be feasible? Wouldn't the rich just find ways around it? Saez and Zucman argue, based on evidence from Denmark and Sweden, both of which used to have significant wealth taxes, that it wouldn't lead to large-scale evasion if the tax applied to all assets and was adequately enforced.

Wouldn't it hurt incentives? Probably not much. Think about it: how much would entrepreneurs be deterred by the prospect that, if their big ideas pan out, they'd have to pay additional taxes on their *second* $50 million?

It's true that the Warren plan would limit the ability of the already incredibly wealthy to make their fortunes even bigger, and pass them on to their heirs. But slowing or reversing our drift toward a society ruled by oligarchic dynasties is a feature, not a bug.

And I've been struck by the reactions of tax experts like Lily Batchelder and David Kamin; while they don't necessarily endorse the Warren plan, they clearly see it as serious and worthy of consideration. It is, writes Kamin, "addressed at a real problem" and "goes big as it should." Warren, says the *Times*, has been "nerding out"; well, the nerds are impressed.

But do ideas this bold stand a chance in 21st-century American politics? The usual suspects are, of course, already comparing Warren to Nicolás Maduro or even Joseph Stalin, despite her actually being more like Teddy Roosevelt or, for that matter, Dwight Eisenhower. More important, my sense is that a lot of conventional political wisdom still assumes that proposals to sharply raise taxes on the wealthy are too left-wing for American voters.

But public opinion surveys show overwhelming support for raising taxes on the rich. One recent poll even found that 45 percent of self-identified

Republicans support Alexandria Ocasio-Cortez's suggestion of a top rate of 70 percent.

By the way, polls also show overwhelming public support for increasing, not cutting, spending on Medicare and Social Security. Strange to say, however, we rarely hear politicians who demand "entitlement reform" dismissed as too right-wing to be taken seriously.

And it's not just polls suggesting that a bold assault on economic inequality might be politically viable. Political scientists studying the behavior of billionaires find that while many of them push for lower taxes, they do so more or less in secret, presumably because they realize just how unpopular their position really is. This "stealth politics" is, by the way, one reason billionaires can seem much more liberal than they actually are—only the handful of liberals among them speak out in public.

The bottom line is that there may be far more scope for a bold progressive agenda than is dreamed of in most political punditry. And Elizabeth Warren has just taken an important step on that agenda, pushing her party to go big. Let's hope her rivals—some of whom are also quite impressive—follow her lead.

11

Trade Wars

GLOBALONEY AND THE BACKLASH

I STARTED MY PROFESSIONAL CAREER WORKING ON INTERNATIONAL trade. My work on that subject and on the related topic of economic geography—trade and the location of production across space generally, within as well as between countries—dominates my top cites on Google Scholar, and got me the Swedish thingie.

So I'm empowered to tell you a dirty little secret: international trade and international trade policy aren't as important as people think they are.

I don't mean that they aren't important. They are, in fact, crucial for many countries—if, say, Bangladesh lost the ability to sell labor-intensive goods, mostly clothing, on world markets the country might quite literally suffer mass starvation. But for big countries like the United States what we do with regard to trade, right or wrong, is a lot less important than, for example, the mess we've made of health care.

Yet international trade occupies a special place in both economic and political discourse, for several reasons.

Economists love to dwell on the benefits of international trade because it's one of those places where economics really does give you insights most people miss.

To many people it seems like common sense that a country wins when it runs a trade surplus, that is, sells more than it buys; that a country can't compete if it's less productive than its trading partners; that if a country does manage to sell goods based on low wages rather than high productivity, it must be dragging other countries' living standards down.

Economists love explaining why none of that is true. Trade generally benefits both sides of the transaction, whether you run a deficit or a surplus (although it doesn't necessarily benefit everyone inside each country). Even low-productivity countries can benefit from trade by concentrating on the things they do least badly (which is where my Bangladesh example is relevant). Such low-productivity countries necessarily offer their workers low wages, but this doesn't hurt richer countries, since those low wages allow them to buy labor-intensive goods cheaply while producing other stuff.

So economists talk a lot about trade—probably more than the subject deserves—because it's someplace where they feel intellectually triumphant.

People who think a lot about international relations also like to talk about trade because the current world trading system is one of the triumphs of international diplomacy. Before World War II, countries imposed tariffs (taxes on imports) and quotas limiting imports whenever they felt like it, usually claiming to be acting in the national interest but often serving domestic special interests too. After the war, however, more and more of the world joined a rules-based system in which nations negotiate tariff rates with each other, and eventually established quasi-judicial procedures to settle disputes when one country accuses another of breaking the rules.

This system was created in the belief that it would make the world richer. But that wasn't all: it was also intended to promote peace. For the American statesmen who created the modern world trading system, notably Cordell Hull, F.D.R.'s long-serving secretary of state, believed that commerce helped secure peace as well as prosperity. So the world trading system was part of the whole set of postwar institutions, like NATO and the U.N., that did indeed seem to help the world avoid huge wars.

And meanwhile, the trading system gradually created a world not of perfectly free trade, but of low tariffs on most manufactured goods.

Finally, discussions of international trade—actually, of almost anything with the word "international" in it—are magnets for people attracted to "globaloney," grand talk about big things.

Naturally, anything that inspires rapture in economists, international relations experts, and globaloneyers will also inspire a backlash. For a number of years this backlash mainly came from the left—from labor groups who claimed, with some justification, that growing trade was putting downward pressure on blue-collar wages, and from more radical groups who saw world trade as a sort of supercharged version of rampant capitalism.

But there's a quite different source of backlash against trade, which has nothing to do with concerns about social justice. It comes instead from business types who do not take well to being told that their common-sense instincts about trade are all wrong, and respond by doubling down on their views, not just rejecting claims about the benefits of trade but demonizing it. Some of us still remember Ross Perot, who warned that free trade with Mexico would produce a "great sucking sound" as U.S. industry moved south.

And in 2016 someone with this sort of anti-intellectual, my-gut-is-smarter-than-the-so-called-experts sensibility became president of the United States. You sometimes see people trying to argue that Donald Trump is more sophisticated than he seems, that he doesn't really believe that every time we run a trade deficit that means someone is stealing America's precious bodily fluids. But all the available evidence suggests that this is exactly what he believes.

And here's the thing: not only is America a huge player in the global economy, our domestic trade law was designed to constrain special-interest politics in Congress—and achieved this by giving huge discretionary authority to the president. So Trump is in a position to wreak a remarkable amount of havoc in the world trade system. The articles in this section describe some of that havoc-wreaking.

OH, WHAT A TRUMPY TRADE WAR!

March 8, 2018

There's near-universal consensus among both economists and business leaders that Donald Trump's tariffs on steel and aluminum are a bad idea, and that the wider trade war those tariffs could trigger would be very destructive. But the chances of heading off this policy disaster are small, because this is a quintessential example of Trump being Trump.

In fact, the tariffs are arguably the Trumpiest thing Trump has done so far.

After all, trade (like racism) is an issue on which Trump has been utterly consistent over the years. He has spent decades railing at other countries that, he claims, hurt America by taking advantage of our relatively open markets. And if his views are based on zero understanding of the issues or even of basic facts, well, Trumpism is all about belligerent ignorance, across the board.

But wait, there's more. There's a reason we have international trade agreements, and it's not to protect us from unfair practices by other countries. The real goal, instead, is to protect us from ourselves: to limit the special-interest politics and outright corruption that used to reign in trade policy.

Trumpocrats, however, don't see corruption and rule by special interests as problems. You could say that the world trading system is, in large part, specifically designed to prevent people like Trump from having too much influence. Of course he wants to wreck it.

Some background: contrary to what some seem to believe, textbook economics doesn't say that free trade is win-win for everyone. Instead, trade policy involves very real conflicts of interest. But these conflicts of interest are overwhelmingly between groups within each country, rather than between countries. For example, a trade war against the European Union would make America as a whole poorer, even if the E.U. didn't retaliate (which it would). It would, however, benefit some industries that happen to face stiff European competition.

And here's the thing: the small groups that benefit from protectionism often have more political influence than the much larger groups that are hurt. That's why Congress used to routinely pass destructive trade bills, culminating in the infamous Smoot-Hawley Tariff Act of 1930: enough members of Congress were bought off, one way or another, to enact legislation that almost everyone knew was bad for the nation as a whole.

In 1934, however, F.D.R. introduced a new approach to trade policy: reciprocal agreements with other countries, in which we exchanged reduced tariffs on their exports for reduced tariffs on ours. This approach introduced a new set of special interests, exporters, who could offer countervailing power against the influence of special interests seeking protection.

F.D.R.'s reciprocal agreement approach led to a rapid unwinding of Smoot-Hawley, and after the war it evolved into a series of global trade deals, creating a world trading system that these days is overseen by the World Trade Organization. In effect, the U.S. remade world trade policy in its own image. And it worked: the global deals that evolved from the reciprocal tariff approach greatly reduced tariff rates around the world, while setting up rules that constrain countries from backtracking on their commitments.

The overall effect of the evolution of the world trading system has been very salutary. Tariff policy, which used to be one of the dirtiest, most corrupt aspects of politics both in the U.S. and elsewhere, has become remarkably (though not perfectly) clean.

And I'd add that global trade agreements are a striking and encouraging example of effective international cooperation. In that sense they make a real if hard to measure contribution to democratic governance and world peace.

But then came Trump.

Under U.S. trade law, which is written to be consonant with our international agreements, the president can impose tariffs under certain narrowly defined conditions. But the steel and aluminum tariffs, justified with an obviously bogus appeal to national security, clearly don't pass the test.

So Trump is in effect both violating U.S. law and throwing the world trading system under the bus. And if this escalates into a full-scale trade war, we'll be back to the bad old days. Tariff policy will once again be driven by influence-peddling and bribery, never mind the national interest.

But that won't bother Trump. After all, we now basically have an Environmental Protection Agency run on behalf of polluters, an Interior Department run by people who want to loot federal land, an Education Department run by the for-profit schools industry, and so on. Why should trade policy be different?

It's true that many big businesses and free-market ideologues, who thought they had Trump in their corner, are horrified by his moves on trade. But what did they expect? There was never any good reason to think that trade policy was safe from Trump's depredations.

A TRADE WAR PRIMER

June 3, 2018

At the moment, the Trumpian trade war appears to be on. And I've been getting some questions from readers about how this is possible. Congress, after all, hasn't voted to back out of our trade agreements, and one suspects that it wouldn't even if Trump asked for such legislation: to all appearances, a lot of Republicans are pretty much O.K. with the near-certainty that he colluded with a hostile foreign power and is currently obstructing justice, but policy actions that might strand and devalue a lot of corporate assets are something else entirely.

So how does Trump have the authority to do this? And what are the consequences for the world? It seems to me that this might be a good time to write down a brief, non-scholarly primer on how the trading system—and U.S. trade policy within that system—work.

The key thing you need to understand about trade policy is that the Econ 101 case for free trade plays very little role in actual policy, certainly in trade negotiations. That's not because policymakers either reject that case or fail to understand it; some do, some don't, but either way it doesn't make that much difference. (In fairness, there's an academic literature arguing that the underlying economics matter more than I'm suggesting, work that I consider admirable but unpersuasive.)

True, for the past eighty years the U.S. has sought to make trade gradually freer; this reflected in part the (very) indirect influence of economic theory, in part the belief that closer economic integration was good for peace and the free world alliance. But the process by which trade liberalization was sought was all about political realism rather than abstract ideals.

And what political realism on trade means is that producer interests matter much more than consumer interests, because producers tend to be far more organized and aware of the stakes in any given trade policy. The classic case was sugar, where for many years U.S. import quotas kept prices here several times above world levels. The benefits of that policy went to a few thousand sugar growers, for each of whom it was worth tens or hundreds of thousands a year. The costs were thinly spread among tens of millions of consumers, the vast majority of whom had no idea there even was an import quota.

Given this asymmetry in representation, you might expect the interests of import-competing industries to predominate in practically everything we could produce here, leading to high levels of protectionism. And that was in fact the way U.S. trade policy tended to work until the 1930s.

But then F.D.R. introduced the Reciprocal Trade Agreements Act—a system, initially, of bilateral negotiations in which America would agree to reduce tariffs on foreign goods if foreign governments reduced tariffs on our goods. What this did was change the political calculus, by bringing the interests of export industries into the picture. U.S. firms competing with imports might still clamor for protection; but they would face the counterweight of U.S. exporters demanding deals that gave them access to foreign markets.

You could say that the RTAA was based on bad economics—that it embodied the mercantilist assumption that exports are good and imports are bad. But it was an enlightened form of mercantilism, creating a process that led to generally good economic outcomes.

For this process to work, Congress needed to step back from the details of trade policy; instead, it would allow the executive branch to negotiate deals, then vote those deals up or down. And the result, even before World War II, was a significant climb-down in tariff rates.

Then, in 1947, the U.S. and its partners established the General Agreement on Tariffs and Trade, which basically created a multilateral version of the same system. I think of the GATT as a system of levers and ratchets. The levers—the mechanism used to make trade gradually freer—consisted of elaborate horse-trading negotiations ("rounds") resulting in tariff reduc-

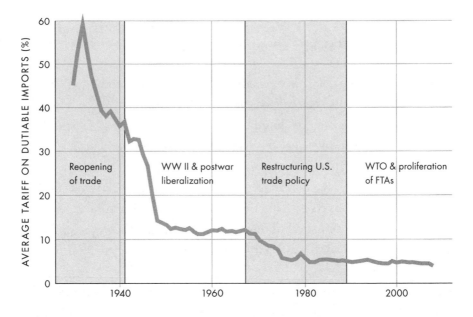

U.S. TRADE-WEIGHTED TARIFFS ON DUTIABLE IMPORTS AND HISTORICAL PERIODS, 1930–2008. *Source: USITC staff compilation from U.S. Department of Commerce statistics.*

tions. The ratchets, preventing backsliding, consisted of rules preventing countries from going back on their previous commitments, except under certain conditions.

Why are there exceptions? Political realism, again. The creators of the trading system realized that it needed some flexibility—that too rigid a system of rules would end up being brittle and would shatter under the press of events. So countries were granted the right to impose new tariffs under the following conditions (real trade lawyers know that I'm oversimplifying, but the essence is right):

- Market disruption—a sudden surge of imports too fast for domestic producers to adjust to, in which case they could be given some breathing room;
- National security—making sure you're not dependent on potential enemies for crucial goods;
- Unfair practices—tariffs to counter, say, subsidized exports;

- Dumping—when foreign firms seem to be selling goods below
  cost in an attempt to establish market dominance.

In the U.S., who determines when one of these justifications applies? Not Congress—that would just reopen the whole can of worms F.D.R. closed in 1934. Instead, the executive branch is supposed to follow a quasi-judicial procedure, in which investigating agencies determine whether one of these conditions is met, then the president decides whether to take action.

But what if the U.S. takes action, but our trading partners don't consider it justified? (Or, conversely, what if the U.S. objects to another country's actions?) They can demand international arbitration, which was very cumbersome until the World Trade Organization was created in 1993, but now usually proceeds quite quickly.

Then what? Suppose the WTO finds that a country has acted inappropriately; what power does it have to enforce that judgment? Directly, none: there isn't a fleet of black helicopters based in Geneva, ready to swoop down on trade miscreants. Instead, the WTO effectively declares the offending nation an outlaw, granting aggrieved trading partners the right to retaliate as they see fit.

And historically that threat has worked: countries that lose WTO cases generally back down and reverse their policies. Why did it work? Because everyone was aware that if things got out of hand, we could devolve into a tit-for-tat trade war that would undo seventy years of progress.

Which brings us to Trump.

The world trading system is actually a quite remarkable construction—a framework that has consistently produced a high level of global cooperation. It has been pretty robust in the face of even severe shocks—notably, the world did not see a major resurgence of protectionism after the 2008 financial crisis. But it was never designed to deal with a major world leader who has contempt for anything resembling the rule of law.

Past presidents have used their authority to impose tariffs, and not always for the best of reasons. Even Obama imposed a temporary "market disruption" tariff on Chinese tires. They have always, however, been circumspect: their tariff actions were limited, and the economic basis for their actions was at least vaguely defensible.

But Trump has gone ahead and imposed tariffs using the national security argument, in a context that makes no sense. There is no coherent argument about why imports of Canadian aluminum pose a national security threat; there will be even less justification if he does the same for autos. In fact, his administration is barely even trying to pretend that real national security concerns are at work. He's just doing this because he can.

Worse, there's no obvious endgame. What can the Chinese, let alone the Europeans and the Canadians, offer that would satisfy him? An end to U.S. trade deficits? That's not something trade policy can or should deliver.

And of course everyone else in the world is furious with the U.S. This matters, because trade policy is inherently political; even if giving Trump big concessions were good economics, which is far from clear, our democratic allies—former allies?—are going to be in no mood to go along.

So now you know why Trump has the power to do what he's doing, and why it's such a big, bad deal.

MAKING TARIFFS CORRUPT AGAIN

September 20, 2018

In normal times, Donald Trump's announcement of tariffs on $200 billion worth of Chinese goods, bringing us closer to an all-out trade war, would have dominated headlines for days. Things being as they are, it was a below-the-fold story, drowned out by all the other scandals underway.

Yet Trump's tariffs really are a big, bad deal. Their direct economic impact will be modest, although hardly trivial. But the numbers aren't the whole story. Trumpian trade policy has, almost casually, torn up rules America itself created more than eighty years ago—rules intended to ensure that tariffs reflected national priorities, not the power of special interests.

You could say that Trump is making tariffs corrupt again. And the damage will be lasting.

Until the 1930s, U.S. trade policy was both dirty and dysfunctional. It wasn't just that overall tariffs were high; who got how much tariff protection was determined through a free-for-all of horse-trading among special interests.

The costs of this free-for-all went beyond economics: they undermined U.S. influence and damaged the world as a whole. Most notably, in the years after World War I, America demanded that European nations repay their war debts, which meant that they had to earn dollars through exports—and at the same time America imposed high tariffs to block those necessary exports.

But the game changed in 1934, when F.D.R. introduced the Reciprocal Trade Agreements Act. Henceforth, tariffs would be negotiated via deals with foreign governments, giving export industries a stake in open markets.

And these deals would be subject to up-or-down votes, reducing the ability of interest groups to buy themselves special treatment.

This U.S. innovation became the template for a global trading system, culminating in the creation of the World Trade Organization. And tariff policy went from being famously dirty to remarkably clean.

Now, the creators of this trading system knew that it needed some flexibility to remain politically viable. So governments were given the right to impose tariffs under a limited set of circumstances: to give industries time to cope with import surges, to respond to unfair foreign practices, to protect national security. And in the U.S. the power to impose these special-case tariffs was vested in the executive branch, on the understanding that this power would be used sparingly and judiciously.

Then came Trump.

So far, Trump has imposed tariffs on about $300 billion worth of U.S. imports, with tariff rates set to rise as high as 25 percent. Although Trump and his officials keep claiming that this is a tax on foreigners, it's actually a tax hike on America. And since most of the tariffs are on raw materials and other inputs into business, the policy will probably have a chilling effect on investment and innovation.

But the pure economic impact is only part of the story. The other part is the perversion of the process. There are rules about when a president may impose tariffs; Trump has obeyed the letter of these rules, barely, but made a mockery of their spirit. Blocking imports from Canada in the name of national security? Really?

Even the big China announcement, supposedly a response to unfair Chinese trade practices, was basically a put-up job. China is often a bad actor in the international economy. But this kind of retaliatory tariff is supposed to be a response to specific policies, and offer the targeted government a clear way to satisfy U.S. demands. What Trump did was instead to lash out based mainly on a vague sense of grievance, with no endgame in sight.

In other words, when it comes to tariffs, as with so many other things, Trump has basically abrogated the rule of law and replaced it with his personal whims. And this will have a couple of nasty consequences.

First, it opens the door for old-fashioned corruption. As I said, most of the tariffs are on inputs into business—and some businesses are getting special treatment. Thus, there are now substantial tariffs on imported steel, but some steel users—including the U.S. subsidiary of a sanctioned Russian company—were granted the right to import steel tariff-free. (The Russian subsidiary's exemption was reversed after it became public knowledge, with officials claiming that it was a "clerical error.")

So what are the criteria for these exemptions? Nobody knows, but there is every reason to believe that political favoritism is running wild.

Beyond that, America has thrown away its negotiating credibility. In the past, countries signing trade agreements with the United States believed that a deal was a deal. Now they know that whatever documents the U.S. may sign supposedly guaranteeing access to its market, the president will still feel free to block their exports, on specious grounds, whenever he feels like it.

In short, while the Trump tariffs may not be that big (yet), they have already turned us into an unreliable partner, a nation whose trade policy is driven by political cronyism, and which is all too likely to default on its promises whenever it's convenient. Somehow, I don't think that's making America great again.

12

Inequality

THE SKEWING OF AMERICA

I GREW UP IN A MIDDLE-CLASS SOCIETY. IT WASN'T EGALITARIAN, BY any means: CEOs of major corporations were paid, on average, about twenty times as much as the average worker. But there was a broad sense that all but a tiny handful of people were living in the same material universe.

That's not true anymore. CEOs now get paid more than three hundred times as much as the average worker. Other high-income groups have also seen huge gains, while the wages of ordinary workers, adjusted for inflation, have grown modestly or not at all for the past four decades.

The skewing of America—the shift of a growing share of income to a small elite—was already clearly visible by the late 1980s. This seemed to many people, myself included, to be a bad thing. Not only did it mean that ordinary families were failing to share in economic progress, it meant a loss of our sense of living in a shared society. So one might have expected a serious discussion of the forces behind rising inequality, and what if anything might be done to reverse the trend.

And there has indeed been a lot of serious scholarship on the causes and consequences of inequality. Some of that work is being done right now by my colleagues at CUNY's Stone Center for the Study of Socioeconomic Inequality, which is where I sit these days.

But there has also, predictably, been an invasion of zombies. After all, acknowledging that there has been a huge rise in inequality might lead to demands that we do something about it. As a result, almost from the beginning there was a sort of inequality-denial industry—more than a bit like the climate-denial industry—which claimed that inequality wasn't really rising, or that it didn't matter. I took on those claims in the first article in this section, published in *The American Prospect* in 1992. You won't be surprised to hear that the same arguments I refuted all those years ago continue to be made today.

A subtler problem that plagued discussions of inequality for many years involved three widespread misperceptions. The first was that rising inequality was mainly about highly-educated workers doing better than the less educated, as opposed to a small subset of the well-educated pulling away from everyone else. I took that one on in "Graduates Versus Oligarchs."

The second was the persistent claim, sometimes although not always made in good faith, that the declining fortunes of blue-collar workers reflected growing social problems like the decline in family values. "Money and Morals" argued that it was the other way around: the symptoms of social decline we see in working-class America are the result, not the cause, of declining opportunity.

The third was that it's all about technology, with the growth of knowledge-based industry demanding highly educated workers, or robots replacing workers in general. This could be true, in principle. But as I argue in "Don't Blame Robots for Low Wages," the evidence suggests that technology has a lot less to do with rising inequality than many want to think, and power relations matter a lot.

Finally, the era of rising inequality has also been an era of widening regional divides, as the poorer parts of America—which had been converging with the richer areas—began sliding back again. These also happened to be areas that went heavily for Donald Trump. The last article in this section takes on the causes and consequences of regional divergence.

THE RICH, THE RIGHT, AND THE FACTS

Deconstructing the Income Distribution Debate

The American Prospect

Fall 1992

During the mid-1980s, economists became aware that something unexpected was happening to the distribution of income in the United States. After three decades during which the income distribution had remained relatively stable, wages and incomes rapidly became more unequal. Academic researchers soon began arguing vigorously about the causes of the growth in inequality: was it global competition, government policy, changing technology, or some other factor? What nobody, whatever his or her political stripe, questioned was the fact that there had been a dramatic change in income distribution.

During 1992 this genteel academic discussion gave way to a public debate, carried out in the pages of *The New York Times*, *The Wall Street Journal*, and assorted popular magazines. This public debate was remarkable in two ways. First, the conservative side displayed great ferocity in presenting its case and attacking its opponents. Second, conservatives chose to take an odd, and ultimately indefensible, position. They could legitimately have challenged those who have called attention to the growing dispersion of income on the grounds that nothing can, or at any rate should, be done about it. But with only a few exceptions they chose instead to make their stand on the facts, to deny that the massive increase in inequality had happened. Since the facts were not on their side, they were forced into an extraordinary series of attempts at statistical distortion.

The whole episode teaches us two lessons. At one level, it is a sort of textbook demonstration of the uses and abuses of statistics. This article reviews that lesson, tracing out how conservatives tried to distort the record and why they were wrong. But the combination of mendacity and sheer incompetence displayed by *The Wall Street Journal*, the U.S. Treasury Department, and a number of supposed economic experts demonstrates something else: the extent of the moral and intellectual decline of American conservatism.

I begin with a review of the basic data, followed by an assessment of the three kinds of conservative attacks on the simple facts about growing inequality: (1) efforts to deny the facts, through a mixture of confused statistical arguments; (2) claims that the growth record of the Reagan years outweighs or negates any apparent increase in inequality; (3) claims that income mobility makes comparisons of the income distribution at a point in time meaningless. A final section tries to put some perspective on the whole debate.

SOME BASIC FACTS

There are some non-official sources that provide evidence for growing inequality of income in the United States. For example, *Fortune* has long carried out annual surveys of executive compensation; and since the mid-1970s compensation of top executives has risen far faster than average or typical wages, a process entertainingly discussed by Graef Crystal in his *In Search of Excess*. Surveys carried out by the University of Michigan have also shed useful light on income distribution, in particular on the dynamics of income over time. There is also anecdotal evidence: Tom Wolfe noted the soaring demand for apartments in Manhattan's "Good Buildings" well before academics had started to take the growing concentration of wealth seriously, and indeed his *Bonfire of the Vanities* arguably tells you all you need to know about the subject.

WHAT THE CENSUS SHOWS

Most academic studies on the distribution of income in the United States rely on Census data, compiled from the Current Population Survey. These data have certain limitations, to which I will turn in a moment. But as a starting point, the Census numbers have one great advantage: they are not controversial. In all the mud-slinging of the income distribution debate, nobody has yet accused the Census of bias or distortion (although that may come next).

Figure 1 shows a picture that ought to be part of the consciousness of anyone who thinks about trends in the U.S. economy since the 1970s. The figure shows the rate of growth of income at selected points in the income distribution over several different periods.

Percentile/years		% Annual Increase (to nearest tenth)
20	1947–73	2.6%
	1973–79	0.4
	1979–89	-0.3
40	1947–73	2.7
	1973–79	0.4
	1979–89	0.3
60	1947–73	2.8
	1973–79	0.7
	1979–89	0.6
80	1947–73	2.7
	1973–79	0.6
	1979–89	1.1
95	1947–73	2.5
	1973–79	1.1
	1979–89	1.6

FIGURE 1. DISTRIBUTION OF INCOME GAINS, 1947–1989. *Source: U.S. Census Bureau.*

The income distribution is measured in percentiles. For example, the first set of bars shows the rate of growth of income of the family at the 20th percentile (the top of the bottom quintile). The choice of percentiles ranging from 20 to 95 means excluding the real extremes. Some very important developments are missed by these exclusions, especially at the top. But this picture still gives us a useful baseline.

The three periods chosen are 1947–1973, 1973–1979, and 1979–1989. The first period represents what Alice Rivlin has called the "good years"—the great postwar boom generation. The remaining two periods show the seventies, the period from the business cycle peak of 1973 to that of 1979, and the eighties, from the 1979 peak to the 1989 peak.

What do we see in the figure? First, the 1947–1973 numbers show what real, broad-based prosperity looks like. Over that period incomes of all groups rose at roughly the same rapid clip, more than 2.5 percent annually. Between 1973 and 1979, as the economy was battered by slow productivity growth and oil shocks, income growth became both much slower and more uneven. Finally, a new pattern emerged after 1979: generally slower income growth, but in particular a strong tilt in the growth pattern, with incomes rising much faster at the top end of the distribution than in the middle, and actually declining at the bottom.

In some of the conservative critiques I will describe below, apologists claim that the 1980s represented a normal process, that there was nothing unusual or distressing about the rise in inequality. As the discussion gets a bit complicated, it will be useful to retain the basic image of Figure 1: "good" growth looks like an all-American picket fence; growth in the 1980s looked like a staircase, with the well-off on the top step.

THE CBO NUMBERS

The Census numbers shown in Figure 1 tell a pretty clear story. Nonetheless, it has been apparent for some time that the story is incomplete, because it fails to give a full picture of gains among families with very high incomes.

Census numbers are of little use in studying high-income families, for two reasons, one major, one minor. The main problem is the arcane technical issue of "top-coding." The questionnaires on which the Current Population Survey is based do not ask for precise incomes; instead, families are asked to place their income within a series of categories, of which the highest is "over x," currently $250,000. This means, of course, that the Census data give no information about changes in the fortunes of families with incomes high enough to be above that top number. The minor problem is that Census data do not count one important source of income for high-income families: capital gains.

It is precisely because Census data are weak when it comes to very high incomes that those who use that data usually look no higher than the 95th percentile; that is, the bottom of the top 5 percent. Over the period 1947–1973, when everyone's income went up at about the same rate, the weakness of Census data at the top end didn't matter much. But it became obvious during the 1980s that incomes were rising even faster among the very well off than at the 95th percentile.

One might have guessed this simply from Figure 1: since the available data show that the higher you go in the income distribution, the bigger the gains, one might reasonably suppose that the same is true for the unavailable data. One might well expect to find that inequality within the top 5 percent has risen, implying larger gains at, say, the 99th percentile than at the 95th.

One could also guess that income was growing especially rapidly at the top from less formal evidence. Notably, Graef Crystal's executive compensation numbers suggested a tripling of the compensation of CEOs relative to ordinary workers, and virtually every social observer has noted an apparent explosion of affluence at the top. All that was lacking was hard statistical evidence.

Work by the Congressional Budget Office fills the gap. The CBO is charged by the House Ways and Means Committee with estimating changes in the incidence of federal taxation, to provide the supporting appendices for that committee's mammoth annual publication, the Green Book. To do this, the CBO has developed a model that pools Census and IRS data. This model allows the CBO to bypass the problem of top-coding, and also allows incorporation of taxable capital gains.

Figure 2 shows the CBO estimates for the gains in income at different parts of the income distribution over the period 1977–1989. (Ideally, we would use 1979–89. Unfortunately, for reasons having to do with its original mandate to focus on tax incidence, the CBO did not do an estimate for 1979.) Here, the data are presented a little differently from those in Figure 1. We are shown changes in, say, average income for families in the bottom quintile, rather than for the individual family at the top of that quintile, and the numbers show the percentage change over the period as a whole, rather than annual rates of change. But the picture is clear: there were truly huge income gains at the very top. In particular, the top 1 percent of families saw their incomes roughly double over a twelve-year period. That's a 6 percent rate of growth, which means that for the very well-off the 1980s really were a very good decade not only compared with the slow growth lower down in the distribution, but even compared with the postwar boom years.

Percentile	% Increase, 1977–89
0–20	-9%
20–40	-2
60–80	8
80–90	13
90–95	18
95–99	24
100	103

FIGURE 2. INCREASES IN INCOME, 1977–1989. *Source: U.S. Census Bureau.*

There is one other important point to be learned from the CBO numbers: how well-off the well-off actually are. The usual story still told by conservatives is that the so-called "rich" are not really all that rich. Conservatives often point out that, according to Census numbers, in 1989 it required an income of only $59,550 to put a family in the top quintile, an income of only $98,963 to put it in the top 5 percent. The implication is that we are essentially a middle-class society, with only an insignificant handful of people rich enough to excite any concern about ill-gotten gains.

But the CBO numbers paint a different picture, because they let us look higher up the scale. According to the CBO, to be classified in the top 1 percent a family of four needed a pre-tax income (in 1993 dollars) of at least $330,000. The average income of four-person families in the top 1 percent was about $800,000. We are no longer talking about the middle class.

THE "KRUGMAN CALCULATION"

It is a remarkable fact that incomes have soared so much at the top of the U.S. income distribution. But is it important? Until recently, most economists thought not; growing poverty might be an important social issue, but the fact that some people are very rich was only a social curiosity.

My own contribution to this discussion was to point out that there is a sense in which the rise in incomes at the top is in fact a major economic issue, and to offer a shorthand way of conveying that point: the now infamous "Krugman calculation" that 70 percent of the rise in average family income has gone to the top 1 percent of families.

Let's begin by recalling that typical incomes grew very slowly during the 1980s. For example, even if one uses a revised consumer price index that shows lower inflation than the standard index, one finds that median family income—the income of the family at the midpoint of the income distribution in 1989—was only 4.2 percent higher than in 1979. That is, median family income rose at only about a 0.4 percent annual rate. And many measures of real wages for typical workers show a decline during the 1980s.

Now one would have expected incomes in the U.S. to grow more slowly than in the good years before 1973, because of the productivity slowdown. Productivity growth in the U.S. economy fell from about 3 percent annually during the postwar boom to about 1 percent annually after 1973; and ordinarily productivity growth determines real income growth.

But although productivity growth is slow, it is not negligible. We are a substantially more productive country now than we were in 1979. So why isn't the typical family significantly better off? Where did the productivity growth go?

The proximate answer is that average incomes went up relative to the median income. Figure 3 shows average versus median family income from 1979 to 1990. It turns out that from 1979 to 1989, average family income rose 11 percent, just about exactly what one would have expected given 1 percent productivity growth. So there is no problem with the accounting.

1979	Average	100
	Median	100
1980	Average	97
	Median	97
1981	Average	95
	Median	94
1982	Average	95
	Median	93
1983	Average	96
	Median	94
1984	Average	99
	Median	96
1985	Average	102
	Median	97
1986	Average	106
	Median	102
1987	Average	107
	Median	103
1988	Average	108
	Median	103
1989	Average	111
	Median	104
1990	Average	108
	Median	102

FIGURE 3. AVERAGE VS. MEDIAN INCOME, 1979–1990. *Source: U.S. Census Bureau.*

The rise in average income relative to median should not be a surprise, given Figures 1 and 2. That is exactly what one would expect to see when incomes become more unequal, because when incomes at the top of the scale are rising faster than the average, incomes farther down must correspondingly grow less rapidly than the average. In an arithmetic sense, we can say that most of the growth in productivity was "siphoned off" to high-income brackets, leaving little room for income growth lower down. I emphasize that this is only an arithmetic point: it says nothing about the economic forces at work, in particular whether something else could or should have happened.

When I say that growth was "siphoned off" to high-income families, however, who am I talking about? Are we talking about two married school-teachers, whose $65,000 income is enough to put them into the top quintile? Or are we talking about Donald Trump?

Figure 2 ought to suggest to you that we are not talking about those schoolteachers: the really big income gains were not near the bottom of the top quintile, but at its top. Indeed, according to the CBO's numbers the share of after-tax income going to the ninth decile: families between the 81st and 90th percentiles actually fell slightly between 1977 and 1989. So all of the siphoning went to families in the top 5 or 10 percent. And given Figure 2, one might well suspect that the bulk went to the top 1 percent.

To get a sense of this and, to be honest, to help attract attention to a trend that I thought had been neglected I proposed the following thought experiment. Imagine two villages, each composed of 100 families representing the percentiles of the family income distribution in a given year in particular, a 1977 village and a 1989 village. According to the CBO numbers, the total income of the 1989 village is about 10 percent higher than that of the 1977 village; but it is not true that the whole distribution is shifted up by 10 percent. Instead, the richest family in the 1989 village has twice the income of its counterpart in the 1977 village, while the bottom forty 1989 families actually have lower incomes than their 1977 counterparts.

Now ask: how much of the difference in the incomes of the two villages is accounted for by the difference in the incomes of the richest family? Equivalently, how much of the rise in average American family income went to the top 1 percent of families? By looking at this measure we get a sense of who was "siphoning off" the growth in average incomes, accounting for the fact that median income went up so little.

The answer is quite startling: 70 percent of the rise in average family income went to the top 1 percent.

What does this tell us? Since the 1970s median income has failed to keep up with average income or, to put it differently, the typical American family has seen little gain in spite of rising productivity. So when we speak of "high income" families, we mean really high income: not garden-variety yuppies, but Tom Wolfe's Masters of the Universe.

Wealth distribution: wealth—the assets that families own—and income are different though related things. Wealth is typically much more concentrated than income: current estimates are that the 1 percent of families with the highest incomes receive about 12 percent of overall pre-tax income, while the wealthiest 1 percent of families has some 37 percent of net worth. Precisely because wealth is so concentrated, it is difficult to measure accurately from sample surveys: a random survey of a few hundred or even a few thousand people will contain only a handful of really wealthy people. Nonetheless, researchers at the Federal Reserve Board have tried to use sophisticated sampling procedures to deal with this problem. For some time their surveys have shown that average wealth was rising much faster than median as in the case of income distribution, a sure sign of growing inequality. In March 1992 they released a working paper that showed a sharp increase in the concentration of wealth even since 1983, with the share of the top 1 percent of families rising from 31 to 37 percent.

Recently, several academic researchers (Claudia Goldin and Brad DeLong of Harvard, together with Edward Wolff of New York University) have put together long-range historical estimates on wealth distribution. They suggest that the concentration of wealth in the U.S. reached a trough in the late 1970s at a level not seen since the nineteenth century, then surged rapidly back to 1920s levels. The point is that the wealth numbers confirm the general picture of a dramatic and rapid increase in economic inequality in the U.S.

POLITICAL IMPLICATIONS

Rising inequality need not have any policy implications. Even if you would prefer to have a flatter distribution, other things equal (and not everyone even shares that goal), what should we do about it? Few people in America would currently support a policy of wage and salary controls (although Claudia Goldin has noted that World War II wage controls seem to have produced a long-term narrowing of wage differentials). One might use growing inequality as an argument for restoring some of the progressivity of the tax system; but most of the growth in inequality has come from changes in pre-tax income, not from regressive tax policies. An honest conservative like Herbert Stein is willing to say "Yes, inequality has increased, but I don't think that calls for any policy response."

Nonetheless, many conservatives were furious when the income distribution story surfaced in early 1992. Above all, the story made the editors of *The Wall Street Journal* and the Bush administration see red.

The reason was pretty clear. Supply-siders like Robert Bartley, the *Journal*'s editorial page editor, believe that their ideology has been justified by what they perceive as the huge economic successes of the Reagan years. The suggestion that these years were not very successful for most people, that most of the gains went to a few well-off families, is a political body blow. And indeed the belated attention to inequality during the spring of 1992 clearly helped the Clinton campaign find a new focus and a new target for public anger: instead of blaming their woes on welfare queens in their Cadillacs, middle-class voters could be urged to blame government policies that favored the wealthy.

So the dismay and anger of conservatives was understandable. The response from the administration, the *Journal*, and other conservative voices was, however, inexcusable: instead of facing up to the fact of rapidly growing inequality under conservative rule, they tried to deny the facts and shoot the messengers.

THE CONSERVATIVE RESPONSE 1: DENIAL

The Number of Families

When *The New York Times* published a story reporting my estimates on the impact of rising inequality, the initial response of a number of conservative economists (including staffers at the Council of Economic Advisers) was to do a different calculation: to ask what share of the growth in total rather than average income went to the top 1 percent. Let's call it the "CEA calculation." This is a very different number, because the number of families in the U.S. grew substantially between 1977 and 1989, as the last of the baby boomers grew up. So total income went up, not by 10 percent, but by about 35 percent. Naturally, the share of this much larger rise that accrued to the richest was a good deal smaller, 25 versus 70 percent. This revised number was widely circulated in Washington as a refutation of the number published in *The New York Times*; indeed, I have been told that one major news magazine almost ran a gleeful story on the *Times*'s blunder, but at the last minute was warned that I was right and the CEA was wrong.

What's wrong with the CEA calculation? Remember the questions we are trying to answer: why didn't the typical American family see much increase in income even though productivity rose substantially, and who was reaping the benefits of rising productivity? If you think about it for a minute, you'll see that using income growth numbers that include sheer growth in working-age population gets us completely away from those questions. Consider, for example, what happened to the bottom 20 percent of the income distribution. Average income among these families fell 10 percent over the CBO period but their numbers went up about 25 percent, and their total income therefore rose about 15 percent. So the CEA calculation has the bottom quintile sharing in economic growth, even though average family income in that group went down!

The CEA also distributed a memo presenting a hypothetical numerical example, too complicated to reproduce here. Its point was that if the labor force were to receive a large influx of inexperienced workers, the experience of the median worker might decline; in that case, stagnation in median income might mask rising wages for a worker with any given degree of experience, and a "Krugman calculation" would erroneously suggest that only the very well-off had gained. The memo was right in principle. As anyone who has looked at labor force and wage data knows, however, the real facts look nothing like the contrived example: the growing inequality of wages represents increased dispersion in wages for workers with given characteristics, not a change in the mix.

The Size of Families

The next issue fits awkwardly into this scheme, since it involves an honest difference of opinion between myself and the CBO, and does not in the end make much difference. This is the question of how, if at all, to deal with the declining size of families in the U.S.

As noted above, the CBO likes to measure, not raw family income, but "adjusted" family income (AFI), measured in multiples of the poverty line. Adjusted family income has been rising faster than income itself, because families have been getting smaller. From 1977 to 1989, AFI grew by 15 percent compared with 10 percent for the raw number.

When you do a Krugman calculation using AFI instead of raw income, the result looks a little bit less extreme: the top 1 percent get 44 instead of 70 percent of the increase. This is still pretty impressive; but is the correction appropriate?

The CBO likes to use adjusted family income because they view it as a better measure of the material standard of living: a family with one child will be able to afford things that a family with three children and the same income cannot. Fair enough. But it seems to be stretching the usefulness of the concept when the decision of U.S. families to have fewer children is considered to be a form of income growth (what would the Republican platform committee say?).

Indeed, the number of hours worked by the typical American family actually rose during the 1980s. So if we are asking why family incomes didn't rise along with productivity, we should if anything be discounting the slight rise in income for the fact that families were working harder to get it. The CBO's adjustment goes in the opposite direction. Or to put it another way: the adjusted family income measure helps explain why so many families are able to afford VCRs, but misses the reason why they feel worse off than their parents.

All this is relatively minor, however. With or without the family size adjustment, the data confirm a radical shift of income to the top 1 percent.

Capital Gains

Many conservative commentators including Paul Craig Roberts, Alan Reynolds, Representative Richard Armey, and the editorial page of *The Wall Street Journal* have bitterly attacked the CBO for including capital gains in its estimates of income. They charge that this inclusion overstates the income of the rich in several ways: it includes one-time sales as if they were persistent income; it counts capital gains on assets held by the rich, but ignores the non-taxable gains of middle-class families on their houses; it counts as income the inflation component of capital gains. And all of these commentators have claimed that the CBO's capital gains estimates are the basis of the conclusion that the rich have done better than you or me.

There are answers to each of these criticisms: asset sales must take place sometime; capital gains on houses are much smaller than the critics imagine; the inflation component has fallen with the rate of inflation, so that if anything the rate of growth of income at the top is understated. The main point, however, is that excluding capital gains from the CBO numbers makes very little difference. With capital gains included, the CBO shows the share of income accruing to the top 1 percent rising from 7 to 12 percent between 1977 and 1989, and shows this group receiving 44 percent of the rise in adjusted family income. Without capital gains, the shift is from 6 to 10 percent, and the share of the rise is 38 percent. Although the CBO does not report this, we can guess that a "Krugman calculation" excluding capital gains would still yield a number in excess of 60 percent. In other words, the capital gains issue is a complete red herring.

Can You Be Too Rich?

When the Federal Reserve wealth study came out, it was immediately attacked by Alan Reynolds in *The Wall Street Journal*, as well as by Republican Congressman Richard Armey. Reynolds's main argument was that the study, based on a survey of three thousand families, could not be reliable about the top 1 percent, since thirty families is too small a sample. This was an interesting reaction, since the Fed study carefully explains that they used a two-stage procedure and that their estimates were based on over four hundred families in the top 1 percent. In fact, the study is written in the form of a working paper on statistical methodology, and the issue of sample size is raised immediately. One can only conclude that Reynolds did not bother to read the study before attacking it.

Rep. Armey, whose results were reported by Reynolds and Paul Craig Roberts in several columns, took a different tack. By careful search through a previous Fed study, he found what he took to be a significant fact: the average wealth of families with incomes above $50,000 rose more slowly over the period 1983–1989 than overall average wealth. He claimed that this fact showed that wealth distribution had actually become more, not less equal. He apparently failed to notice that the size of the "over $50,000" group had increased over the period, from 17 to 20 percent of the population. Suppose that I told you that the average SAT scores of the top 20 percent of students today are lower than those of the top 17 percent a few years ago. Would you worry, or would you simply point out that the extra students I added to the sample obviously dragged down the average?

The wealth dispute was a minor part of the distribution controversy, but it was revealing about the desperation, unscrupulousness, and sheer lack of competence of today's conservatives.

THE CONSERVATIVE RESPONSE 2: TAKING CREDIT FOR GROWTH

The second line of conservative defense has become a familiar one: they claim that the growth record of the Reagan years shows that supply-side policies produce gains for everyone, and that it is destructive to worry about or even to notice the distribution of income.

Look again at Figure 3. It is clear that from the recession year of 1982 to the business cycle peak in 1989, median income rose substantially (12.5 percent, versus 16.8 percent for average income). If you use these years as the basis of comparison, the lag of median behind average income doesn't look very important. The question is whether these are really the right years to compare.

If there is one really solid contribution of macroeconomic theory to human knowledge, it is the distinction between the business cycle and long-term growth. Long-term growth is achieved by expanding the economy's productive capacity; recessions and recoveries represent fluctuations in the degree to which that capacity is being utilized. It is a bad thing to be in a recession, and a good thing to recover, but one should never confuse the rapid growth that takes place during a recovery with an improvement in the economy's long-term performance: once the economy is near capacity, growth is bound to slow down. Moreover, recessions and recoveries depend far more on the Federal Reserve than on the administration in power, and happen to Republicans and Democrats alike. That is why a sensible assessment of economic trends involves comparing business cycle peaks or, even better, asking what has happened to the level of income associated with any given unemployment rate.

It is therefore ironic that supply-side ideologues, who originally crusaded against the traditional Keynesian focus on the business cycle, now rest their claims for success entirely on the business cycle recovery from 1982 to 1989. But of course they must, for their program failed to produce any acceleration in long-term growth.

The rise in median income from 1982 to 1989, Robert Bartley's "seven fat years," represented almost entirely a transitory business cycle recovery, which reached its inevitable limit at a level only 4 percent above the 1979 peak. And the subsequent recession, which is no more George Bush's fault than the 1980 slump was Jimmy Carter's, has probably dropped median income back to within less than 4 percent above the 1980 level.

The basic proposition that the "Krugman calculation" was meant to convey is that income inequality has been increasing so rapidly that most families have failed to get much benefit out of long-term growth. This proposition stands. One need not take seriously the efforts by supply-siders to chop the past fifteen years into little slices, and claim the good ones while disclaiming the bad ones.

THE CONSERVATIVE RESPONSE 3: INCOME MOBILITY

America is not a static society. People who have high incomes one year may have lower incomes the next, and vice versa. In the two hypothetical villages that I described earlier, one would not necessarily suppose that the same people (or their children) occupied the same positions in 1977 and 1989. And economic welfare depends more on the average income you earn over a long period than on your income in any given year. So there are some risks in drawing too many conclusions about the distribution of economic welfare from statistics on the distribution of income in any one year.

There are two ways in which income mobility—the shuffling of the economic deck that takes place as families move up or down the income ranking—could offset the proposition that inequality has increased sharply. First, if income mobility were very high, the degree of inequality in any given year would be unimportant, because the distribution of lifetime income would be very even. I think of this as the blender model: whatever the current position of the bubbles in your Mixmaster, over the course of a few minutes each bubble will on average be halfway up.

Second, if income mobility had increased over time, this could offset the increased inequality at each point in time. An increase in income mobility tends to make the distribution of lifetime income more equal, since those who are rich have nowhere to go but down, while those who are poor have nowhere to go but up.

Unfortunately, neither of these possibilities actually characterizes the U.S. economy. There is considerable income mobility in the U.S., but by no means enough to make the distribution of income irrelevant. For example, Census data show that 81.6 percent of those families who were in the bottom quintile of the income distribution in 1985 were still in that bottom quintile the next year; for the top quintile the fraction was 76.3 percent. Over longer time periods, there is more mixing, but still not that much. Studies by the Urban Institute and the U.S. Treasury have both found that about half of the families who start in either the top or the bottom quintile of the income distribution are still there after a decade, and that only 3 to 6 percent rise from bottom to top or fall from top to bottom.

Even this overstates income mobility, since (1) those who slip out of the top quintile (say) are typically at the bottom of that category, and (2) much of the movement up and down represents fluctuations around a fairly fixed long-term distribution. Joel Slemrod of the University of Michigan has provided a useful indicator that suggests how persistent high incomes tend to be: the average income of families whose income exceeded $100,000 in 1983 was $176,000 in that year; their average income over the seven-year period ending in 1985 was $153,000.

Nor is there any indication that income mobility increased significantly during the 1980s. Table 1 shows some evidence from a study by Greg Duncan of the University of Michigan on transitions over a five-year period into and out of a somewhat arbitrary but reasonable definition of the "middle class." This middle-class category shrank in the 1980s, so that middle-class families became more likely both to rise and to fall; but correspondingly fewer poor families moved up or rich families down into the middle class. (Vanishingly few poor families became rich or vice versa). The overall picture suggests little change in mobility.

	Period Effects			Cyclical Effects	
	All Years	Before 1980	1980 and After	Nonrecession Years	Recession Years
High-Income Transitions					
Percent of Middle-Income Individuals Climbing Out	6.7	6.3	7.5	6.9	6.2
Percent of High-Income Individuals Falling Out	29.7	31.1	27.1	28.5	31.8
Low-Income Transitions					
Percent of Low-Income Individuals Climbing Out	33.6	33.5	30.4	35.0	32.3
Percent of Middle-Income Individuals Falling Out	7.0	6.2	8.5	6.2	8.5

TABLE 1. PERCENT OF ADULTS MAKING KEY INCOME TRANSITIONS.
Source: Dimitri B. Papadimitriou and Edward N. Wolff, Poverty and Prosperity in the USA in the Late Twentieth Century (Palgrave Macmillan, 1993), reproduced with permission of SNCSC. Note: Recession years are defined by five-year growth in per-capita real disposable personal income. They include 1974–1975 and 1979–1981.

Income mobility might in principle be an important offset to the growth in inequality, but in practice it turns out that it isn't. That did not stop conservatives from trying to use it as a debating point.

THE HUBBARD STUDY

In June [1992] the Treasury's Office of Tax Analysis, under the direction of Glenn Hubbard, an economist on leave from Columbia, released a report claiming that there is actually huge upward mobility in the U.S. In particular, it claimed that 86 percent of individuals who started in the bottom quintile in 1979 had moved out by 1988, and indeed that an individual who started in the bottom quintile was more likely to end up in the top quintile than to stay where he was.

But this report was based on what we may charitably call a strange procedure. Here's what Hubbard's report did: it tracked a group of individuals who paid income taxes in all ten years from 1979 to 1988, and compared their incomes not with each other but with those of the population at large. The restriction to individuals who paid taxes in all years immediately introduced a strong bias toward including only the economically successful; only about half of families paid income taxes in all ten years. This bias toward the successful was apparent in the fact that by the end of the sample period the group contained very few poor people and a lot of affluent ones: indeed, only 7 percent of the sample were in the bottom quintile by the sample's end, while 28 percent were in the top quintile. More important, by comparing the sample with the population at large rather than with each other, the report essentially treated the normal tendency of earnings to rise with age as representing social mobility. The median age of those whom the study classified as being in the bottom quintile in 1979 was only twenty-two.

Kevin Murphy, a labor economist at the University of Chicago, neatly summed up what the Treasury study had found: "This isn't your classic income mobility. This is the guy who works in the college bookstore and has a real job by his early thirties."

INCOME GAINS

We have finally come to the last, and perhaps most effectively confusing, conservative argument.

Let's give the fact first: families who start out with high income on average have low or negative income growth over the next decade, while families who start out with low income on average see their incomes rise rapidly. This is true in both the Urban Institute and the Treasury data. In the Urban Institute's numbers, families in the bottom quintile in 1977 saw their income rise 77 percent by 1986, while families in the top quintile saw their income rise only 5 percent. The editorial page of *The Wall Street Journal*, Paul Craig Roberts, and others have seized upon this kind of number as evidence that the poor actually did better than the rich in the 1980s. Let me call this the "*WSJ* calculation."

The *WSJ* calculation seems striking; but on reflection it is completely consistent with the conclusion that the U.S. has rapidly growing inequality. It shows only that there is indeed some income mobility, but nobody denied that. And it is no more a sign that supply-side policies helped the poor than the fact that very few people win the lottery several years in a row.

Unfortunately, it is hard to explain this without a numerical example: imagine an economy in which in any given year half of the families earn

$100,000 and the other half earn $200,000. And imagine also that this economy fits the blender model, so that a family that starts in the bottom half has a 50 percent chance of being in the top half ten years later, and conversely.

Now do the *WSJ* calculation. Families that start in the bottom half begin with $100,000; ten years later, on average they have $150,000, so they gain 50 percent. Families that start in the top half begin with $200,000; ten years later, on average they also have $150,000, so they lose 33 percent.

But has the distribution of income gotten more equal? No: it is unchanged. All that we see is the familiar statistical phenomenon of "regression toward the mean." Essentially, the initially rich have nowhere to go but down, the initially poor nowhere to go but up. So if the income distribution were stable, any income mobility would inevitably produce the *WSJ* result; and it is not surprising that we still get it even when income inequality is rising.

If income mobility were as high as in this example, of course, the income distribution at a point in time wouldn't matter very much. But as we have already seen, income mobility isn't that high: most poor or rich people stay that way. So we have enough income mobility to make the *WSJ* calculation seem right, but not enough to change the real story that inequality is rising.

If you want a more concrete image, think of it this way. In any given year, some of the people with low incomes are just having a bad year. They are workers on temporary layoff, small businessmen taking writeoffs, farmers hit by bad weather. These people will be doing much better in a few years, so that the average income of people who are currently low-income will rise a lot looking forward. But that does not mean that people who are persistently poor have rising incomes; they don't. Perhaps the most revealing way to show what is wrong with the *WSJ* calculation is to do it in reverse, as Isabel Sawhill of the Urban Institute did. In her data, families who were in the top quintile in 1977 had experienced an 11 percent fall in income by 1986. But when she instead looked at families who were in the top quintile in 1986, she found that they had experienced a 65 percent gain! Conservatives like to emphasize income mobility, because they can evoke the historical image of America as a land of opportunity, an image that has always been partially if not completely true. But when all is said and done, mobility in the 1980s was neither increasing, nor high enough to make any difference to the overwhelming picture of growing inequality.

The growth in income inequality in the United States since the 1970s is hardly an inconspicuous part of the economic landscape. On the contrary, it is apparent in virtually every economic statistic, and colors nearly everything about our national life. You may accept this trend or deplore it, but one might have thought that nobody could seriously deny it.

The surprise lesson of the income distribution controversy, then, is what it says about today's conservative mind-set. It turns out that many conservatives, for all their anti-totalitarian rhetoric, have Orwellian instincts: if the record doesn't say what you wish it did, hide it or fudge it.

There are substantive issues about income distribution. Nobody really knows all the reasons why incomes at the top have soared while those at the bottom have plunged. Still less is there a consensus about what kinds of policies might limit or reverse the trend. But it seems that many conservatives not only don't want to discuss substance: they prefer not to face reality, and to live in a fantasy world in which the 1980s turned out the way they were supposed to, not the way they did.

GRADUATES VERSUS OLIGARCHS

February 27, 2006

Ben Bernanke's maiden Congressional testimony as chairman of the Federal Reserve was, everyone agrees, superb. He didn't put a foot wrong on monetary or fiscal policy.

But Mr. Bernanke did stumble at one point. Responding to a question from Representative Barney Frank about income inequality, he declared that "the most important factor" in rising inequality "is the rising skill premium, the increased return to education."

That's a fundamental misreading of what's happening to American society. What we're seeing isn't the rise of a fairly broad class of knowledge workers. Instead, we're seeing the rise of a narrow oligarchy: income and wealth are becoming increasingly concentrated in the hands of a small, privileged elite.

I think of Mr. Bernanke's position, which one hears all the time, as the 80–20 fallacy. It's the notion that the winners in our increasingly unequal society are a fairly large group—that the 20 percent or so of American workers who have the skills to take advantage of new technology and globalization are pulling away from the 80 percent who don't have these skills.

The truth is quite different. Highly educated workers have done better than those with less education, but a college degree has hardly been a ticket to big income gains. The 2006 Economic Report of the President tells us that the real earnings of college graduates actually fell more than 5 percent between 2000 and 2004. Over the longer stretch from 1975 to 2004 the average earnings of college graduates rose, but by less than 1 percent per year.

So who are the winners from rising inequality? It's not the top 20 percent, or even the top 10 percent. The big gains have gone to a much smaller, much richer group than that.

A new research paper by Ian Dew-Becker and Robert Gordon of Northwestern University, "Where Did the Productivity Growth Go?," gives the details. Between 1972 and 2001 the wage and salary income of Americans at the 90th percentile of the income distribution rose only 34 percent, or about 1 percent per year. So being in the top 10 percent of the income distribution, like being a college graduate, wasn't a ticket to big income gains.

But income at the 99th percentile rose 87 percent; income at the 99.9th percentile rose 181 percent; and income at the 99.99th percentile rose 497 percent. No, that's not a misprint.

Just to give you a sense of who we're talking about: the nonpartisan Tax Policy Center estimates that this year the 99th percentile will correspond to an income of $402,306, and the 99.9th percentile to an income of $1,672,726. The center doesn't give a number for the 99.99th percentile, but it's probably well over $6 million a year.

Why would someone as smart and well informed as Mr. Bernanke get the nature of growing inequality wrong? Because the fallacy he fell into tends to dominate polite discussion about income trends, not because it's true, but because it's comforting. The notion that it's all about returns to education suggests that nobody is to blame for rising inequality, that it's just a case of supply and demand at work. And it also suggests that the way to mitigate inequality is to improve our educational system—and better education is a value to which just about every politician in America pays at least lip service.

The idea that we have a rising oligarchy is much more disturbing. It suggests that the growth of inequality may have as much to do with power relations as it does with market forces. Unfortunately, that's the real story.

Should we be worried about the increasingly oligarchic nature of American society? Yes, and not just because a rising economic tide has failed to lift most boats. Both history and modern experience tell us that highly unequal societies also tend to be highly corrupt. There's an arrow of causation that runs from diverging income trends to Jack Abramoff and the K Street project.

And I'm with Alan Greenspan, who—surprisingly, given his libertarian roots—has repeatedly warned that growing inequality poses a threat to "democratic society."

It may take some time before we muster the political will to counter that threat. But the first step toward doing something about inequality is to abandon the 80–20 fallacy. It's time to face up to the fact that rising inequality is driven by the giant income gains of a tiny elite, not the modest gains of college graduates.

MONEY AND MORALS

February 9, 2012

L
ately inequality has re-entered the national conversation. Occupy
Wall Street gave the issue visibility, while the Congressional Budget Office supplied hard data on the widening income gap. And the
myth of a classless society has been exposed: among rich countries, America
stands out as the place where economic and social status is most likely to be
inherited.

So you knew what was going to happen next. Suddenly, conservatives
are telling us that it's not really about money; it's about morals. Never mind
wage stagnation and all that, the real problem is the collapse of working-class
family values, which is somehow the fault of liberals.

But is it really all about morals? No, it's mainly about money.

To be fair, the new book at the heart of the conservative pushback,
Charles Murray's *Coming Apart: The State of White America, 1960–2010*,
does highlight some striking trends. Among white Americans with a high
school education or less, marriage rates and male labor force participation
are down, while births out of wedlock are up. Clearly, white working-class
society has changed in ways that don't sound good.

But the first question one should ask is: Are things really that bad on
the values front?

Mr. Murray and other conservatives often seem to assume that the
decline of the traditional family has terrible implications for society as a
whole. This is, of course, a longstanding position. Reading Mr. Murray, I
found myself thinking about an earlier diatribe, Gertrude Himmelfarb's
1996 book, *The De-Moralization of Society: From Victorian Virtues to Mod-*

ern Values, which covered much of the same ground, claimed that our society was unraveling, and predicted further unraveling as the Victorian virtues continued to erode.

Yet the truth is that some indicators of social dysfunction have improved dramatically even as traditional families continue to lose ground. As far as I can tell, Mr. Murray never mentions either the plunge in teenage pregnancies among all racial groups since 1990 or the 60 percent decline in violent crime since the mid-nineties. Could it be that traditional families aren't as crucial to social cohesion as advertised?

Still, something is clearly happening to the traditional working-class family. The question is what. And it is, frankly, amazing how quickly and blithely conservatives dismiss the seemingly obvious answer: a drastic reduction in the work opportunities available to less-educated men.

Most of the numbers you see about income trends in America focus on households rather than individuals, which makes sense for some purposes. But when you see a modest rise in incomes for the lower tiers of the income distribution, you have to realize that all—yes, all—of this rise comes from the women, both because more women are in the paid labor force and because women's wages aren't as much below male wages as they used to be.

For lower-education working men, however, it has been all negative. Adjusted for inflation, entry-level wages of male high school graduates have fallen 23 percent since 1973. Meanwhile, employment benefits have collapsed. In 1980, 65 percent of recent high-school graduates working in the private sector had health benefits, but, by 2009, that was down to 29 percent.

So we have become a society in which less-educated men have great difficulty finding jobs with decent wages and good benefits. Yet somehow we're supposed to be surprised that such men have become less likely to participate in the work force or get married, and conclude that there must have been some mysterious moral collapse caused by snooty liberals. And Mr. Murray also tells us that working-class marriages, when they do happen, have become less happy; strange to say, money problems will do that.

One more thought: The real winner in this controversy is the distinguished sociologist William Julius Wilson.

Back in 1996, the same year Ms. Himmelfarb was lamenting our moral collapse, Mr. Wilson published *When Work Disappears: The World of the*

New Urban Poor, in which he argued that much of the social disruption among African-Americans popularly attributed to collapsing values was actually caused by a lack of blue-collar jobs in urban areas. If he was right, you would expect something similar to happen if another social group—say, working-class whites—experienced a comparable loss of economic opportunity. And so it has.

So we should reject the attempt to divert the national conversation away from soaring inequality toward the alleged moral failings of those Americans being left behind. Traditional values aren't as crucial as social conservatives would have you believe—and, in any case, the social changes taking place in America's working class are overwhelmingly the consequence of sharply rising inequality, not its cause.

DON'T BLAME ROBOTS FOR LOW WAGES

March 14, 2019

The other day I found myself, as I often do, at a conference discussing lagging wages and soaring inequality. There was a lot of interesting discussion. But one thing that struck me was how many of the participants just assumed that robots are a big part of the problem—that machines are taking away the good jobs, or even jobs in general. For the most part this wasn't even presented as a hypothesis, just as part of what everyone knows.

And this assumption has real implications for policy discussion. For example, a lot of the agitation for a universal basic income comes from the belief that jobs will become ever scarcer as the robot apocalypse overtakes the economy.

So it seems like a good idea to point out that in this case what everyone knows isn't true. Predictions are hard, especially about the future, and maybe the robots really will come for all our jobs one of these days. But automation just isn't a big part of the story of what happened to American workers over the past forty years.

We do have a big problem—but it has very little to do with technology, and a lot to do with politics and power.

Let's back up for a minute, and ask: What is a robot, anyway? Clearly, it doesn't have to be something that looks like C-3PO, or rolls around saying "Exterminate! Exterminate!" From an economic point of view, a robot is anything that uses technology to do work formerly done by human beings.

And robots in that sense have been transforming our economy literally for centuries. David Ricardo, one of the founding fathers of economics, wrote about the disruptive effects of machinery in 1821!

These days, when people talk about the robot apocalypse, they don't usually think of things like strip mining and mountaintop removal. Yet these technologies utterly transformed coal mining: coal production almost doubled between 1950 and 2000 (it only began falling a few years ago), yet the number of coal miners fell from 470,000 to fewer than 80,000.

Or consider freight containerization. Longshoremen used to be a big part of the scene in major port cities. But while global trade has soared since the 1970s, the share of U.S. workers engaged in "marine cargo handling" has fallen by two-thirds.

Technological disruption, then, isn't a new phenomenon. Still, is it accelerating? Not according to the data. If robots really were replacing workers en masse, we'd expect to see the amount of stuff produced by each remaining worker—labor productivity—soaring. In fact, productivity grew a lot faster from the mid-1990s to the mid-2000s than it has since.

So technological change is an old story. What's new is the failure of workers to share in the fruits of that technological change.

I'm not saying that coping with change was ever easy. The decline of coal employment had devastating effects on many families, and much of what used to be coal country has never recovered. The loss of manual jobs in port cities surely contributed to the urban social crisis of the seventies and eighties.

But while there have always been some victims of technological progress, until the 1970s rising productivity translated into rising wages for a great majority of workers. Then the connection was broken. And it wasn't the robots that did it.

What did? There is a growing though incomplete consensus among economists that a key factor in wage stagnation has been workers' declining bargaining power—a decline whose roots are ultimately political.

Most obviously, the federal minimum wage, adjusted for inflation, has fallen by a third over the past half century, even as worker productivity has risen 150 percent. That divergence was politics, pure and simple.

The decline of unions, which covered a quarter of private-sector workers in 1973 but only 6 percent now, may not be as obviously political. But other countries haven't seen the same kind of decline. Canada is as unionized now as the U.S. was in 1973; in the Nordic nations unions cover two-thirds of the work force. What made America exceptional was a political environment deeply hostile to labor organizing and friendly toward union-busting employers.

And the decline of unions has made a huge difference. Consider the case of trucking, which used to be a good job but now pays a third less than it did in the 1970s, with terrible working conditions. What made the difference? De-unionization was a big part of the story.

And these easily quantifiable factors are just indicators of a sustained, across-the-board anti-worker bias in our politics.

Which brings me back to the question of why we're talking so much about robots. The answer, I'd argue, is that it's a diversionary tactic—a way to avoid facing up to the way our system is rigged against workers, similar to the way talk of a "skills gap" was a way to divert attention from bad policies that kept unemployment high.

And progressives, above all, shouldn't fall for this facile fatalism. American workers can and should be getting a much better deal than they are. And to the extent that they aren't, the fault lies not in our robots, but in our political leaders.

WHAT'S THE MATTER WITH TRUMPLAND?

April 2, 2018

These days almost everyone has the (justified) sense that America is coming apart at the seams. But this isn't a new story, or just about politics. Things have been falling apart on multiple fronts since the 1970s: political polarization has marched side by side with economic polarization, as income inequality has soared.

And both political and economic polarization have a strong geographic dimension. On the economic side, some parts of America, mainly big coastal cities, have been getting much richer, but other parts have been left behind. On the political side, the thriving regions by and large voted for Hillary Clinton, while the lagging regions voted for Donald Trump.

I'm not saying that everything is great in coastal cities: many people remain economically stranded even within metropolitan areas that look successful in the aggregate. And soaring housing costs, thanks in large part to Nimbyism, are a real and growing problem. Still, regional economic divergence is real and correlates closely, though not perfectly, with political divergence.

But what's behind this divergence? What's the matter with Trumpland?

Regional disparities aren't a new phenomenon in America. Indeed, before World War II the world's richest, most productive nation was also a nation with millions of dirt-poor farmers, many of whom didn't even have electricity or indoor plumbing. But until the 1970s those disparities were rapidly narrowing.

Take, for example, the case of Mississippi, America's poorest state. In the 1930s, per-capita income in Mississippi was only 30 percent as high as per-capita income in Massachusetts. By the late 1970s, however, that figure was almost 70 percent—and most people probably expected this process of convergence to continue.

But the process went into reverse instead: these days, Mississippi is back down to only about 55 percent of Massachusetts income. To put this in international perspective, Mississippi now is about as poor relative to the coastal states as Sicily is relative to northern Italy.

Mississippi isn't an isolated case. As a new paper by Benjamin Austin, Edward Glaeser, and Lawrence Summers documents, regional convergence in per-capita incomes has stopped dead. And the relative economic decline of lagging regions has been accompanied by growing social problems: a rising share of prime-aged men not working, rising mortality, high levels of opioid consumption.

An aside: One implication of these developments is that William Julius Wilson was right. Wilson famously argued that the social ills of the non-white inner-city poor had their origin not in some mysterious flaws of African-American culture but in economic factors—specifically, the disappearance of good blue-collar jobs. Sure enough, when rural whites faced a similar loss of economic opportunity, they experienced a similar social unraveling.

So what *is* the matter with Trumpland?

For the most part I'm in agreement with Berkeley's Enrico Moretti, whose 2012 book, *The New Geography of Jobs*, is must reading for anyone trying to understand the state of America. Moretti argues that structural changes in the economy have favored industries that employ highly educated workers—and that these industries do best in locations where there are already a lot of these workers. As a result, these regions are experiencing a virtuous circle of growth: their knowledge-intensive industries prosper, drawing in even more educated workers, which reinforces their advantage.

And at the same time, regions that started with a poorly educated work force are in a downward spiral, both because they're stuck with the wrong industries and because they're experiencing what amounts to a brain drain.

While these structural factors are surely the main story, however, I think we have to acknowledge the role of self-destructive politics.

That new Austin et al. paper makes the case for a national policy of aiding lagging regions. But we already have programs that would aid these

WHAT'S THE MATTER WITH TRUMPLAND?

regions—but which they won't accept. Many of the states that have refused to expand Medicaid, even though the federal government would foot the great bulk of the bill—and would create jobs in the process—are also among America's poorest.

Or consider how some states, like Kansas and Oklahoma—both of which were relatively affluent in the 1970s, but have now fallen far behind—have gone in for radical tax cuts, and ended up savaging their education systems. External forces have put them in a hole, but they're digging it deeper.

And when it comes to national politics, let's face it: Trumpland is in effect voting for its own impoverishment. New Deal programs and public investment played a significant role in the great postwar convergence; conservative efforts to downsize government will hurt people all across America, but it will disproportionately hurt the very regions that put the G.O.P. in power.

The truth is that doing something about America's growing regional divide would be hard even with smart policies. The divide will only get worse under the policies we're actually likely to get.

13

Conservatives

MOVEMENT CONSERVATISM

"I DON'T BELONG TO ANY ORGANIZED POLITICAL PARTY," QUIPPED WILL Rogers. "I'm a Democrat." The joke had some truth when he said it; it has even more truth now. Don't take my word for it: political scientists will tell you that the two parties are fundamentally different in structure.

The Democratic Party isn't necessarily hapless or ineffective, but it has always been a loose coalition of interest groups. It's not as loose as it was in the days when it incorporated both northern union leaders and southern segregationists, and it seems to have become more ideologically cohesive in recent years. But no single group is in charge.

The modern Republican Party, by contrast, is best seen as just one part of a highly organized movement that includes the Murdoch media empire, a dizzying array of think tanks and advocacy groups that are mostly funded by the same group of billionaires, and more. Observers both inside and outside often refer to this collective as "movement conservatism."

Movement conservatism wasn't always an important force in U.S. politics. It barely existed before the 1970s, and it didn't fully take over the G.O.P. until the 1990s. But now it's the only kind of conservatism that matters—and it's the driving force behind America's deep political polarization. Again, the political scientists have found ways to measure these things. At least until recently, Democrats had moved only slightly to the left—but Republicans moved very far to the right. There is polarization in our politics but, as the political scientists say, it's "asymmetric."

Many people who opine on U.S. politics and policy, however, either don't recognize or refuse to acknowledge the fundamental asymmetry between the parties. We even have a name for it: bothsidesism. It's the insistence that whatever excesses of partisanship you may see on the right have an equivalent on the left, that the way forward to solving America's problems is for good centrists of both parties to come together and work things out. All of this is willfully naïve.

There are, of course, leftist radicals in America, but they don't control the Democratic Party; rightist radicals basically *are* the Republican Party. There are some politicians one might describe as centrists, in the sense that their policy views broadly match public opinion—although public opinion is actually much further to the left on economic issues than is widely acknowledged. In any case, however, at this point virtually every politician one might call a centrist is a Democrat; Republican centrists have been driven out of the G.O.P.

And you can't write realistically about either politics or policy—because policy ideas depend, at least in part, on what has some realistic chance of happening—without taking asymmetric polarization into account. The articles in this section all deal, one way or another, with the realities of U.S. politics in the age of movement conservatism.

SAME OLD PARTY

October 8, 2007

There have been a number of articles recently that portray President Bush as someone who strayed from the path of true conservatism. Republicans, these articles say, need to return to their roots.

Well, I don't know what true conservatism is, but while doing research for my forthcoming book I spent a lot of time studying the history of the American political movement that calls itself conservatism—and Mr. Bush hasn't strayed from the path at all. On the contrary, he's the very model of a modern movement conservative.

For example, people claim to be shocked that Mr. Bush cut taxes while waging an expensive war. But Ronald Reagan also cut taxes while embarking on a huge military buildup.

People claim to be shocked by Mr. Bush's general fiscal irresponsibility. But conservative intellectuals, by their own account, abandoned fiscal responsibility thirty years ago. Here's how Irving Kristol, then the editor of *The Public Interest*, explained his embrace of supply-side economics in the 1970s: he had a "rather cavalier attitude toward the budget deficit and other monetary or fiscal problems" because "the task, as I saw it, was to create a new majority, which evidently would mean a conservative majority, which came to mean, in turn, a Republican majority—so political effectiveness was the priority, not the accounting deficiencies of government."

People claim to be shocked by the way the Bush administration outsourced key government functions to private contractors yet refused to exert effective oversight over these contractors, a process exemplified by the failed reconstruction of Iraq and the Blackwater affair.

But back in 1993, Jonathan Cohn, writing in *The American Prospect*, explained that "under Reagan and Bush, the ranks of public officials necessary to supervise contractors have been so thinned that the putative gains of contracting out have evaporated. Agencies have been left with the worst of both worlds—demoralized and disorganized public officials and unaccountable private contractors."

People claim to be shocked by the Bush administration's general incompetence. But disinterest in good government has long been a principle of modern conservatism. In *The Conscience of a Conservative*, published in 1960, Barry Goldwater wrote that "I have little interest in streamlining government or making it more efficient, for I mean to reduce its size."

People claim to be shocked that the Bush Justice Department, making a mockery of the Constitution, issued a secret opinion authorizing torture despite instructions by Congress and the courts that the practice should stop. But remember Iran-Contra? The Reagan administration secretly sold weapons to Iran, violating a legal embargo, and used the proceeds to support the Nicaraguan contras, defying an explicit Congressional ban on such support.

Oh, and if you think Iran-Contra was a rogue operation, rather than something done with the full knowledge and approval of people at the top— who were then protected by a careful cover-up, including convenient presidential pardons—I've got a letter from Niger you might want to buy.

People claim to be shocked at the Bush administration's efforts to disenfranchise minority groups, under the pretense of combating voting fraud. But Reagan opposed the Voting Rights Act, and as late as 1980 he described it as "humiliating to the South."

People claim to be shocked at the Bush administration's attempts— which, for a time, were all too successful—to intimidate the press. But this administration's media tactics, and to a large extent the people implementing those tactics, come straight out of the Nixon administration. Dick Cheney wanted to search Seymour Hersh's apartment, not last week, but in 1975. Roger Ailes, the president of Fox News, was Nixon's media adviser.

People claim to be shocked at the Bush administration's attempts to equate dissent with treason. But Goldwater—who, like Reagan, has been reinvented as an icon of conservative purity but was a much less attractive figure in real life—staunchly supported Joseph McCarthy, and was one of only twenty-two senators who voted against a motion censuring the demagogue.

Above all, people claim to be shocked by the Bush administration's authoritarianism, its disdain for the rule of law. But a full half century has passed since *The National Review* proclaimed that "the White community in the South is entitled to take such measures as are necessary to prevail," and dismissed as irrelevant objections that might be raised after "consulting a catalogue of the rights of American citizens, born Equal"—presumably a reference to the document known as the Constitution of the United States.

Now, as they survey the wreckage of their cause, conservatives may ask themselves: "Well, how did we get here?" They may tell themselves: "This is not my beautiful Right." They may ask themselves: "My God, what have we done?"

But their movement is the same as it ever was. And Mr. Bush is movement conservatism's true, loyal heir.

ERIC CANTOR AND THE DEATH OF A MOVEMENT

June 12, 2014

How big a deal is the surprise primary defeat of Representative Eric Cantor, the House majority leader? Very. Movement conservatism, which dominated American politics from the election of Ronald Reagan to the election of Barack Obama—and which many pundits thought could make a comeback this year—is unraveling before our eyes.

I don't mean that conservatism in general is dying. But what I and others mean by "movement conservatism," a term I think I learned from the historian Rick Perlstein, is something more specific: an interlocking set of institutions and alliances that won elections by stoking cultural and racial anxiety but used these victories mainly to push an elitist economic agenda, meanwhile providing a support network for political and ideological loyalists.

By rejecting Mr. Cantor, the Republican base showed that it has gotten wise to the electoral bait-and-switch, and, by his fall, Mr. Cantor showed that the support network can no longer guarantee job security. For around three decades, the conservative fix was in; but no more.

To see what I mean by bait-and-switch, think about what happened in 2004. George W. Bush won re-election by posing as a champion of national security and traditional values—as I like to say, he ran as America's defender against gay married terrorists—then turned immediately to his real priority: privatizing Social Security. It was the perfect illustration of the strategy famously described in Thomas Frank's book *What's the Matter with Kansas?* in which Republicans would mobilize voters with social issues, but invariably turn postelection to serving the interests of corporations and the 1 percent.

In return for this service, businesses and the wealthy provided both lavish financial support for right-minded (in both senses) politicians and a safety net—"wing-nut welfare"—for loyalists. In particular, there were always comfortable berths waiting for those who left office, voluntarily or otherwise. There were lobbying jobs; there were commentator spots at Fox News and elsewhere (two former Bush speechwriters are now *Washington Post* columnists); there were "research" positions (after losing his Senate seat, Rick Santorum became director of the "America's Enemies" program at a think tank supported by the Koch brothers, among others).

The combination of a successful electoral strategy and the safety net made being a conservative loyalist a seemingly low-risk professional path. The cause was radical, but the people it recruited tended increasingly to be apparatchiks, motivated more by careerism than by conviction.

That's certainly the impression Mr. Cantor conveyed. I've never heard him described as inspiring. His political rhetoric was nasty but low-energy, and often amazingly tone-deaf. You may recall, for example, that in 2012 he chose to celebrate Labor Day with a Twitter post honoring business owners. But he was evidently very good at playing the inside game.

It turns out, however, that this is no longer enough. We don't know exactly why he lost his primary, but it seems clear that Republican base voters didn't trust him to serve their priorities as opposed to those of corporate interests (and they were probably right). And the specific issue that loomed largest, immigration, also happens to be one on which the divergence between the base and the party elite is wide. It's not just that the elite believes that it must find a way to reach Hispanics, whom the base loathes. There's also an inherent conflict between the base's nativism and the corporate desire for abundant, cheap labor.

And while Mr. Cantor won't go hungry—he'll surely find a comfortable niche on K Street—the humiliation of his fall is a warning that becoming a conservative apparatchik isn't the safe career choice it once seemed.

So whither movement conservatism? Before the Virginia upset, there was a widespread media narrative to the effect that the Republican establishment was regaining control from the Tea Party, which was really a claim that good old-fashioned movement conservatism was on its way back. In reality, however, establishment figures who won primaries did so only by reinventing themselves as extremists. And Mr. Cantor's defeat shows that lip service to extremism isn't enough; the base needs to believe that you really mean it.

In the long run—which probably begins in 2016—this will be bad news for the G.O.P., because the party is moving right on social issues at a time when the country at large is moving left. (Think about how quickly the ground has shifted on gay marriage.) Meanwhile, however, what we're looking at is a party that will be even more extreme, even less interested in participating in normal governance, than it has been since 2008. An ugly political scene is about to get even uglier.

THE GREAT CENTER-RIGHT DELUSION

October 31, 2018

W hat's driving American politics off a cliff? Racial hatred and the cynicism of politicians willing to exploit it play a central role. But there are other factors. And an opinion piece by Alexander Hertel-Fernandez, Matto Mildenberger, and Leah Stokes in today's *Times* (which is actually social science, not opinion!) seems to confirm something I already suspected. misunderstanding of what voters want is distorting both political positioning and public policy.

What the authors of the piece show is that congressional aides grossly misperceive the views of their bosses' constituents; this is true in both parties, but more so of Republicans. What they don't point out explicitly is that with the exception of A.C.A. repeal, Democrats err in the *same direction* as Republicans, just less so. Specifically, both parties believe that the public is to the right of where it really is.

An aside on A.C.A. repeal: I wonder what's really going on here. Lots of polling suggests that voters overwhelmingly want protection for pre-existing conditions and subsidies to help lower-income Americans afford insurance—that is, they want the substance of the A.C.A., even if they say they disapprove of the law. So I'd take this result with a grain of salt: Democrats may not be as wrong here as it appears.

Anyway, what I'd really like to see are comparable surveys of other groups—say, political analysts for major media organizations. Why? Because I suspect we'd see a similar result: people who opine on politics also imagine that voters are farther to the right than they really are. What I'm suggesting, in other words, is that there's a shared inside-the-Beltway delusion: that

America is a conservative, or at most center-right nation, a view that isn't grounded in reality.

It's true that Republicans, who are increasingly a far-right party, have been more than competitive politically, controlling the White House, the House of Representatives, or both for all but four of the past twenty-four years. But this owes a lot to a tilted playing field—they only won the popular vote for president once over that stretch, and can hold the House even when Democrats get a lot more votes.

And it also reflects a political strategy in which Republicans run on anything but their policies. Trump's frantic attempt to make next week's election about scary brown people rather than health care or tax cuts is cruder and uglier than anything we've seen for a long time, but it's not fundamentally out of character. Bush the elder ran against Willie Horton. Bush the younger ran on national security. Their actual policies, not so much.

In fact, we got an object lesson in the dissonance between G.O.P. electioneering and public preferences in 2004–2005. Bush made it a national security election, with a tinge of culture war; as I used to joke, he ran as the enemy of gay married terrorists. Then, with victory under his belt, he proclaimed that he had a mandate to privatize Social Security. He didn't.

But many pundits thought he did. For several months after the 2004 election it was conventional wisdom in the commentariat that of course Bush would get his way on Social Security, and that people like Nancy Pelosi who were trying to stop his push were on the wrong side of history. The overwhelming backlash from voters, who really, really like Social Security (and Medicare, and Medicaid) completely surprised many self-proclaimed political experts.

So what are the effects of this delusion of America as a center-right nation? It has clearly inhibited Democrats from taking bold policy positions, out of fear that they'll be too far left for voters—a fear fed by journalists who keep insisting that the public wants centrists who are somewhere between the parties. Remember the Bloomberg for president bandwagon, which consisted of a number of prominent pundits and maybe three nonjournalist voters.

But Republicans are even further out of touch. Hertel-Fernandez et al note correctly that the Trump tax cut has proved consistently unpopular;

they don't point out that at first Republicans were sure that it would be a big political winner: "If we can't sell this to the American people, we ought to go into another line of work," declared Mitch McConnell. But they couldn't sell it, and the tax cut has virtually disappeared from G.O.P. messaging.

And Republicans appear to have been completely blindsided by the public backlash against their attempts to remove protection for pre-existing conditions, which is amazing if you think about it. How could they not realize that this is a sore spot?

Which brings me to something David Roberts wrote yesterday, which complements something I've been thinking for a while. He notes, in regard to the frame-Mueller debacle, that we're dealing with the "second generation of Fox News conservatives," who grew up entirely inside the right-wing bubble and don't understand how people outside that bubble talk, think, and behave.

I'd say that this goes even more for professional G.O.P. politicos, who are all apparatchiks. That is, they grew up inside the apparatus of movement conservatism, and really imagine that everyone except a few leftist losers shares their ideology. They don't even realize that their party's success has been based on racial antagonism, that most people want to raise taxes on the rich and maintain social benefits.

And this, by the way, is where Trump has an advantage. He didn't grow up in the conservative hothouse; his very crudity means that he understands that his electoral chances depend not on repeating conservative pieties but on maximum ugliness.

THE EMPTY QUARTERS OF U.S. POLITICS

February 1, 2019

Howard Schultz, the coffee billionaire, who imagined that he could attract broad support as a "centrist," turns out to have an approval rating of 4 percent, versus 40 percent disapproval.

Ralph Northam, a Democrat who won the governorship of Virginia in a landslide, is facing a firestorm of denunciation from his own party over racist images on his medical school yearbook page.

Donald Trump, who ran on promises to expand health care and raise taxes on the rich, began betraying his working-class supporters the moment he took office, pushing through big tax cuts for the rich while trying to take health coverage away from millions.

These are, it turns out, related stories, all of them tied to the two great absences in American political life.

One is the absence of socially liberal, economically conservative voters. These were the people Schultz thought he could appeal to; but basically they don't exist, accounting for only around, yes, 4 percent of the electorate.

The other is the absence of economically liberal, socially conservative politicians—let's be blunt and just say "racist populists." There are plenty of voters who would like that mix, and Trump pretended to be their man; but he wasn't, and neither is anyone else.

Understanding these empty quarters is, I'd argue, the key to understanding U.S. politics.

Once upon a time there were racist populists in Congress: the New Deal coalition relied on a large contingent of segregationist Dixiecrats. But this was always unstable. In practice, advocating economic inclusion seems to spill over into advocacy of racial and social inclusion, too. By the 1940s, northern Democrats were already more pro-civil rights than northern Republicans, and as the Northam affair shows, the party now has very little tolerance for even the appearance of racism.

Meanwhile, the modern Republican Party is all about cutting taxes on the rich and benefits for the poor and the middle class. And Trump, despite his campaign posturing, has turned out to be no different.

Hence the failure of our political system to serve socially conservative/racist voters who also want to tax the rich and preserve Social Security. Democrats won't ratify their racism; Republicans, who have no such compunctions, will—remember, the party establishment solidly backed Roy Moore's Senate bid—but won't protect the programs they depend on.

But why are there so few voters holding the reverse position, combining social/racial liberalism and economic conservatism? The answer, I'd argue, lies in just how far to the right the G.O.P. has gone.

Polling is unambiguous here. If you define the "center" as a position somewhere between those of the two parties, when it comes to economic issues the public is overwhelmingly left of center; if anything, it's to the left of the Democrats. Tax cuts for the rich are the G.O.P.'s defining policy, but two-thirds of voters believe that taxes on the rich are actually too low, while only 7 percent believe that they're too high. Voters support Elizabeth Warren's proposed tax on large fortunes by a three-to-one majority. Only a small minority want to see cuts in Medicaid, even though such cuts have been central to every G.O.P. health care proposal in recent years.

Why did Republicans stake out a position so far from voters' preferences? Because they could. As Democrats became the party of civil rights, the G.O.P. could attract working-class whites by catering to their social and racial illiberalism, even while pursuing policies that hurt ordinary workers.

The result is that to be an economic conservative in America means advocating policies that, on their merits, only appeal to a small elite. Basically nobody wants these policies on their own; they only sell if they're packaged with racial hostility.

So what do the empty quarters of U.S. politics mean for the future?

First, of course, that Schultz is a fool—and so are those who dream of a reformed G.O.P. that remains conservative but drops its association with racists. There's hardly anyone who wants that mix of positions.

Second, fears that Democrats are putting their electoral prospects in danger by moving too far left, for example by proposing higher taxes on the rich and Medicare expansion, are grossly exaggerated. Voters want an economic move to the left—it's just that some of them dislike Democratic support for civil rights, which the party can't drop without losing its soul.

What's less clear is whether there's room for politicians willing to be true racist populists, unlike Trump, who was faking the second part. There's a substantial bloc of racist-populist voters, and you might think that someone would try to serve them. But maybe the gravitational attraction of big money—which has completely captured the G.O.P., and has arguably kept Democrats from moving as far left as the electorate really wants—is too great.

In any case, if there's a real opening for an independent, that candidate will look more like George Wallace than like Howard Schultz. Billionaires who despise the conventional parties should beware of what they wish for.

14

Eek! Socialism!

RED-BAITING IN THE 21ST CENTURY

SHOULD AMERICA HAVE A MEDICARE-TYPE PROGRAM FOR ALL ITS LEGAL residents? That's a real question you can ask voters, and get meaningful responses. (People generally like the idea of being able to buy into Medicare, but not the idea of being required to give up private insurance if they're happy with it.)

Should America adopt socialism? That's not a real question, because "socialism" can mean different things to different people. The classic definition is "government ownership of the means of production," and clearly voters don't favor that. But there's a long tradition in American politics of trying to conflate socialism in that sense with what Europeans call "social democracy"—a market economy, but with a strong public social safety net and regulations that limit the range of actions businesses can take in pursuit of profit. Indeed, before it went into effect and became immensely popular, Medicare itself was denounced as "socialized medicine," amid dire warnings that it would destroy American freedom.

Or to put it another way, if you think we should be a bit more like Denmark—a market economy, but one with a much stronger social safety net than we have here—conservatives will insist that you want to turn us into Venezuela, where contempt for market forces has produced economic disaster.

As I write this, Republicans are clearly trying to make fear of socialism a central theme of their 2020 campaign, hoping to take advantage of the fact that the Democratic Party—which is basically social-democratic at this point—includes politicians who have defiantly, but I'd say inaccurately, taken to calling themselves socialists. I have no idea how well this scare tactic will work. But to the extent it gets traction, it will do so partly because too few people understand what social democracy does, or what life is like in countries that have gone further down the social-democratic road than we have.

The articles in this section try to take on that lack of knowledge from a variety of angles: describing what life is really like in Western Europe, but also trying to dispel some myths about how our own society works—especially the persistent but false claim that free markets always foster personal freedom.

CAPITALISM, SOCIALISM, AND UNFREEDOM

August 26, 2018

T here are two articles currently on the *Times* home page—an opinion piece by Corey Robin, and a news analysis by Neil Irwin—that I think should be read together. Taken as a pair, they get at a lot of what's wrong with the neoliberal ideology (and yes, I do think that's the right term here) that has dominated so much public discourse since the 1970s.

What, after all, were and are the selling points for low taxes and minimal regulation? Partly, of course, the claim that small government is the key to great economic performance, a rising tide that raises all boats. This claim persists—because there are powerful interests that want it to persist—even though the era of neoliberal dominance has in fact been marked by so-so economic growth that hasn't been shared with ordinary workers:

The other claim, however, has been that free markets translate into personal freedom: that an unregulated market economy liberates ordinary people from the tyranny of bureaucracies. In a free market, the story goes, you don't need to flatter your boss or the company selling you stuff, because they know you can always go to someone else.

What Robin points out is that the reality of a market economy is nothing like that. In fact, the daily experience of tens of millions of Americans—especially but not only those who don't make a lot of money—is one of constant dependence on the good will of employers and other more powerful economic players.

Employed full time: Median usual weekly real earnings: Wage and Salary workers: 16 years and over: Men

Source: U.S. Bureau of Labor Statistics.

It's true that, as Brad DeLong says, many of Robin's examples would actually apply in any complex economic system: I've wasted time dealing with both Verizon and the Social Security Administration, and in both cases my socioeconomic status surely made it a lot easier than it would have been for a minimum-wage worker. (I have, on the other hand, had consistently good experiences at the much-maligned DMV.) But the idea that free markets remove power relations from the equation is just naïve.

And it's even more naïve now than it was a few decades ago, because, as Irwin points out, large economic players are dominating more and more of the economy. It's increasingly clear, for example, that monopsony power is depressing wages; but that's not all it does. Concentration of hiring among a few firms, plus things like noncompete clauses and tacit collusion that reinforce their market power, don't just reduce your wage if you're hired. They also reduce or eliminate your options if you're mistreated: quit because you have an abusive boss or have problems with company policy, and you may have real trouble getting a new job.

But what can be done about it? Corey Robin says "socialism"—but as far as I can tell he really means social democracy: Denmark, not Venezuela. Government-mandated employee protections may restrict the ability of corporations to hire and fire, but they also shield workers from some very real forms of abuse. Unions do somewhat limit workers' options, but they also offer an important counterweight against corporate monopsony power.

Oh, and social safety net programs can do more than limit misery: they can be liberating. I've known many people who stuck with jobs they disliked for fear of losing health coverage; Obamacare, flawed as it is, has noticeably reduced that kind of "lock in," and a full guarantee of health coverage would make our society visibly freer.

The other day I had some fun with the Cato Institute index of economic freedom across states, which finds Florida the freest and New York the least free. (Is it O.K. for me to write this, comrade commissar?) As I pointed out, freedom Cato-style seems to be associated with, among other things, high infant mortality. Live free and die! (New Hampshire is just behind Florida.)

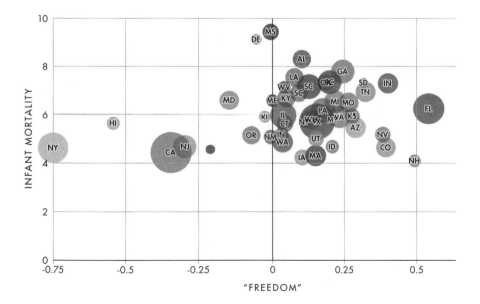

Source: William P. Ruger and Jason Sorens, Freedom in the 50 States: An Index of Personal and Economic Freedom (Cato Institute, 2018).

But seriously, do the real differences between New York and Florida make New Yorkers less free? New York is a highly unionized state—25.3 percent of the work force—while only 6.6 percent of Florida workers are represented by unions. Does this make New York workers less free, or does it empower them in the face of corporate power?

Also, New York has expanded Medicaid and tried to make the A.C.A. exchanges work, so that only 8 percent of nonelderly adults are uninsured, compared with 18 percent in Florida. Are New Yorkers chafing under the heavy hand of health law, or do they feel freer knowing that they're at much less risk of being ruined by medical emergency—or cast into the abyss if they lose their job?

If you're a highly paid professional, it probably doesn't make much difference. But my guess is that most workers feel at least somewhat freer in New York than they do in Florida.

Now, there are no perfect answers to the inevitable sacrifice of some freedom that comes with living in a complex society; utopia is not on the menu. But the advocates of unrestricted corporate power and minimal worker protection have been getting away for far too long with pretending that they're the defenders of freedom—which is not, in fact, just another word for nothing left to lose.

SOMETHING NOT ROTTEN IN DENMARK

August 16, 2018

To be or not to be a socialist hellhole, that is the question. Sorry, I couldn't help myself.

Last weekend, Trish Regan, a Fox Business host, created a bit of an international incident by describing Denmark as an example of the horrors of socialism, right along with Venezuela. Denmark's finance minister suggested that she visit his country and learn some facts.

Indeed, Regan couldn't have picked a worse example—or, from the point of view of U.S. progressives, a better one.

For Denmark has indeed taken a very different path from the United States over the past few decades, veering (modestly) to the left where we've veered right. And it has done just fine.

American politics has been dominated by a crusade against big government; Denmark has embraced an expansive government role, with public spending more than half of G.D.P. American politicians fear talk about redistribution of income from the rich to the less well-off; Denmark engages in such redistribution on a scale unimaginable here. American policy has been increasingly hostile to organized labor, and unions have virtually disappeared from the private sector; two-thirds of Danish workers are unionized.

Conservative ideology says that Denmark's policy choices should be disastrous, that grass should be growing in the streets of Copenhagen. Regan was, in effect, describing what her employers think must be happening there. But if Denmark is a hellhole, it's doing a very good job of hiding that fact: I was just there, and it looks awfully prosperous.

And the data agree with that impression. Danes are more likely to have jobs than Americans, and in many cases they earn substantially more. Overall G.D.P. per capita in Denmark is a bit lower than in America, but that's basically because the Danes take more vacations. Income inequality is much lower, and life expectancy is higher.

The simple fact is that life is better for most Danes than it is for their U.S. counterparts. There's a reason Denmark consistently ranks well ahead of America in measures of happiness and life satisfaction.

But is Denmark socialist?

The libertarian Cato Institute says no: "Denmark has quite a free-market economy, apart from its welfare state transfers and high government consumption." That's some qualification.

It's true that Denmark doesn't at all fit the classic definition of socialism, which involves government ownership of the means of production. It is, instead, social-democratic: a market economy where the downsides of capitalism are mitigated by government action, including a very strong social safety net.

But U.S. conservatives—like Fox's Regan—continually and systematically blur the distinction between social democracy and socialism. In 2008, John McCain accused Barack Obama of wanting socialism, basically because Obama called for an expansion of health coverage. In 2012, Mitt Romney declared that Obama got his ideas from "socialist democrats in Europe."

In other words, in American political discourse, anyone who wants to make life in a market economy less nasty, brutish, and short gets denounced as a socialist.

And this smear campaign has had a predictable effect: sooner or later, if you call any attempt to improve American lives "socialism," a lot of people will conclude that socialism is O.K.

A recent Gallup poll found that majorities both of young voters and of self-identified Democrats prefer socialism to capitalism. But this doesn't mean that tens of millions of Americans want the government to seize the economy's commanding heights. It just means that many people, told that wanting America to be a bit more like Denmark is socialist, end up believing that socialism isn't so bad, after all.

The same may be said for some Democratic politicians. Much has been made of Alexandria Ocasio-Cortez, not just because of her upset primary victory, but because she's a self-proclaimed socialist. Her platform, however, isn't socialist at all by the traditional definition. It's just unabashedly social-democratic.

And that puts her in line with the rest of her party. Whenever I read articles questioning what Democrats stand for, I wonder if the writers are paying any attention to what candidates are saying about policy. For today's Democratic Party is actually impressively unified around social-democratic goals, far more so than in the past.

True, there are differences over both policy and rhetorical strategy. Should the push for universal health coverage involve Medicare for All, or simply the right for everyone to buy into an enhanced Medicare program? Should Democrats simply ignore Republican slander of their social-democratic ideas, or should they try to turn the "socialist" smear into a badge of honor?

But these aren't very deep divisions, certainly nothing like the divisions between liberals and centrists that wracked the party a couple of decades ago.

The simple fact is that there is far more misery in America than there needs to be. Every other advanced country has universal health care and a much stronger social safety net than we do. And it doesn't have to be that way.

TRUMP VERSUS THE SOCIALIST MENACE

February 7, 2019

In 1961, America faced what conservatives considered a mortal threat: calls for a national health insurance program covering senior citizens. In an attempt to avert this awful fate, the American Medical Association launched what it called Operation Coffee Cup, a pioneering attempt at viral marketing.

Here's how it worked: Doctors' wives (hey, it was 1961) were asked to invite their friends over and play them a recording in which Ronald Reagan explained that socialized medicine would destroy American freedom. The housewives, in turn, were supposed to write letters to Congress denouncing the menace of Medicare.

Obviously the strategy didn't work; Medicare not only came into existence, but it became so popular that these days Republicans routinely (and falsely) accuse *Democrats* of planning to cut the program's funding. But the strategy—claiming that any attempt to strengthen the social safety net or limit inequality will put us on a slippery slope to totalitarianism—endures.

And so it was that Donald Trump, in his State of the Union address, briefly turned from his usual warnings about scary brown people to warnings about the threat from socialism.

What do Trump's people, or conservatives in general, mean by "socialism"? The answer is, it depends.

Sometimes it means any kind of economic liberalism. Thus after the SOTU, Steven Mnuchin, the Treasury secretary, lauded the Trump economy and declared that "we're not going back to socialism"—i.e., apparently America itself was a socialist hellhole as recently as 2016. Who knew?

Other times, however, it means Soviet-style central planning, or Venezuela-style nationalization of industry, never mind the reality that there is essentially nobody in American political life who advocates such things.

The trick—and "trick" is the right word—involves shuttling between these utterly different meanings, and hoping that people don't notice. You say you want free college tuition? Think of all the people who died in the Ukraine famine! And no, this isn't a caricature: read the strange, smarmy report on socialism that Trump's economists released last fall; that's pretty much how its argument goes.

So let's talk about what's really on the table.

Some progressive U.S. politicians now describe themselves as socialists, and a significant number of voters, including a majority of voters under thirty, say they approve of socialism. But neither the politicians nor the voters are clamoring for government seizure of the means of production. Instead, they've taken on board conservative rhetoric that describes anything that tempers the excesses of a market economy as socialism, and in effect said, "Well, in that case I'm a socialist."

What Americans who support "socialism" actually want is what the rest of the world calls social democracy: a market economy, but with extreme hardship limited by a strong social safety net and extreme inequality limited by progressive taxation. They want us to look like Denmark or Norway, not Venezuela.

And in case you haven't been there, the Nordic countries are not, in fact, hellholes. They have somewhat lower G.D.P. per capita than we do, but that's largely because they take more vacations. Compared with America, they have higher life expectancy, much less poverty, and significantly higher overall life satisfaction. Oh, and they have high levels of entrepreneurship—because people are more willing to take the risk of starting a business when they know that they won't lose their health care or plunge into abject poverty if they fail.

Trump's economists clearly had a hard time fitting the reality of Nordic societies into their anti-socialist manifesto. In some places they say that the Nordics aren't really socialist; in others they try desperately to show that despite appearances, Danes and Swedes are suffering—for example, it's expensive for them to operate a pickup truck. I am not making this up.

What about the slippery slope from liberalism to totalitarianism? There's absolutely no evidence that it exists. Medicare didn't destroy freedom. Stalinist Russia and Maoist China didn't evolve out of social democracies. Venezuela was a corrupt petrostate long before Hugo Chávez came along. If there's a road to serfdom, I can't think of any nation that took it.

So scare-mongering over socialism is both silly and dishonest. But will it be politically effective?

Probably not. After all, voters overwhelmingly support most of the policies proposed by American "socialists," including higher taxes on the wealthy and making Medicare available to everyone (although they don't support plans that would force people to give up private insurance—a warning to Democrats not to make single-payer purity a litmus test).

On the other hand, we should never discount the power of dishonesty. Right-wing media will portray whomever the Democrats nominate for president as the second coming of Leon Trotsky, and millions of people will believe them. Let's just hope that the rest of the media report the clean little secret of American socialism, which is that it isn't radical at all.

15

Climate

THE MOST IMPORTANT THING

TO BE HONEST, SOMETIMES I WONDER WHETHER I'M WASTING MY TIME talking about any issue other than climate change. I mean, civilization faces an existential threat; if we don't take action to limit emissions of greenhouse gases, in the long run nothing else—not health reform, not income inequality, not even financial crisis—will matter.

There are, of course, some pretty good reasons not to write every column about the menace of climate change. Life and policymaking must go on, in at least the hope that we'll do enough to avert the climate threat before it's too late. There's also the point that the impact of writing depends on how much you can add as well as the importance of the issue you address. As Raymond Chandler put it in his essay *The Simple Art of Murder*, "some very dull books have been written about God, and some very fine ones about how to make a living and stay fairly honest."

Also, like it or not, while climate is a growing political issue, winning support for action will require bundling climate policy with other things people care about. More about that in a minute.

So I don't write about climate all the time, or even remotely in proportion to its importance in the larger scheme of things. But this then raises the question, what does an economist have to contribute on this issue? I think there are three answers.

First, while I am not a climate scientist, the political debates over climate change bear a strong resemblance to political debates over economic policy. Like the economy, global climate is a complex system; like economic policy, climate policy is an area where some people are sincerely trying to understand how the world works, but others have a vested interest in promoting their views whether or not they're supported by the evidence.

So I know from decades of experience what both serious research and politically motivated fake scholarship look like. When I look at the work of a researcher like Michael Mann, originator of the famous "hockey stick" graph on global temperatures, on one side, and the furious attempts on the part of climate deniers to demonize and discredit him, on the other, it's not hard at all to see which side is which.

Second, one of the arguments against doing anything on climate change is the claim that any serious attempt to limit greenhouse gas emissions would inflict huge damage on the economy. So there's a straight economics dimension to the debate too.

Finally, I like to think that years spent watching the politics of economic policy have given me some insights into the politics of policy in general. In particular, the path of health care reform seems to me to have been an object lesson in the principle that the perfect is the enemy of the good. There are valid arguments for the superiority of a single-payer, Medicare for All–type health system over hybrid public-private alternatives like Obamacare. But in 2009, when there was the first real chance at health reform in fifteen years, it was clear that the country wasn't ready for single-payer (and probably still isn't). So we went for something second-best—and 20 million people got coverage.

What does this have to do with climate change? Every Economics 101 student is taught that the efficient way to deal with pollution is to put a price on it, say with a carbon tax. And some of my colleagues seem fixated on a purist approach: we should have a carbon tax and only a carbon tax. Meanwhile, some progressives have been calling for a so-called Green New Deal, which would mix climate policy with other objectives, and would rely heavily on other policies besides a carbon tax. In the last article here I argue that a Christmas tree approach to climate policy—lots of things for various interested parties—would in fact be O.K.

DONALD AND THE DEADLY DENIERS

October 15, 2018

C limate change is a hoax.

Climate change is happening, but it's not man-made.

Climate change is man-made, but doing anything about it would destroy jobs and kill economic growth.

These are the stages of climate denial. Or maybe it's wrong to call them stages, since the deniers never really give up an argument, no matter how thoroughly it has been refuted by evidence. They're better described as cockroach ideas—false claims you may think you've gotten rid of, but keep coming back.

Anyway, the Trump administration and its allies—put on the defensive by yet another deadly climate change–enhanced hurricane and an ominous United Nations report—have been making all of these bad arguments over the past few days. I'd say it was a shocking spectacle, except that it's hard to get shocked these days. But it was a reminder that we're now ruled by people who are willing to endanger civilization for the sake of political expediency, not to mention increased profits for their fossil-fuel friends.

About those cockroaches: details aside, the very multiplicity of climate-denial arguments—the deniers' story keeps changing, but the bottom line that we should do nothing remains the same—is a sign that the opponents of climate action are arguing in bad faith. They aren't seriously trying to engage with the reality of climate change or the economics of reduced emissions; their goal is to keep polluters free to pollute as long as possible, and they'll grab onto anything serving that goal.

Still, it's worth pointing out how thoroughly all their arguments have collapsed in recent years.

These days, climate deniers seem to have temporarily backed down a bit on claims that nothing is happening. The old dodge of comparing temperatures to an unusually warm year in 1998 to deny that the planet is getting warmer—which is like comparing days in early July with a warm day in May, and denying that there's such a thing as summer—has been undermined by a string of new temperature records. And massive tropical storms fed by a warming ocean have made the consequences of climate change increasingly visible to the public.

So the new strategy is to downplay what has happened. Climate-change models "have not been very successful," declared Larry Kudlow, the top White House economic adviser. Actually, they have: global warming to date is well in line with past projections. "Something's changing and it'll change back again," asserted Donald Trump on *60 Minutes*, based upon, well, nothing.

Having grudgingly conceded that maybe the planet is indeed getting a bit warmer, the climate deniers claim to be unconvinced that greenhouse gases are responsible. "I don't know that it's man-made," said Trump. And while he has sort-of-kind-of backed down on his earlier claims that climate change is a hoax concocted by the Chinese, he's still seeing vast conspiracies on the part of climate scientists, who he says "have a very big political agenda."

Think about that. Decades ago experts predicted, based on fundamental science, that emissions would raise global temperatures. People like Trump scoffed. Now the experts' prediction has come true. And the deniers insist that emissions aren't the culprit, that something else must be driving the change, and it's all a conspiracy. Come on.

Why, it's as if Trump were to suggest that the Saudis had nothing to do with the disappearance of Jamal Khashoggi, who vanished after entering a Saudi embassy—that he was killed by some mysterious third party. Oh, wait.

Finally, about the cost of climate policy: I've noted in the past how strange it is that conservatives have total faith in the power and flexibility of market economies, but claim that these economies will be completely destroyed if the government creates incentives to reduce greenhouse gas emissions.

Apocalyptic claims about the cost of reducing emissions are especially strange given tremendous technological progress in renewable energy: The costs of wind and solar power have plummeted. Meanwhile, coal-fired power plants have become so uncompetitive that the Trump administration wants to subsidize them at the expense of cleaner energy.

In short, while the arguments of climate deniers were always weak, they've gotten much weaker. Even if you were genuinely persuaded by the deniers five or ten years ago, subsequent developments should have made you reconsider.

In reality, of course, climate denial has never had much to do with either logic or evidence; as I said, deniers are clearly arguing in bad faith. They don't really believe what they're saying. They're just looking for excuses that will let people like the Koch brothers keep making money. Besides, liberals want to limit emissions, and modern conservatism is largely about owning the libs.

One way to think about what's happening here is that it's the ultimate example of Trumpian corruption. We have good reason to believe that Trump and his associates are selling out America for the sake of personal gain. When it comes to climate, however, they aren't just selling out America; they're selling out the whole world.

THE DEPRAVITY OF CLIMATE-CHANGE DENIAL

November 26, 2018

The Trump administration is, it goes without saying, deeply anti-science. In fact, it's anti-objective reality. But its control of the government remains limited; it didn't extend far enough to prevent the release of the latest National Climate Assessment, which details current and expected future impacts of global warming on the United States.

True, the report was released on Black Friday, clearly in the hope that it would get lost in the shuffle. The good news is that the ploy didn't work.

The assessment basically confirms, with a great deal of additional detail, what anyone following climate science already knew: climate change poses a major threat to the nation, and some of its adverse effects are already being felt. For example, the report, written before the latest California disaster, highlights the growing risks of wildfire in the Southwest; global warming, not failure to rake the leaves, is why the fires are getting ever bigger and more dangerous.

But the Trump administration and its allies in Congress will, of course, ignore this analysis. Denying climate change, no matter what the evidence, has become a core Republican principle. And it's worth trying to understand both how that happened and the sheer depravity involved in being a denialist at this point.

Wait, isn't depravity too strong a term? Aren't people allowed to disagree with conventional wisdom, even if that wisdom is supported by overwhelming scientific consensus?

Yes, they are—as long as their arguments are made in good faith. But there are almost no good-faith climate-change deniers. And denying science for profit, political advantage, or ego satisfaction is not O.K.; when failure to act on the science may have terrible consequences, denial is, as I said, depraved.

The best recent book I've read on all this is *The Madhouse Effect* by Michael E. Mann, a leading climate scientist, with cartoons by Tom Toles. As Mann explains, climate denial actually follows in the footsteps of earlier science denial, beginning with the long campaign by tobacco companies to confuse the public about the dangers of smoking.

The shocking truth is that by the 1950s, these companies already knew that smoking caused lung cancer; but they spent large sums propping up the appearance that there was a real controversy about this link. In other words, they were aware that their product was killing people, but they tried to keep the public from understanding this fact so they could keep earning profits. That qualifies as depravity, doesn't it?

In many ways, climate denialism resembles cancer denialism. Businesses with a financial interest in confusing the public—in this case, fossil-fuel companies—are prime movers. As far as I can tell, every one of the handful of well-known scientists who have expressed climate skepticism has received large sums of money from these companies or from dark money conduits like Donors Trust—the same conduit, as it happens, that supported Matthew Whitaker, the new acting attorney general, before he joined the Trump administration.

But climate denial has sunk deeper political roots than cancer denial ever did. In practice, you can't be a modern Republican in good standing unless you deny the reality of global warming, assert that it has natural causes, or insist that nothing can be done about it without destroying the economy. You also have to either accept or acquiesce in wild claims that the overwhelming evidence for climate change is a hoax, that it has been fabricated by a vast global conspiracy of scientists.

Why would anyone go along with such things? Money is still the main answer: almost all prominent climate deniers are on the fossil-fuel take. However, ideology is also a factor: If you take environmental issues seriously, you are led to the need for government regulation of some kind, so rigid free-market ideologues don't want to believe that environmental concerns are real (although apparently forcing consumers to subsidize coal is fine).

Finally, I have the impression that there's an element of tough-guy posturing involved—real men don't use renewable energy, or something.

And these motives matter. If important players opposed climate action out of good-faith disagreement with the science, that would be a shame but not a sin, calling for better efforts at persuasion. As it is, however, climate denial is rooted in greed, opportunism, and ego. And opposing action for those reasons *is* a sin.

Indeed, it's depravity, on a scale that makes cancer denial seem trivial. Smoking kills people, and tobacco companies that tried to confuse the public about that reality were being evil. But climate change isn't just killing people; it may well kill civilization. Trying to confuse the public about that is evil on a whole different level. Don't some of these people have children?

And let's be clear: while Donald Trump is a prime example of the depravity of climate denial, this is an issue on which his whole party went over to the dark side years ago. Republicans don't just have bad ideas; at this point, they are, necessarily, bad people.

CLIMATE DENIAL WAS THE CRUCIBLE FOR TRUMPISM

December 3, 2018

Many observers seem baffled by Republican fealty to Donald Trump—the party's willingness to back him on all fronts, even after severe defeats in the midterm elections. What kind of party would show such support for a leader who is not only evidently corrupt and seemingly in the pocket of foreign dictators, but also routinely denies facts and tries to criminalize anyone who points them out?

The answer is, the kind of the party that, long before Trump came on the scene, committed itself to denying the facts on climate change and criminalizing the scientists reporting those facts.

The G.O.P. wasn't always an anti-environment, anti-science party. George H. W. Bush introduced the cap-and-trade program that largely controlled the problem of acid rain. As late as 2008, John McCain called for a similar program to limit emissions of the greenhouse gases that cause global warming.

But McCain's party was already well along in the process of becoming what it is today—a party that is not only completely dominated by climate deniers, but is hostile to science in general, that demonizes and tries to destroy scientists who challenge its dogma.

Trump fits right in with this mind-set. In fact, when you review the history of Republican climate denial, it looks a lot like Trumpism. Climate denial, you might say, was the crucible in which the essential elements of Trumpism were formed.

Take Trump's dismissal of all negative information about his actions and their consequences as either fake news invented by hostile media or the products of a sinister "deep state." That kind of conspiracy theorizing has long been standard practice among climate deniers, who began calling the evidence for global warming—evidence that has convinced 97 percent of climate scientists—a "gigantic hoax."

What was the evidence for this vast conspiracy? A lot of it rested on, you guessed it, hacked emails. The credulousness of all too many journalists about the supposed misconduct revealed by "Climategate," a pseudo-scandal that relied on selective, out-of-context quotes from emails at a British university, prefigured the disastrous media handling of hacked Democratic emails in 2016. (All we learned from those emails was that scientists are people—occasionally snappish, and given to talking in professional shorthand that hostile outsiders can willfully misinterpret.)

Oh, and what is supposed to be motivating the thousands of scientists perpetrating this hoax? We've become accustomed to the spectacle of Donald Trump, the most corrupt president in history, leading the most corrupt administration of modern times, routinely calling his opponents and critics "crooked." Much the same thing happens in climate debate.

The truth is that most prominent climate deniers are basically paid to take that position, receiving large amounts of money from fossil-fuel companies. But after the release of the recent National Climate Assessment detailing the damage we can expect from global warming, a parade of Republicans went on TV to declare that scientists were only saying these things "for the money." Projection much?

Finally, Trump has brought a new level of menace to American politics, inciting his followers to violence against critics and trying to order the Justice Department to prosecute Hillary Clinton and James Comey.

But climate scientists have faced harassment and threats, up to and including death threats, for years. And they've also faced efforts by politicians to, in effect, criminalize their work. Most famously, Michael E. Mann, creator of the "hockey stick" graph, was for years the target of an anti-climate science jihad by Ken Cuccinelli, at the time Virginia's attorney general.

And on it goes. Recently a judge in Arizona, responding to a suit from a group linked to the Koch brothers (and obviously not understanding how research works), ordered the release of all emails from climate scientists at the University of Arizona. To forestall the inevitable selective misrepresentation, Mann has released all the emails he exchanged with his Arizona colleagues, with explanatory context.

There are three important morals to this story.

First, if we fail to meet the challenge of climate change, with catastrophic results—which seems all too likely—it won't be the result of an innocent failure to understand what was at stake. It will, instead, be a disaster brought on by corruption, willful ignorance, conspiracy theorizing, and intimidation.

Second, that corruption isn't a problem of "politicians" or the "political system." It's specifically a problem of the Republican Party, which has burrowed ever deeper into climate denial even as the damage from a warming planet becomes more and more obvious.

Third, we can now see climate denial as part of a broader moral rot. Donald Trump isn't an aberration, he's the culmination of where his party has been going for years. You could say that Trumpism is just the application of the depravity of climate denial to every aspect of politics. And there's no end to the depravity in sight.

HOPE FOR A GREEN NEW YEAR

December 31, 2018

Let's be honest with ourselves: the new Democratic majority in the House won't be able to enact new legislation. I'll be astonished if there are bipartisan deals on anything important—even on infrastructure, where both sides claim to want action but what the G.O.P. really wants is an excuse to privatize public assets.

So the immediate consequences of the power shift in Washington won't involve actual policymaking; they'll come mainly from Democrats' new, subpoena-power-armed ability to investigate the fetid swamp of Trumpian corruption.

But that doesn't mean that Democrats should ignore policy issues. On the contrary, the party should spend the next two years figuring out what, exactly, it will try to do if it gains policymaking power in 2021. Which brings me to the big policy slogan of the moment: the so-called Green New Deal. Is this actually a good idea?

Yes, it is. But it's important to go beyond the appealing slogan, and hash out many of the details. You don't want to be like the Republicans, who spent years talking big about repealing Obamacare, but never worked out a realistic alternative.

So what does the Green New Deal mean? It's not entirely clear, which is what makes it a good slogan: it could mean a number of good things. But the main thrust, as I understand it, is that we should make a big move to tackle climate change, and that this move should accentuate the positive, not the negative. In particular, it should emphasize investments and subsidies, not carbon taxes.

But wait, *shouldn't* we be considering a carbon tax? In principle, yes. As any card-carrying economist can tell you, there are big advantages to discouraging pollution by putting a price on emissions, which you can do either by imposing a tax or by creating a cap-and-trade system in which people buy and sell emission permits.

It's Economics 101: a pollution tax or equivalent creates broad-based incentives in a way less comprehensive policies can't. Why? Because it encourages people to reduce their carbon footprint in all possible ways, from using renewable energy, to conservation, to shifting consumption away from energy-intensive products.

A carbon tax is, however, a tax—which will upset the people who have to pay it. Yes, the revenue from a carbon tax could be used to cut other taxes, but convincing enough people that they will be better off overall would be a very hard sell. And claims that a carbon tax high enough to make a meaningful difference would attract significant bipartisan support are a fantasy at best, a fossil-fuel-industry ploy to avoid major action at worst.

The point is that going for a less-than-ideal but salable policy, at least initially, is better than letting the best be the enemy of the good. That was the lesson of health care reform: single payer had no chance of being enacted under President Barack Obama, but a somewhat awkward public-private hybrid system that preserved employer-based insurance was (just) doable— and 20 million Americans gained coverage.

Now that the principle of universal coverage is out there, a gradual transition to some version of Medicare for All is starting to look politically possible; but it was important to start with policies that achieved big progress without greatly disrupting people's lives.

Can we similarly make big progress on climate change without disrupting Americans' lives too much? My read of the data says yes.

The majority of U.S. greenhouse-gas emissions come from electricity generation and transportation. We could cut generation-related emissions by two-thirds or more simply by ending the use of coal and making more use of renewables (whose prices have fallen drastically), without requiring that Americans consume less power. We could almost surely reduce transportation emissions by a comparable amount by raising mileage and increasing the use of electric vehicles, even if we didn't reduce the number of miles we drive each year.

These are gains that could be achieved with a combination of positive incentives like tax credits and not-too-onerous regulation. Add in investments in technology and infrastructure that supports alternative energy, and a Green New Deal that dramatically reduces emissions seems entirely practical, even without carbon taxes. And these policies would visibly create jobs in renewable energy, which already employs a lot more people than coal mining.

Of course, some people would be hurt. The 53,000 Americans still employed in coal mining would eventually have to find other employment (and aid for workers in transition industries should be a part of the Green New Deal). Profits of fossil-fuel companies would also go down, although these companies now give almost all their money to the G.O.P., so it's not clear why Democrats should care.

Overall, however, Democrats can surely do for climate change what they did for health care: devise policies that hugely improve the situation while producing far more winners than losers. They can't enact a Green New Deal right away—but they should start preparing now, and be ready to move in two years.

16

Trump

WHY NOT THE WORST?

I WAS AS SHOCKED AS ANYONE BY DONALD TRUMP'S ELECTION, ALTHOUGH the sneering media treatment of Hillary Clinton had me worried—but that's a tale for the next section of this book, on the problems of the media. But I wasn't shocked by the fact that the G.O.P. would nominate him, nor was I surprised either that his behavior in office has been every bit as bad as pessimists warned it would be, or that Republicans in Congress—who have always had the power to rein him in—have effectively collaborated in his miasma of corruption and cruelty.

For the fact is that something like Trumpism was coming. Trump's victory required that a lot of things go wrong—mainly the toxic combination of misbehavior by James Comey and the pettiness of the media, which sniped at Clinton in the belief that she couldn't lose. But America's right wing has been moving toward Trump-style governance for a long time.

Think about it. How could white nationalism not be on the rise, when movement conservatism has depended on white resentment to win elections despite following policies that benefit a wealthy elite at the expense of most Americans? How could the paranoid mind-set of Trump followers not emerge from a political movement that sees everything that doesn't confirm its preconceptions—from the reality of climate change to low inflation—as the product of vast conspiracies? And although people tend to forget it, the corruption and cronyism of the Trump administration were prefigured in the Bush years. In many ways, what Trump has done to America since 2016 is similar to what the Bush team did to Iraq in the disastrous first year of occupation.

And an international perspective also helps. I had been following the rise of the white nationalist right in Europe, and the de facto collapse of democracy in Hungary and Poland. I was all too aware that it could, in fact, happen here.

Anyway, the columns in this section are mainly about U.S. politics from 2016 to 2018. They're mostly about the terrible things that have happened and why they have happened, but they're not all negative. Of all the pieces here, my sense is that my column on the unsung greatness of Nancy Pelosi struck the deepest nerve. Her achievements were there for all to see; even if you didn't like her policy direction, her spectacular effectiveness should have been obvious. Yet nobody was saying it at the time. Of course, more people were saying it after the 2018 midterms, when Democrats gained forty House seats.

THE PARANOID STYLE IN G.O.P. POLITICS

October 8, 2018

Many people are worried, rightly, about what the appointment of Brett Kavanaugh means for America in the long term. He's a naked partisan who clearly lied under oath about many aspects of his personal history; that's as important as, and related to, the question of what he did to Christine Blasey Ford, a question that remains unresolved because the supposed investigation was such a transparent sham. Putting such a man on the Supreme Court has, at a stroke, destroyed the court's moral authority for the foreseeable future.

But such long-term worries should be a secondary concern right now. The more immediate threat comes from what we saw on the Republican side during and after the hearing: not just contempt for the truth, but also a rush to demonize any and all criticism. In particular, the readiness with which senior Republicans embraced crazy conspiracy theories about the opposition to Kavanaugh is a deeply scary warning about what might happen to America, not in the long run, but just a few weeks from now.

About that conspiracy theorizing: it began in the first moments of Kavanaugh's testimony, when he attributed his problems to "a calculated and orchestrated political hit" motivated by people seeking "revenge on behalf of the Clintons." This was a completely false, hysterical accusation, and making it should in itself have disqualified Kavanaugh for the court.

But Donald Trump quickly made it much worse, attributing protests against Kavanaugh to George Soros and declaring, falsely (and with no evidence), that the protesters were being paid.

And here's the thing: major figures in the G.O.P. quickly backed Trump up. Charles Grassley, chairman of the Senate committee that heard Blasey and Kavanaugh, insisted that the protesters were indeed employed by Soros. Senator John Cornyn declared, "We will not be bullied by the screams of paid protesters." No, the protesters aren't being paid to protest, let alone by George Soros. But to be a good Republican, you now have to pretend they are.

What's going on here? At one level, this isn't new. Conspiracy theorizing has been a part of American politics from the beginning. Richard Hofstadter published his famous essay "The Paranoid Style in American Politics" back in 1964 and cited examples running back to the 18th century. Segregationists fighting civil rights routinely blamed "outside agitators"—especially northern Jews—for African-American protests.

But the significance of conspiracy theorizing depends on who does it.

When people on the political fringe blame shadowy forces—often, as it happens, sinister Jewish financiers—for their frustrations, you can write it off as delusional. When people who hold most of the levers of power do the same thing, their fantasizing isn't a delusion, it's a tool: a way to delegitimize opposition, to create excuses not just for disregarding but for punishing anyone who dares to criticize their actions.

That's why conspiracy theories have been central to the ideology of so many authoritarian regimes, from Mussolini's Italy to Erdogan's Turkey. It's why the governments of Hungary and Poland, former democracies that have become de facto one-party states, love to accuse outsiders in general and Soros in particular of stirring up opposition to their rule. Because, of course, there can't be legitimate complaints about their actions and policies.

And now senior figures in the Republican Party, which controls all three branches of the federal government—if you had any questions about whether the Supreme Court was a partisan institution, they should be gone now—are sounding just like the white nationalists in Hungary and Poland. What does this mean?

The answer, I submit, is that the G.O.P. is an authoritarian regime in waiting.

Trump himself clearly has the same instincts as the foreign dictators he so openly admires. He demands that public officials be loyal to him personally, not to the American people. He threatens political opponents with retribution—two years after the last election, he's still leading chants of "Lock her up." He attacks the news media as enemies of the people.

Add in the investigations closing in on Trump's many scandals, from tax cheating to self-dealing in office to possible collusion with Russia, all of which give him every incentive to shut down freedom of the press and independence of law enforcement. Does anyone doubt that Trump would like to go full authoritarian, given the chance?

And who's going to stop him? The senators parroting conspiracy theories about Soros-paid protesters? The newly rigged Supreme Court? What we've learned in the past few weeks is that there is no gap between Trump and his party, nobody who will say stop in the name of American values.

But as I said, the G.O.P. is an authoritarian regime in waiting, not yet one in practice. What's it waiting for?

Well, think of what Trump and his party might do if they retain both houses of Congress in the coming election. If you aren't terrified of where we might be in the very near future, you aren't paying attention.

TRUMP AND THE ARISTOCRACY OF FRAUD

October 4, 2018

I t turns out that I may have done Donald Trump an injustice.

You see, I've always been skeptical of his claims to be a great deal-maker. But what we've just learned is that his negotiating prowess began early. Indeed, it was so amazing that he was already making $200,000 a year in today's dollars at a very young age.

Specifically, that's what he was making when he was 3 years old. He was a millionaire by the age of 8. Of course, the money came from his father—who spent decades evading the taxes he was legally required to pay on money given to his children.

The blockbuster *New York Times* report on the Trump family's history of fraud is really about two distinct although linked kinds of fraudulence.

On one side, the family engaged in tax fraud on a huge scale, using a variety of money-laundering techniques to avoid paying what it owed. On the other, the story Donald Trump tells about his life—his depiction of himself as a self-made businessman who made billions starting from humble roots—has always been a lie: Not only did he inherit his wealth, receiving the equivalent of more than $400 million from his father, but Fred Trump bailed his son out after deals went bad.

One implication of these revelations is that Trump supporters who imagine that they've found a straight-talking champion who will drain the swamp while using his business acumen to make America great again have been suckered, bigly.

But the tale of the Trump money is part of a bigger story. Even among those unhappy at the extent to which we live in an era of soaring inequality and growing concentration of wealth at the top, there has been a tendency to believe that great wealth is, more often than not, earned more or less honestly. It's only now that the amounts of sheer corruption and lawbreaking that underlie our march toward oligarchy have started to come into focus.

Until recently, my guess is that most economists, even tax experts, would have agreed that tax *avoidance* by corporations and the wealthy—which is legal—was a big issue, but tax *evasion*—hiding money from the tax man—was a lesser one. It was obvious that some rich people were exploiting legal if morally dubious loopholes in the tax code, but the prevailing view was that simply defrauding the tax authorities and hence the public wasn't that widespread in advanced countries.

But this view always rested on shaky foundations. After all, tax evasion, almost by definition, doesn't show up in official statistics, and the super-wealthy aren't in the habit of mouthing off about what great tax cheats they are. To get a real picture of how much fraud is going on, you either have to do what the *Times* did—exhaustively investigate the finances of a particular family—or rely on lucky breaks that reveal what was previously hidden.

Two years ago, a huge lucky break came in the form of the Panama Papers, a trove of data leaked from a Panamanian law firm that specialized in helping people hide their wealth in offshore havens, and a smaller leak from HSBC. While the unsavory details revealed by these leaks made headlines right away, their true significance has only become clear with work done by Berkeley's Gabriel Zucman and associates in cooperation with Scandinavian tax authorities.

Matching information from the Panama Papers and other leaks with national tax data, these researchers found that outright tax evasion actually is a big deal at the top. The truly wealthy end up paying a much lower effective tax rate than the merely rich, not because of loopholes in tax law, but because they break the law. The wealthiest taxpayers, the researchers found, pay on average 25 percent less than they owe—and, of course, many individuals pay even less.

This is a big number. If America's wealthy evade taxes on the same scale (which they almost surely do), they're probably costing the government around as much as the food stamp program does. And they're also using tax evasion to entrench their privilege and pass it on to their heirs, which is the real Trump story.

The obvious question is, what are our elected representatives doing about this epidemic of cheating? Well, Republicans in Congress have been on the case for years: they've been systematically defunding the Internal Revenue Service, crippling its ability to investigate tax fraud. We don't just have government by tax cheats; we have government of tax cheats, for tax cheats.

What we're learning, then, is that the story of what's happening to our society is even worse than we thought. It's not just that the president of the United States is, as veteran tax reporter David Cay Johnston put it, a "financial vampire," cheating taxpayers the way he has cheated just about everyone else who deals with him.

Beyond that, our trend toward oligarchy—rule by the few—is also looking more and more like kakistocracy—rule by the worst, or at least the most unscrupulous. The corruption isn't subtle; on the contrary, it's cruder than almost anyone imagined. It also runs deep, and it has infected our politics, quite literally up to its highest levels.

STOP CALLING TRUMP A POPULIST

August 2, 2018

Message to those in the news media who keep calling Donald Trump a "populist": I do not think that word means what you think it means.

It's true that Trump still, on occasion, poses as someone who champions the interests of ordinary working Americans against those of the elite. And I guess there's a sense in which his embrace of white nationalism gives voice to ordinary Americans who share his racism but have felt unable to air their prejudice in public.

But he's been in office for a year and a half, time enough to be judged on what he does, not what he says. And his administration has been relentlessly anti-worker on every front. Trump is about as populist as he is godly—that is, not at all.

Start with tax policy, where Trump's major legislative achievement is a tax cut that mainly benefits corporations—whose tax payments have fallen off a cliff—and has done nothing at all to raise wages. The tax plan does so little for ordinary Americans that Republicans have stopped campaigning on it. Yet the administration is floating the (probably illegal) idea of using executive action to cut taxes on the rich by an extra $100 billion.

There's also health policy, where Trump, having failed to repeal Obamacare—which would have been a huge blow to working families—has engaged instead in a campaign of sabotage that has probably raised premiums by almost 20 percent relative to what they would have been otherwise. Inevitably, the burden of these higher premiums falls most heavily on families earning just a bit too much to be eligible for subsidies, that is, the upper part of the working class.

And then there's labor policy, where the Trump administration has moved on multiple fronts to do away with regulations that had protected workers from exploitation, injury, and more.

But immediate policy doesn't tell the whole story. You also want to look at Trump's appointments. When it comes to policies that affect workers, Trump has created a team of cronies: almost every important position has gone to a lobbyist or someone with strong financial connections to industry. Labor interests have received no representation at all.

And the nomination of Brett Kavanaugh for the Supreme Court deserves special attention. There's a lot we don't know about Kavanaugh, partly because Senate Republicans are blocking Democratic requests for more information. But we do know he's starkly, extremely, anti-labor—way to the right of the mainstream, and well to the right even of most Republicans.

The best-known example of his radically anti-worker views is his argument that SeaWorld shouldn't face any liability after a captive killer whale killed one of its workers, because the victim should have known the risks when she took the job. But there's much more anti-labor extremism in his record.

When you bear in mind that Kavanaugh, if confirmed, will be around for a long time, this extremism is enough to justify rejecting his nomination—especially when added to his support for unrestricted presidential power and whatever it is in his record that Republicans are trying to hide.

But why would Trump, the self-proclaimed champion of American workers, choose someone like that? Why would he do all the things he's doing to hurt the very people who gave him the White House?

I don't know the answer, but I do think that the conventional explanation—that Trump, who is both lazy and supremely ignorant about policy details, was unwittingly captured by G.O.P. orthodoxy—both underestimates the president and makes him seem nicer than he is.

Watching Trump in action, it's hard to escape the impression that he knows very well that he's inflicting punishment on his own base. But he's a man who likes to humiliate others, in ways great and small. And my guess is that he actually takes pleasure in watching his supporters follow him even as he betrays them.

In fact, sometimes his contempt for his working-class base comes right out into the open. Remember "I love the poorly educated"? Remember his boast that he could shoot somebody on Fifth Avenue and not lose any voters?

Anyway, whatever his motivations, Trump in action is the opposite of populist. And no, his trade war doesn't change that judgment. William McKinley, the quintessential Gilded Age president who defeated a populist challenger, was also a protectionist. Furthermore, the Trumpian trade war is being carried out in a way that produces maximum harm to U.S. workers in return for minimum benefits.

While he isn't a populist, however, Trump is a pathological liar, the most dishonest man ever to hold high office in America. And his claim to stand with working Americans is one of his biggest lies.

Which brings me back to media use of the term "populist." When you describe Trump using that word, you are in effect complicit in his lie—especially when you do it in the context of supposedly objective reporting.

And you don't have to do this. You can describe what Trump is doing without using words that give him credit where it isn't due. He's scamming his supporters; you don't have to help him do it.

PARTISANSHIP, PARASITES, AND POLARIZATION

August 21, 2018

Parasites are a huge force in the natural world. For the most part they simply feed on their hosts. But there are a number of cases in which they exert a more insidious influence: they actually change their hosts' behavior, in ways that benefit the parasites but damage and perhaps eventually kill their victims.

And lately I've been wondering if that's what's happening to America. How much of our political sickness is the result of a parasitic infection? What I have in mind specifically is an infestation of direct-marketing scams that exploit and reinforce political partisanship, largely on the right, basically to sell merchandise.

If this sounds absurd to you, bear with me a bit. I'm not the first person to make this suggestion—Rick Perlstein, our leading historian of modern conservatism, made basically the same argument (without the biological analogy) back in 2012 and, as I'll explain, a lot of things have happened since then to reinforce his point.

What set me on this trail initially was learning that Ben Shapiro, the Young Conservative Intellectual du jour, is using his talk-show presence to market dietary supplements.

I'll come back to that. First, some notes on political economy.

When I try to understand political behavior, I, like many others, often find myself thinking about Mancur Olson's classic *The Logic of Collective Action*. Olson's simple yet profound insight was that political action on behalf of a group is, from the point of view of members of that group, a public good.

What do we mean by that? A public good is something that, if provided, benefits many people—but whoever provides it has no way to limit the bene-fits to himself or herself, and hence no way to cash in on the good's provision. The classic example is a lighthouse that steers everyone away from shoals, whether or not they've paid the fee; public health measures that limit dis-ease are in the same category. As a result, the fact that a public good is worth providing from society's point of view is no guarantee that it will actually be provided; it has to be worth some *individual's* while.

As Olson pointed out, the same goes for political action. Just because a political candidate's victory would be good for, say, farmers doesn't mean that farmers will give him or her money; each individual farmer will have an incentive to free ride on everyone else's contributions. So political action is normally undertaken by individuals or small, organized groups that stand to benefit directly. Either that, or it's a byproduct of other activities that are advantageous for their own reasons and can also be harnessed for political action, like memberships in trade associations or unions.

But don't rich people give money to support the interests of their class? Actually, a lot of the money we see in politics ends up being money spent in the givers' own, personal interests. For example, you can think of the Koch brothers' political spending as an investment in themselves: they have ben-efited immensely from the recent tax cut, with a payoff that far exceeds the amount they spent promoting it.

So a lot of political action is driven by people trying to shape policy in a way that benefits them personally. But what the Shapiro/brain pills story drives home to me is that there's another important factor in our current political scene: the use of political action as a marketing ploy, by people out to make a buck selling stuff that has little to do with politics per se.

As I said, Rick Perlstein has already written the basic text here. As he documents, right-wing Web sites largely act as marketing centers for stuff like this:

> Dear Reader, I'm going to tell you something, but you must prom-ise to keep it quiet. You have to understand that the "elite" would not be at all happy with me if they knew what I was about to tell you. That's why we have to tread carefully. You see, while most peo-ple are paying attention to the stock market, the banks, brokerages

and big institutions have their money somewhere else . . . [in] what
I call the hidden money mountain . . . All you have to know is the
insider's code (which I'll tell you) and you could make an extra
$6,000 every single month.

And some of the most influential voices on the right haven't just sold
advertising space to purveyors of snake oil, they've gotten directly into the
snake-oil business themselves.

Thus:

- Glenn Beck in his heyday juiced up his viewers by telling them
  that Obama was going to unleash hyperinflation any day now; he
  personally cashed in by hawking overpriced gold coins.
- Alex Jones makes a splash by claiming that school massacres are
  fake news, and the victims are really actors. But he makes his
  money by selling diet supplements.
- Ben Shapiro writes critiques of liberal academics that conservatives consider erudite (remember Ezra Klein's line about a stupid person's idea of what a thoughtful person sounds like?), but
  makes his money the same way Alex Jones does.

Why should marketing scams be linked to political extremism? It's all
about affinity fraud: once you establish a persona that appeals to angry, aging
white guys, you can sell them stuff that will supposedly protect their virility,
their waistline, and their wealth.

And at a grander level, isn't that what Fox News is really about? Consider it not as an ideological organization per se but as a business: it offers
cheap programming (because there isn't much reporting) that appeals to the
prejudices of angry old white guys who like to sit on the couch and rant at
their TV, and uses its viewership to help advertisers selling weight-loss plans.

Now, normally we think of individuals' views and interests as the forces
driving politics, including the ugly polarization increasingly dominating
the scene. The commercial exploitation of that polarization, if we mention
it at all, is treated as a sort of surface phenomenon that feeds off the fundamental dynamic.

But are we sure that's right? The Alex Joneses, Ben Shapiros, and Fox Newses of the world couldn't profit from extremism unless there were some underlying predisposition of angry old white guys to listen to this stuff. But maybe the commercial exploitation of political anger is what has concentrated and weaponized that anger. In other words, going back to where I started this essay, maybe the reason we're in a political nightmare is that our political behavior has, in effect, been parasitized by marketing algorithms.

I know I'm not the only one thinking along these lines. Charlie Stross argues that "paperclip maximizers"—not people, but social systems and algorithms that try to maximize profits, market share, or whatever—have increasingly been directing the direction of society, in ways that hurt humanity. He's mostly focused on corporate influence over policy, as opposed to mobilization of angry people in the service of direct-order scams, but both could be operating.

Anyway, I think it's really important to realize the extent to which peddling political snake oil, whether it's about the economy, race, the effects of immigration, or whatever, is to an important extent a way to peddle actual snake oil: magic pills that will let you lose weight without ever feeling hungry and restore your youthful manhood.

WHY IT CAN HAPPEN HERE

August 27, 2018

As I mentioned earlier, soon after the fall of the Berlin Wall, a friend of mine—an expert on international relations—made a joke: "Now that Eastern Europe is free from the alien ideology of Communism, it can return to its true historical path—fascism." Even at the time, his quip had a real edge.

And as of 2018 it hardly seems like a joke at all. What Freedom House calls illiberalism is on the rise across Eastern Europe. This includes Poland and Hungary, both still members of the European Union, in which democracy as we normally understand it is already dead.

In both countries the ruling parties—Law and Justice in Poland, Fidesz in Hungary—have established regimes that maintain the forms of popular elections, but have destroyed the independence of the judiciary, suppressed freedom of the press, institutionalized large-scale corruption, and effectively delegitimized dissent. The result seems likely to be one-party rule for the foreseeable future.

And it could all too easily happen here. There was a time, not long ago, when people used to say that our democratic norms, our proud history of freedom, would protect us from such a slide into tyranny. In fact, some people still say that. But believing such a thing today requires willful blindness. The fact is that the Republican Party is ready, even eager, to become an American version of Law and Justice or Fidesz, exploiting its current political power to lock in permanent rule.

Just look at what has been happening at the state level.

In North Carolina, after a Democrat won the governorship, Republicans used the incumbent's final days to pass legislation stripping the governor's office of much of its power.

In Georgia, Republicans tried to use transparently phony concerns about access for disabled voters to close most of the polling places in a mainly black district.

In West Virginia, Republican legislators exploited complaints about excessive spending to impeach the entire State Supreme Court and replace it with party loyalists.

And these are just the cases that have received national attention. There are surely scores if not hundreds of similar stories across the nation. What all of them reflect is the reality that the modern G.O.P. feels no allegiance to democratic ideals; it will do whatever it thinks it can get away with to entrench its power.

What about developments at the national level? That's where things get really scary. We're currently sitting on a knife edge. If we fall off it in the wrong direction—specifically, if Republicans retain control of both houses of Congress in November—we will become another Poland or Hungary faster than you can imagine.

This week Axios created a bit of a stir with a scoop about a spreadsheet circulating among Republicans in Congress, listing investigations they think Democrats are likely to carry out if they take the House. The thing about the list is that every item on it—starting with Donald Trump's tax returns—is something that obviously *should* be investigated, and would have been investigated under any other president. But the people circulating the document simply take it for granted that Republicans won't address any of these issues: party loyalty will prevail over constitutional responsibility.

Many Trump critics celebrated last week's legal developments, taking the Manafort conviction and the Cohen guilty plea as signs that the walls may finally be closing in on the lawbreaker in chief. But I felt a sense of deepened dread as I watched the Republican reaction: faced with undeniable evidence of Trump's thuggishness, his party closed ranks around him more tightly than ever.

A year ago it seemed possible that there might be limits to the party's complicity, that there would come a point where at least a few representatives or senators would say, no more. Now it's clear that there are no limits: They'll do whatever it takes to defend Trump and consolidate power.

This goes even for politicians who once seemed to have some principles. Senator Susan Collins of Maine was a voice of independence in the health care debate; now she sees no problem with having a president who's an unindicted co-conspirator appoint a Supreme Court justice who believes that presidents are immune from prosecution. Senator Lindsey Graham denounced Trump in 2016, and until recently seemed to be standing up against the idea of firing the attorney general to kill the Mueller investigation; now he's signaled that he's O.K. with such a firing.

But why is America, the birthplace of democracy, so close to following the lead of other countries that have recently destroyed it?

Don't tell me about "economic anxiety." That's not what happened in Poland, which grew steadily through the financial crisis and its aftermath. And it's not what happened here in 2016: study after study has found that racial resentment, not economic distress, drove Trump voters.

The point is that we're suffering from the same disease—white nationalism run wild—that has already effectively killed democracy in some other Western nations. And we're very, very close to the point of no return.

WHO'S AFRAID OF NANCY PELOSI?

August 13, 2018

Normally, a party that gives away $2 trillion without worrying about where the money will come from can buy itself at least a few votes. But Donald Trump's tax cut remains remarkably unpopular, and Republicans barely mention it on the campaign trail—in fact, Democrats are running against the tax cut more than Republicans are running on it.

Nor are Republicans talking much about Trump's trade war, which also remains unpopular.

What, then, does the G.O.P. have to run on? It can hype the supposed menace from illegal immigrants—but that hasn't been gaining much traction, either. Instead, Republicans' attack ads have increasingly focused on one of their usual boogeymen—or, rather, a boogeywoman: Nancy Pelosi, the former and possibly future speaker of the House.

So this seems like a good time to remind everyone that Pelosi is by far the greatest speaker of modern times and surely ranks among the most impressive people ever to hold that position. And it's interesting to ask why she gets so little credit with the news media, and hence with the general public, for her accomplishments.

What has Pelosi achieved?

First, as House minority leader, she played a crucial role in turning back George W. Bush's attempt to privatize Social Security.

Then she was the key figure, arguably even more crucial than President Barack Obama, in passing the Affordable Care Act, which produced a spectacular fall in the number of uninsured Americans and has proved surprisingly robust even in the face of Trumpian sabotage. She helped enact financial reform, which has turned out to be more vulnerable to being under-mined, but still helped stabilize the economy and protected many Americans from fraud.

Pelosi also helped pass the Obama stimulus plan, which economists overwhelmingly agree mitigated job losses from the financial crisis, as well as playing a role in laying the foundation for a green energy revolution.

It's quite a record. Oh, and whenever you hear Republicans claim that Pelosi is some kind of wild-eyed leftist, ask yourself, what's so radical about protecting retirement income, expanding health care, and reining in runaway bankers?

It's probably also worth noting that Pelosi has been untouched by allegations of personal scandal, which is amazing given the right's ability to manufacture such allegations out of thin air.

So how does Pelosi stack up against the four Republicans who have held the speaker's position since the G.O.P. took control of the House in 1994?

Newt Gingrich was a blowhard who shut down the government in a failed attempt to blackmail Bill Clinton into cutting Medicare, then led the impeachment of Clinton over an affair even as he himself was cheating on his wife.

Dennis Hastert, we now know, had a history of molesting teenage boys. Personal behavior aside, the "Hastert rule," under which Republicans could support only legislation approved by a majority of their own party, empowered extremists and made America less governable.

John Boehner didn't do much except oppose everything Obama proposed, including measures that were crucial to dealing with the aftermath of the financial crisis.

And Paul Ryan, the current but departing speaker, is a flimflam man: a fake deficit hawk whose one legislative achievement is a budget-busting tax cut, a fake policy wonk whose budget proposals were always obvious smoke and mirrors, pretending to address the budget deficit but actually just redistributing income from the poor to the rich. In the final act of his political career he has also shown himself to be a coward, utterly unwilling to stand up to Trump's malfeasance.

Looking at modern House speakers, then, Pelosi stands out as a giant among dwarfs. But you'd never know that from her media coverage.

While in office, Hastert was generally portrayed as a stolid embodi-
ment of middle-American values. Ryan was for years the recipient of fawning
media coverage, which lauded him as the ultimate serious, honest conservative long after his phoniness was obvious to anyone who paid attention. But
Pelosi is typically referred to as "divisive." Why?

I mean, it's true that she's a political partisan—but no more so than any
of the Republicans who preceded and followed her. Her policy stances are
far less at odds with public opinion than, say, Ryan's attempts to privatize
Medicare and slash its funding. So what makes her "divisive"? The fact that
Republicans keep attacking her? That would happen to any Democrat.

Or maybe it's just the fact that she's a woman—a woman who happens
to have been far better at her job than any man in recent memory.

Does all this mean that Pelosi should become speaker again if Democrats retake the House? Not necessarily: you can make an argument for a
new face despite her extraordinary record.

But her achievements really have been remarkable. It's a sad commentary on Republicans that they have nothing to run on except demonizing a
politician whose track record makes them look pathetic. And it's a sad commentary on the news media that so much reporting echoes these baseless
attacks.

TRUTH AND VIRTUE IN THE AGE OF TRUMP

November 12, 2018

Remember when freedom was just another word for nothing left to lose? These days it's just another word for giving lots of money to Donald Trump.

What with the midterm elections—and the baseless Republican cries of voting fraud—I don't know how many people heard about Trump's decision to award the Presidential Medal of Freedom to Miriam Adelson, wife of casino owner and Trump megadonor Sheldon Adelson. The medal is normally an acknowledgment of extraordinary achievement or public service; on rare occasions this includes philanthropy. But does anyone think the Adelsons' charitable activities were responsible for this honor?

Now, this may seem like a trivial story. But it's a reminder that the Trumpian attitude toward truth—which is that it's defined by what benefits Trump and his friends, not by verifiable facts—also applies to virtue. There is no heroism, there are no good works, except those that serve Trump.

About truth: Trump, of course, lies a lot—in the run-up to the midterms he was lying in public more than one hundred times each week. But his assault on truth goes deeper than the frequency of his lies, because Trump and his allies don't accept the very notion of objective facts. "Fake news" doesn't mean actual false reporting; it means any report that hurts Trump, no matter how solidly verified. And conversely, any assertion that helps Trump, whether it's about job creation or votes, is true precisely because it helps him.

The attempt by Trump and his party to shut down the legally mandated Florida recount with claims, based on no evidence, of large-scale voting fraud fits right into this partisan epistemology. Do Republicans really believe that there were vast numbers of fraudulent or forged ballots? Even asking that question is a category error. They don't "really believe" anything, except that they should get what they want. Any vote count that might favor a Democrat is bad for them; therefore it's fraudulent, no evidence needed.

The same worldview explains Republicans' addiction to conspiracy theories. After all, if people keep insisting on the truth of something that hurts their party, it can't be out of respect for the facts—because in their world, there are no neutral facts.

So the people making inconvenient assertions must be in the pay of sinister forces. In Arizona, Democrat Kyrsten Sinema won a Senate seat on the strength of late-counted ballots. Did you know that the state G.O.P. has filed a freedom of information request for information on interactions between election officials and, you guessed it, George Soros?

It's worth pointing out, by the way, that this rejection of objective facts and insistence that anyone insisting on inconvenient truths must be part of a left-wing conspiracy dominated the Republican psyche long before Trump. Most notably, the claim that the overwhelming evidence for global warming is a giant hoax, the product of a vast plot involving thousands of scientists around the world, has been G.O.P. orthodoxy for years.

True, the party's presidential candidates used to be mealy-mouthed about rejecting facts and endorsing conspiracy theories, rather than being full-throated crazy. But Trump is only going where many of his party's senior figures have been for a long time.

Anyway, my point is that the rejection of any standard besides whether it helps or hurts Trump extends beyond true or false to basic values. In Trump-World, which is now indistinguishable from G.O.P.-World, good and bad are defined solely by whether the interests of The Leader are served. Thus, Trump attacks and insults our closest allies while praising brutal dictators who flatter him (and declares neo-Nazis "very fine people").

And the same goes for heroism and cowardice. A genuine hero like John McCain, who was critical of Trump, gets dismissed as a failure: "He's not a war hero. . . . I like people who weren't captured." Meanwhile, Miriam Adelson, whose service to the nation basically consists of giving Trump campaign contributions, gets the Presidential Medal of Freedom.

Oh, and this, too, predates Trump. Remember how Republicans denigrated John Kerry's war record?

As with so much about the current political scene, it's essential to realize and acknowledge that this is not a symmetric, both-sides-do-it situation. If you say something along the lines of "truth and virtue are now defined by partisanship," you're actually enabling the bad guys, because only one party thinks that way.

Democrats, being human, sometimes have biased views and engage in motivated reasoning. But they haven't abandoned the whole notion of objective facts and nonpolitical goodness; Republicans have.

What all of this means is that what's going on in America right now isn't politics as usual. It's much more existential than that. You have to be truly delusional to see the Republicans' response to their party's midterm setback as anything but an attempted power grab by a would-be authoritarian movement, which rejects any opposition or even criticism as illegitimate. Our democracy is still very much in danger.

CONSERVATISM'S MONSTROUS ENDGAME

December 17, 2018

T he midterm elections were, to an important extent, a referendum on the Affordable Care Act; health care, not Donald Trump, dominated Democratic campaigning. And voters delivered a clear verdict: they want Obamacare's achievements, the way it expanded coverage to roughly 20 million people who would otherwise have been uninsured, to be sustained.

But on Friday, Reed O'Connor, a partisan Republican Judge known for "weaponizing" his judicial power, declared the A.C.A. as a whole—protection for pre-existing conditions, subsidies to help families afford coverage, and the Medicaid expansion—unconstitutional. Legal experts from both right and left ridiculed his reasoning and described his ruling as "raw political activism." And that ruling probably won't be sustained by higher courts.

But don't be too sure that his sabotage will be overturned. O'Connor's abuse of power may be unusually crude, but that sort of behavior is becoming increasingly common. And it's not just health care, nor is it just the courts. What Nancy Pelosi called the "monstrous endgame" of the Republican assault on health care is just the leading edge of an attack on multiple fronts, as the G.O.P. tries to overturn the will of the voters and undermine democracy in general.

For while we may congratulate ourselves on the strength of our political institutions, in the end institutions consist of people and fulfill their roles only as long as the people in them respect their intended purpose. Rule of law depends not just on what is written down, but also on the behavior of those who interpret and enforce that rule.

If these people don't regard themselves as servants of the law first, partisans second, if they won't subordinate their political goals to their duty to preserve the system, laws become meaningless and only power matters.

And what we're seeing in America—what we've actually been seeing for years, although much of the news media and political establishment has refused to acknowledge it—is an invasion of our institutions by right-wing partisans whose loyalty is to party, not principle. This invasion is corroding the Republic, and the corrosion is already very far advanced.

I say "right-wing" advisedly. There are bad people in both parties, as there are in all walks of life. But the parties are structurally different. The Democratic Party is a loose coalition of interest groups, but the modern Republican Party is dominated by "movement conservatism," a monolithic structure held together by big money—often deployed stealthily—and the closed intellectual ecosystem of Fox News and other partisan media. And the people who rise within this movement are, to a far greater degree than those on the other side, apparatchiks, political loyalists who can be counted on not to stray from the party line.

Republicans have been stuffing the courts with such people for decades; O'Connor was appointed by George W. Bush. That's why his ruling, no matter how bad the legal reasoning, wasn't a big surprise. The only question was whether he would imagine himself able to get away with such a travesty. Obviously he did, and he may well have been right.

But as I said, it's not just the courts. Even as Trump and his allies spin fantasies about sabotage by the "deep state," the reality is that a growing number of positions in government agencies are being occupied by right-wing partisans who care nothing for, or actively oppose, their agencies' missions. The Environmental Protection Agency is now run by people who don't want to protect the environment, Health and Human Services by people who want to deny Americans health care.

The same takeover by apparatchiks is taking place in politics. Remember when the role of the Senate was supposed to be to "advise and consent"? Under Republican control it's just plain consent—there is almost literally nothing Trump can do, up to and including clear evidence of corruption and criminality, that will induce senators from his party to exercise any kind of oversight.

So how do people who think and behave this way respond when the public rejects their agenda? They attempt to use their power to overrule the democratic process. When Democrats threaten to win elections, they rig the voting process, as they did in Georgia. When Democrats win despite election rigging, they strip the offices Democrats win of power, as they did in Wisconsin. When Democratic policies prevail despite all of that, they use apparatchik-stuffed courts to strike down legislation on the flimsiest of grounds.

As David Frum, the author of *Trumpocracy*, warned a year ago: "If conservatives become convinced that they cannot win democratically, they will not abandon conservatism. They will reject democracy." That's happening as we speak.

So Pelosi was right about Reed O'Connor's ruling being a symptom of a "monstrous endgame," but the game in question isn't just about perpetuating the assault on health care, it's about assaulting democracy in general. And the current state of the endgame is probably just the beginning; the worst, I fear, is yet to come.

MANHOOD, MOOLA, McCONNELL, AND TRUMPISM

December 13, 2018

After Tuesday's testy exchange between Donald Trump and Democratic leaders, it seems quite possible that the tweeter in chief will shut down the government in an attempt to get funding for a wall on the Mexican border. What's remarkable about this prospect is that the wall is an utterly stupid idea. Even if you're bitterly opposed to immigration, legal or otherwise, spending tens of billions of dollars on an ostentatious physical barrier is neither a necessary nor an effective way to stop immigrants from coming.

So what's it about? Nancy Pelosi, almost sure to be the next speaker of the House, reportedly told colleagues that for Trump, the wall is a "manhood thing." That sounds right. But that got me thinking. What other policies are driven by Trump's insecurity? What's driving this administration's policy in general?

The answer to these questions, I'd argue, is that there are actually three major motives behind Trumpist policy, which we can label Manhood, McConnell, and Moola.

By McConnell I mean the standard G.O.P. agenda, which basically serves the interests of big donors, both wealthy individuals and corporations. This agenda consists, above all, of tax cuts for the donor class, with cuts in social programs to make up for some of the lost revenue. It also includes deregulation, especially for polluters but also for financial institutions and dubious players like for-profit colleges.

During the 2016 campaign, Trump posed as a different kind of Republican, someone who would protect the safety net and raise taxes on the rich.

In office, however, his domestic policy has been totally orthodox. His only significant legislative victory in the first two years has been a tax cut that heavily favored the rich; he has done all he can to undermine health care for lower- and middle-income Americans; he has gutted both environmental protection and financial regulation.

Trump's foreign policy has, however, made a break, not just with previous Republican practice, but with everything America used to stand for. Previous presidents may have made realpolitik accommodations with unsavory regimes, but we've never seen anything like Trump's obvious preference for brutal despots over democratic allies, his willingness to make excuses for whatever people like Vladimir Putin or Mohammed bin Salman do, up to and including murder.

Some of this may reflect personal values: Putin, bin Salman, and other strongmen are just Trump's kind of people. But it's hard to escape the suspicion that Moola—financial payoffs to Trump personally via the Trump Organization—plays an important role. After all, unlike leaders of democracies, dictators and absolute monarchs can direct lots of cash to Trump properties and offer the Trump family investment opportunities without having to explain their actions to pesky elected representatives.

So where does Manhood come in? The wall is an obvious example. The giveaway is the administration's focus on how the "big, beautiful wall" will look, as opposed to what it will do. When Customs and Border Protection solicited bids from contractors, it specified that the wall be "physically imposing," and further that "the north side of wall (i.e., U.S.-facing side) shall be aesthetically pleasing." It didn't say that the structure should bear huge signs reading TRUMP WALL, but that may have been an oversight.

But I'd argue that Trump's desire to assert his manhood is playing a big role in other areas, too, most notably trade policy.

I've been tracking the adventures of Tariff Man, and what strikes me is not just the overwhelming view on the part of economists that the Trump tariffs are a bad idea, but the fact that the tariffs are a political dud. That is, there doesn't seem to be any large constituency demanding a confrontation with our trading partners.

Who wants a trade war? Not corporate interests—stocks fall whenever trade rhetoric heats up and rise when it cools down. Not farmers, hit hard by retaliatory foreign tariffs. Not working-class voters in the Rust Belt states that were crucial to Trump's 2016 victory: a plurality of likely voters in those states say that tariffs hurt their families. Belligerence on trade, it turns out, is pretty much a one-man affair: it's what Trump wants, and that's about it.

True, given how U.S. trade law works, a president can have a trade war (as opposed to, say, a border wall) without congressional approval. But what's Trump's motivation? Well, he made trade his signature issue, and he wants to claim that he's achieved big things. It's telling that even when he leaves policy mostly the same he insists on a name change. That way he can go around pretending that the "U.S.-Mexico-Canada Agreement"—or as Pelosi calls it, the "trade agreement formerly known as Prince"—is completely different from NAFTA, and that he had a big win.

So major affairs of state are being decided not by the national interest, nor even by the interests of major groups within the nation, but by the financial interests and/or ego of the man in the White House. Is America amazing, or what?

17

On the Media

BEYOND FAKE NEWS

AFTER THE 2016 ELECTION, AS PEOPLE ASKED HOW SUCH A THING COULD happen, there was a lot of talk about the role of "fake news"—conspiracy theories and false claims spreading through social media. For example, Pizzagate—the claim, based on nothing, that high-ranking Democratic officials were connected with a child sex ring involving a Washington pizzeria—spread widely over the Internet, leading among other things to death threats to restaurant owners.

Such false claims have overwhelmingly favored Donald Trump. But the times being what they are, Trump and his followers quickly hijacked the term "fake news" to mean any reporting, no matter how factual, that reflected badly on the Trump administration. And a lot of people have bought in: the number of people who consider major news media outlets credible has fallen sharply, mainly because of plunging trust among Republicans.

The truth is that major media outlets (other than those owned by Rupert Murdoch) are pretty careful about getting their facts right, and the constant attacks they face for doing their job should scare you. Yet this doesn't mean that the media are unbiased. On the contrary, there are some strong biases in what gets reported and how it gets reported—biases that have played a major role in our political dysfunction.

I'm not talking about straight political bias, either liberal or conservative. Instead, I'm talking about things like false equivalence—giving two sides of a dispute equal treatment even when one is clearly telling lies. A fair number of people now refer to this as "views differ on shape of planet," after the first column in this section, which was written during the 2000 campaign. On the rare occasions when the media don't engage in bothsidesism, it tends to be because the Very Serious People all agree on something—which happens to be wrong.

I'm also talking about the tendency to replace policy discussion with the-ater criticism—focusing on how candidates supposedly come across rather than on what they're actually proposing, which I went after in "Triumph of the Trivial." And factually accurate reporting can still be effectively biased against a candidate who for whatever reason reporters don't like, which hap-pened both to Al Gore in 2000 and Hillary Clinton in 2016.

The columns in this section, then, are about the real failings of the news media, and how they have contributed to our political descent.

BAIT-AND-SWITCH

November 1, 2000

Thehe big lesson of this year's campaign—a lesson that we can be sure politicians will take to heart—is that a candidate can get away with saying things that are demonstrably untrue, as long as the untruths involve big numbers.

George W. Bush has repeatedly declared, among other things, that he intends to spend about a trillion dollars on new programs; his budget actually earmarks less than half that much. But his repetition of this claim has not led the public to question his credibility.

Mr. Bush has also promised to use a trillion dollars of Social Security money for two conflicting purposes: putting it into private accounts for young workers, while still using it to pay benefits to older workers. And his favorite argument for privatization involves similar double dipping. When he compares the rate of return people can get on their money with the implied rate of return on Social Security contributions, he seems to have misunderstood why Social Security offers lower returns: it has to set young workers' contributions aside, or it will run out of money before today's middle-aged workers have retired.

But it's not a misunderstanding. Since warnings about his accounting have come from many places, including the American Academy of Actuaries, Mr. Bush's continuing use of this comparison is not a mistake—it's a ploy. Still, this exercise in double counting has caused remarkably few problems for a campaign that promises to bring "honor and integrity" back to the White House.

How has he gotten away with it? One answer is that voters can't relate to big numbers. But it's also true that the media haven't helped them make sense of these numbers.

Partly this is a matter of marketing—insider gossip makes better TV than budget arithmetic. But there has also been a political aspect: the mainstream media are fanatically determined to seem evenhanded. One of the great jokes of American politics is the insistence by conservatives that the media have a liberal bias. The truth is that reporters have failed to call Mr. Bush to account on even the most outrageous misstatements, presumably for fear that they might be accused of partisanship. If a presidential candidate were to declare that the earth is flat, you would be sure to see a news analysis under the headline "Shape of the Planet: Both Sides Have a Point." After all, the earth isn't perfectly spherical.

What we don't know, however, is how the story ends. If Mr. Bush wins, he will have to produce an actual budget, not to mention an actual Social Security plan. At that point rhetorical flourishes won't be enough. So what would he really do?

Many analysts seem to hope—hope!—that Mr. Bush is actually playing bait-and-switch. That is, they hope that if he wins the election he will actually unveil a program very different from anything he has suggested in the campaign. Conservatives, in particular, not so secretly believe that the real program will involve drastic cuts in social spending to make room for reductions in income and estate taxes, and large cuts in Social Security benefits to offset the diversion of taxes into private accounts.

But the needed spending cuts would make a mockery of any claim to compassionate conservatism. And we have a pretty good idea what a realistic plan for partial Social Security privatization would look like. It would involve some combination of substantially raising the retirement age, sharply reducing cost-of-living adjustments, and heavily taxing those private accounts when they are cashed in. ("It's your money"—but under the plan proposed by one of Mr. Bush's advisers, you get to keep only 25 percent of any gains you make.)

Would Mr. Bush dare to present such a tough-minded plan, after promising a free lunch in his campaign? Think of the reaction to the original Clinton health plan, and ask whether Mr. Bush would be prepared to face a similar firestorm.

My guess is that if elected, Mr. Bush will try to govern as he has campaigned. The accounts will simply be fudged until the financial markets, alarmed by America's rapidly deteriorating finances, deliver a message that cannot be ignored.

But maybe I've underestimated Mr. Bush's willingness to cast aside his campaign promises. Sad to say, if he wins we must indeed hope that he actually was playing bait-and-switch.

TRIUMPH OF THE TRIVIAL

July 30, 2004

Under the headline "Voters Want Specifics from Kerry," *The Washington Post* recently quoted a voter demanding that John Kerry and John Edwards talk about "what they plan on doing about health care for middle-income or lower-income people. I have to face the fact that I will never be able to have health insurance, the way things are now. And these millionaires don't seem to address that."

Mr. Kerry proposes spending $650 billion extending health insurance to lower- and middle-income families. Whether you approve or not, you can't say he hasn't addressed the issue. Why hasn't this voter heard about it?

Well, I've been reading sixty days' worth of transcripts from the places four out of five Americans cite as where they usually get their news: the major cable and broadcast TV networks. Never mind the details—I couldn't even find a clear statement that Mr. Kerry wants to roll back recent high-income tax cuts and use the money to cover most of the uninsured. When reports mentioned the Kerry plan at all, it was usually horse-race analysis—how it's playing, not what's in it.

On the other hand, everyone knows that Teresa Heinz Kerry told someone to "shove it," though even there, the context was missing. Except for a brief reference on MSNBC, none of the transcripts I've read mention that the target of her ire works for Richard Mellon Scaife, a billionaire who financed smear campaigns against the Clintons—including accusations of murder. (CNN did mention Mr. Scaife on its Web site, but described him only as a donor to "conservative causes.") And viewers learned nothing about Mr. Scaife's long vendetta against Mrs. Heinz Kerry herself.

There are two issues here, trivialization and bias, but they're related.

Somewhere along the line, TV news stopped reporting on candidates' policies, and turned instead to trivia that supposedly reveal their personalities. We hear about Mr. Kerry's haircuts, not his health care proposals. We hear about George Bush's brush-cutting, not his environmental policies.

Even on its own terms, such reporting often gets it wrong, because journalists aren't especially good at judging character. ("He is, above all, a moralist," wrote George Will about Jack Ryan, the Illinois Senate candidate who dropped out after embarrassing sex-club questions.) And the character issues that dominate today's reporting have historically had no bearing on leadership qualities. While planning D-Day, Dwight Eisenhower had a close, though possibly platonic, relationship with his female driver. Should that have barred him from the White House?

And since campaign coverage as celebrity profiling has no rules, it offers ample scope for biased reporting.

Notice the voter's reference to "these millionaires." A *Columbia Journalism Review* Web site called campaigndcsk.org says its analysis "reveals a press prone to needlessly introduce Senators Kerry and Edwards and Kerry's wife, Teresa Heinz Kerry, as millionaires or billionaires, without similar labels for President Bush or Vice President Cheney."

As the site points out, the Bush campaign has been "hammering away with talking points casting Kerry as out of the mainstream because of his wealth, hoping to influence press coverage." The campaign isn't claiming that Mr. Kerry's policies favor the rich—they manifestly don't, while Mr. Bush's manifestly do. Instead, we're supposed to dislike Mr. Kerry simply because he's wealthy (and not notice that his opponent is, too). Republicans, of all people, are practicing the politics of envy, and the media obediently go along.

In short, the triumph of the trivial is not a trivial matter. The failure of TV news to inform the public about the policy proposals of this year's presidential candidates is, in its own way, as serious a journalistic betrayal as the failure to raise questions about the rush to invade Iraq.

P.S.: Another story you may not see on TV: Jeb Bush insists that electronic voting machines are perfectly reliable, but the *St. Petersburg Times* says the Republican Party of Florida has sent out a flier urging supporters to use absentee ballots because the machines lack a paper trail and cannot "verify your vote."

P.P.S.: Three weeks ago, *The New Republic* reported that the Bush administration was pressuring Pakistan to announce a major terrorist capture during the Democratic convention. Hours before Mr. Kerry's acceptance speech, Pakistan announced, several days after the fact, that it had apprehended an important Al Qaeda operative.

IS THERE ANY POINT TO ECONOMIC ANALYSIS?

New York Times *Blog*

August 4, 2013

A few further thoughts inspired by the sad revelation that Beltway conventional wisdom has settled on the proposition that high unemployment is structural, not cyclical, even though there is now a bipartisan consensus among economists that the opposite is true.

First, about the meaning of terms: when economists talk about rising "structural" unemployment, what they actually mean is something quite specific—it's not vague hand-waving, it's the assertion that the "full-employment" rate of unemployment, the level of unemployment at which prices and wages start to rise and you risk a wage-price spiral, has increased. When that happens, you can't solve the unemployment problem just by getting someone to spend more and thereby increasing demand; when it hasn't happened, you can.

What about all the other things we talk about, like the variation of unemployment across regions or occupations or skills? Well, since the usual story about rising structural unemployment involves some kind of "mismatch" between workers and jobs, you'd expect the "signature" of this mismatch to be the emergence of shortages of workers somewhere or of some kind; so the fact that you don't see this militates against structural stories. But the ultimate question is, always, how low can we push unemployment before inflation becomes a problem—and there is essentially no evidence that this number has gone up since 2007, let alone that it is somewhere near the current unemployment level.

And as I said, there is now a much stronger consensus that unemployment is cyclical, not structural, than there was a couple of years ago. In another blog post I mentioned Eddie Lazear's paper at Jackson Hole; there was also Narayana Kocherlakota's change of heart (for which he deserves major props—the number of economic analysts willing to change their views in the face of evidence is much too small).

So what we have here is an economic discussion working the way things are supposed to work—slower than I'd like, but, still, in the end we did have the professionals concluding that one popular story about the nature of our troubles was wrong.

And the pundit class, it seems, paid no attention. Talking about "structural" sounds serious, or maybe Serious, so that's what they say, even though the evidence is all the other way. And it's not even "views differ on the shape of the planet" territory: PBS viewers weren't even given a hint that the professional consensus exists. It's as if you had a program on climate and only climate-change deniers were represented.

And maybe we should put this in the context of another debate, the big one over austerity. Here too there has been a rather decisive turn in professional opinion; there are a lot of dead-enders even within the economics profession, but the fact remains that both pillars of the pro-austerity position—claims of expansionary austerity, and claims that terrible things happen when debt crosses some rather low threshold—have collapsed, spectacularly. Yet policy hasn't changed at all; at best there have been tiny adjustments at the margin in Europe, and in the U.S. we're still slashing spending in the face of a weak economy.

It's pretty depressing for those who would like to believe that analysis and evidence matter. The recent evolution of both policy and conventional wisdom on macroeconomics seems to suggest otherwise.

THE YEAR OF LIVING STUPIDLY

New York Times *Blog*

August 7, 2013

I didn't realize it, but just before my lament over the imperviousness of conventional wisdom to evidence, Simon Wren-Lewis made a similar point, but more broadly. Reading his post, I had some further thoughts.

To this day, one often hears pundits and establishment types in general talking as if we had a clear distinction between the elite, who know How Things Work, and the great unwashed who need to be led to elite wisdom. The reality, however, is nothing like this. It's true that there are crank doctrines—goldbuggery, the Laffer curve, etc.—that play a substantial role in popular opinion but have no traction with the elite. But the elite itself has spent much of the past five years committed to economic doctrines—the prevalence of structural unemployment, the urgency of deficit reduction and entitlement reform, the destructive effects of "uncertainty"—that may not be quite as contrary to the evidence as fears of hyperinflation just around the corner, but are pretty bad. And the influence of these doctrines has remained almost unscathed even though this past year should have driven them completely out of respectable discussion.

It has, after all, been quite a year—not just the sea change in professional opinion on structural unemployment, but the collapse of the expansionary austerity doctrine and its replacement by the view that multipliers are quite large, the collapse of the 90 percent debt threshold view, the plunging deficit, and the vanishing of medium-term debt concerns, and more.

Yet policy hasn't changed at all, and elite views have hardly shifted. How is this possible? Wren-Lewis hits the main points: politicians seek out economists who reinforce their prejudices; news media are either propaganda organs or desperately afraid of declaring, in any straightforward way, that politicians are wrong, no matter how much what they say is at odds with the truth.

That is, by the way, where the PolitiFact deficit bungle comes in. Eric Cantor says that the deficit is growing when it's actually falling fast; Politi-Fact rules this "half true" because projections suggest that the deficit will rise (modestly) after 2015. It's as if I said it was raining when it was actually sunny, and you declared my statement half true because (unreliable) weather forecasts call for rain later in the week. The reality, surely, is that the so-called fact checkers thought they were playing it safe, avoiding calling a top G.O.P. official either uninformed or a liar; as it turns out, they're getting a different kind of grief, and that's a good thing.

But back to the frustrations of policy analysis. Obviously economists have to do what they can to get things right, and get the word out. But the past five years have been a disappointing revelation: knowledge, it seems, isn't power, and actual power is all too eager to ignore actual knowledge in favor of stuff that sounds Serious and/or serves an agenda.

HILLARY CLINTON GETS GORED

September 5, 2016

Americans of a certain age who follow politics and policy closely still have vivid memories of the 2000 election—bad memories, and not just because the man who lost the popular vote somehow ended up in office. For the campaign leading up to that endgame was nightmarish too.

You see, one candidate, George W. Bush, was dishonest in a way that was unprecedented in U.S. politics. Most notably, he proposed big tax cuts for the rich while insisting, in raw denial of arithmetic, that they were targeted for the middle class. These campaign lies presaged what would happen during his administration—an administration that, let us not forget, took America to war on false pretenses.

Yet throughout the campaign most media coverage gave the impression that Mr. Bush was a bluff, straightforward guy, while portraying Al Gore—whose policy proposals added up, and whose critiques of the Bush plan were completely accurate—as slippery and dishonest. Mr. Gore's mendacity was supposedly demonstrated by trivial anecdotes, none significant, some of them simply false. No, he never claimed to have invented the Internet. But the image stuck.

And right now I and many others have the sick, sinking feeling that it's happening again.

True, there aren't many efforts to pretend that Donald Trump is a paragon of honesty. But it's hard to escape the impression that he's being graded on a curve. If he manages to read from a TelePrompter without going off script, he's being presidential. If he seems to suggest that he wouldn't round up all 11 million undocumented immigrants right away, he's moving into the mainstream. And many of his multiple scandals, like what appear to be clear payoffs to state attorneys general to back off investigating Trump University, get remarkably little attention.

Meanwhile, we have the presumption that anything Hillary Clinton does must be corrupt, most spectacularly illustrated by the increasingly bizarre coverage of the Clinton Foundation.

Step back for a moment, and think about what that foundation is about. When Bill Clinton left office, he was a popular, globally respected figure. What should he have done with that reputation? Raising large sums for a charity that saves the lives of poor children sounds like a pretty reasonable, virtuous course of action. And the Clinton Foundation is, by all accounts, a big force for good in the world. For example, Charity Watch, an independent watchdog, gives it an "A" rating—better than the American Red Cross.

Now, any operation that raises and spends billions of dollars creates the potential for conflicts of interest. You could imagine the Clintons using the foundation as a slush fund to reward their friends, or, alternatively, Mrs. Clinton using her positions in public office to reward donors. So it was right and appropriate to investigate the foundation's operations to see if there were any improper quid pro quos. As reporters like to say, the sheer size of the foundation "raises questions."

But nobody seems willing to accept the answers to those questions, which are, very clearly, "no."

Consider the big Associated Press report suggesting that Mrs. Clinton's meetings with foundation donors while secretary of state indicate "her possible ethics challenges if elected president." Given the tone of the report, you might have expected to read about meetings with, say, brutal foreign dictators or corporate fat cats facing indictment, followed by questionable actions on their behalf.

But the prime example the A.P. actually offered was of Mrs. Clinton meeting with Muhammad Yunus, a winner of the Nobel Peace Prize who also happens to be a longtime personal friend. If that was the best the investigation could come up with, there was nothing there.

So I would urge journalists to ask whether they are reporting facts or simply engaging in innuendo, and urge the public to read with a critical eye. If reports about a candidate talk about how something "raises questions," creates "shadows," or anything similar, be aware that these are all too often weasel words used to create the impression of wrongdoing out of thin air.

And here's a pro tip: the best ways to judge a candidate's character are to look at what he or she has actually done, and what policies he or she is proposing. Mr. Trump's record of bilking students, stiffing contractors, and more is a good indicator of how he'd act as president; Mrs. Clinton's speaking style and body language aren't. George W. Bush's policy lies gave me a much better handle on who he was than all the up-close-and-personal reporting of 2000, and the contrast between Mr. Trump's policy incoherence and Mrs. Clinton's carefulness speaks volumes today.

In other words, focus on the facts. America and the world can't afford another election tipped by innuendo.

18

Economic Thoughts

THE DISMAL SCIENCE

ALTHOUGH I'VE BEEN WRITING FOR *THE NEW YORK TIMES* FOR ALMOST two decades, in some sense I still feel that I'm a college professor moonlighting as a journalist. In this final section of the book I offer a few samples of me sounding more like an academic than I usually do in the pages of the *Times*.

About that: the biggest problem even quite good academic writers have when they try to address a broader public is that even well-informed readers who aren't specialists in the field don't come in with the shared background you can presume on when talking to insiders.

Talk to a group of economists, and you can use a phrase like "increasing returns," and expect them not just to know what it means—that the more you produce, the lower your cost per unit—but to be aware of the whole penumbra of associated issues. For example, they'll know that increasing returns normally lead to the breakdown of perfect competition, in which many small firms produce the same thing. They'll also know how important perfect competition is to standard economic models. And so on. It's easy to condemn jargon, but when specialized language is used as a quick way to refer to fairly complex concepts, it's crucial to communication among professionals.

Unfortunately, using specialized language also means that non-professionals have no idea what you're talking about.

If you're careful and you work very hard, you can often convey important economic insights in plain English, to readers who come at it from a standing start. For example, just before writing this essay I published a column on the decline of rural America that was, in effect, a sort of stealth restatement of the thesis of my most cited academic paper, "Increasing Returns and Economic Geography" (1991). And putting in the work of translating economics into ordinary language is both important and gratifying.

But sometimes I want to kick up my heels a bit, and write something that isn't a technical research paper, but uses more jargon than I usually allow myself. This section contains a selection of examples.

I start with an essay I was asked to write in 1991. It was supposed to be about my "life philosophy," but I decided that this was silly. It made far more sense to talk about my strategy for doing economic research. And I think the essay may give even general readers who are willing to bear with a bit of jargon some sense of what that other side of my life looked like, and perhaps what it was about how I did research that helped me transition to writing for an audience of millions.

A significant part of my research has involved macroeconomics, especially ideas associated with the work of John Maynard Keynes. Unfortunately, faced with a crisis that called for unabashed Keynesian policies, both Europe and America fell short. "The Instability of Moderation" is an essay on why we bungled policy, in which I argue that the Keynesian stance—value the market economy, but be ready for strong government action when necessary—although wise, was hard to sustain both intellectually and politically.

Finally, you couldn't write about economics in the 20-teens without being expected to weigh in on Bitcoin and other cryptocurrencies. I've been very much a skeptic, and explain why in the essay reproduced here.

HOW I WORK

Sage

October 1, 1993

My formal charge in this essay is to talk about my "life philosophy." Let me make it clear at the outset that I have no intention of following instructions, since I don't know anything special about life in general. I believe it was Schumpeter who claimed to be not only the best economist, but also the best horseman and the best lover in his native Austria. I don't ride horses, and have few illusions on other scores. (I am, however, a pretty good cook.)

What I want to talk about in this essay is something more restricted: some thoughts about thinking, and particularly how to go about doing interesting economics. I think that among economists of my generation I can claim to have a fairly distinctive intellectual style—not necessarily a better style than my colleagues, for there are many ways to be a good economist, but one that has served me well. The essence of that style is a general research strategy that can be summarized in a few rules; I also view my more policy-oriented writing and speaking as ultimately grounded in the same principles. I'll get to my rules for research later in this essay. I think I can best introduce those rules, however, by describing how (it seems to me) I stumbled into the way I work.

ORIGINS

Most young economists today enter the field from the technical end. Originally intending a career in hard science or engineering, they slip down the scale into the most rigorous of the social sciences. The advantages of entering economics from that direction are obvious: one arrives already well trained in mathematics, one finds the concept of formal modeling natural. It is not, however, where I come from. My first love was history; I studied little math, picking up what I needed as I went along.

Nonetheless, I got deeply involved in economics early, working as a research assistant (on world energy markets) to William Nordhaus while still only a junior at Yale. Graduate school followed naturally, and I wrote my first really successful paper—a theoretical analysis of balance-of-payments crises—while still at M.I.T. I discovered that I was facile with small mathematical models, with a knack for finding simplifying assumptions that made them tractable. Still, when I left graduate school I was, in my own mind at least, somewhat directionless. I was not sure what to work on; I was not even sure whether I really liked research.

I found my intellectual feet quite suddenly, in January 1978. Feeling somewhat lost, I paid a visit to my old advisor Rudi Dornbusch. I described several ideas to him, including a vague notion that the monopolistic competition models I had studied in a short course offered by Bob Solow—especially the lovely little model of Dixit and Stiglitz—might have something to do with international trade. Rudi flagged that idea as potentially very interesting indeed; I went home to work on it seriously; and within a few days I realized that I had hold of something that would form the core of my professional life.

What had I found? The point of my trade models was not particularly startling once one thought about it: economies of scale could be an independent cause of international trade, even in the absence of comparative advantage. This was a new insight to me, but had (as I soon discovered) been pointed out many times before by critics of conventional trade theory. The models I worked out left some loose ends hanging; in particular, they typically had many equilibria. Even so, to make the models tractable I had to make obviously unrealistic assumptions. And once I had made those assumptions, the models were trivially simple; writing them up left me no opportunity to display any high-powered technique. So one might have concluded that I was doing nothing very interesting (and that was what some of my colleagues were to tell me over the next few years). Yet what I saw—and for some reason saw almost immediately—was that all of these features were virtues, not vices, that they added up to a program that could lead to years of productive research.

I was, of course, only saying something that critics of conventional theory had been saying for decades. Yet my point was not part of the mainstream of international economics. Why? Because it had never been expressed in nice models. The new monopolistic competition models gave me a tool to open cleanly what had previously been regarded as a can of worms. More important, however, I suddenly realized the remarkable extent to which the methodology of economics creates blind spots. We just don't see what we can't formalize. And the biggest blind spot of all has involved increasing returns. So there, right at hand, was my mission: to look at things from a slightly different angle, and in so doing to reveal the obvious, things that had been right under our noses all the time.

The models I wrote down that winter and spring were incomplete, if one demanded of them that they specify exactly who produced what. And yet they told meaningful stories. It took me a long time to express clearly what I was doing, but eventually I realized that one way to deal with a difficult problem is to change the question—in particular by shifting levels. A detailed analysis may be extremely nasty, yet an aggregative or systemic description that is far easier may tell you all you need to know.

To get this system or aggregate level description required, of course, accepting the basically silly assumptions of symmetry that underlay the Dixit-Stiglitz and related models. Yet these silly assumptions seemed to let me tell stories that were persuasive, and that could not be told using the hallowed assumptions of the standard competitive model. What I began to realize was that in economics we are always making silly assumptions; it's just that some of them have been made so often that they come to seem natural. And so one should not reject a model as silly until one sees where its assumptions lead.

Finally, the simplicity of the models may have frustrated my lingering urge to show off the technical skills I had so laboriously acquired in graduate school, but was, I soon realized, central to the enterprise. Trade theorists had failed to address the role of increasing returns, not out of empirical conviction, but because they thought it was too hard to model. How much more effective, then, to show that it could be almost childishly simple?

And so, before my twenty-fifth birthday, I basically knew what I was going to do with my professional life. I don't know what would have happened if my grand project had met with rejection from other economists—perhaps I would have turned cranky, perhaps I would have lost faith and abandoned the effort. But in fact all went astonishingly well. In my own mind, the curve of my core research since that January of 1978 has followed a remarkably consistent path. Within a few months, I had written up a basic monopolistic competition trade model—as it turned out, simultaneously and independently with similar models by Avinash Dixit and Victor Norman, on one side, and Kelvin Lancaster, on the other. I had some trouble getting that paper published—receiving the dismissive rejection by a flagship journal (the *Quarterly Journal of Economics*) that seems to be the fate of every innovation in economics—but pressed on. From 1978 to roughly the end of 1984 I focused virtually all my research energies on the role of increasing returns and imperfect competition in international trade. (I took one year off to work in the U.S. government; but more about that below). What had been a personal quest turned into a movement, as others followed the same path. Above all, Elhanan Helpman—a deep thinker whose integrity and self-discipline were useful counterparts to my own flakiness and disorganization—first made crucial contributions himself, then talked me into collaborative work. Our magnum opus, *Market Structure and Foreign Trade*, served the purpose of making our ideas not only respectable but almost standard: iconoclasm to orthodoxy in seven years.

For whatever reason, I allowed my grand project on increasing returns to lie fallow for a few years in the 1980s, and turned my attention to international finance. My work in this area consisted primarily of small models inspired by current policy issues; although these models lacked the integrating theme of my trade models, I think that my finance work is to some extent unified by its intellectual style, which is very similar to that of my work on trade.

In 1990 I returned to the economics of increasing returns from a new direction. I suddenly realized that the techniques that had allowed us to legitimize the role of increasing returns in trade could also be used to reclaim a whole outcast field: that of economic geography, the location of activity in space. Here, perhaps even more than in trade, was a field full of empirical insights, good stories, and obvious practical importance, lying neglected right under our noses because nobody had seen a good way to formalize it. For me, it was like reliving the best moments of my intellectual childhood. Doing geography is hard work; it requires a lot of hard thinking to make the models look trivial, and I am increasingly finding that I need the computer as an aid not just to data analysis but even to theorizing. Yet it is immensely rewarding. For me, the biggest thrill in theory is the moment when your model tells you something that should have been obvious all along, something that you can immediately relate to what you know about the world, and yet which you didn't really appreciate. Geography still has that thrill.

My work on geography seems, at the time of writing, to be leading me even further afield. In particular, there are obvious affinities between the concepts that arise naturally in geographic models and the language of traditional development economics—the "high development theory" that flourished in the 1940s and 1950s, then collapsed. So I expect that my basic research project will continue to widen in scope.

RULES FOR RESEARCH

In the course of describing my formative moment in 1978, I have already implicitly given my four basic rules for research. Let me now state them explicitly, then explain. Here are the rules:

1. Listen to the Gentiles
2. Question the question
3. Dare to be silly
4. Simplify, simplify

Listen to the Gentiles

What I mean by this rule is "Pay attention to what intelligent people are saying, even if they do not have your customs or speak your analytical language." The point may perhaps best be explained by example. When I began my rethinking of international trade, there was already a sizeable literature criticizing conventional trade theory. Empiricists pointed out that trade took place largely between countries with seemingly similar factor endowments, and that much of this trade involved intra-industry exchanges of seemingly similar products. Acute observers pointed to the importance of economies of scale and imperfect competition in actual international markets. Yet all of this intelligent commentary was ignored by mainstream trade theorists— after all, their critics often seemed to have an imperfect understanding of comparative advantage, and had no coherent models of their own to offer; so why pay attention to them? The result was that the profession overlooked evidence and stories that were right under its nose.

The same story is repeated in geography. Geographers and regional scientists have amassed a great deal of evidence on the nature and importance of localized external economies, and organized that evidence intelligently if not rigorously. Yet economists have ignored what they had to say, because it comes from people speaking the wrong language.

I do not mean to say that formal economic analysis is worthless, and that anybody's opinion on economic matters is as good as anyone else's. On the contrary! I am a strong believer in the importance of models, which are to our minds what spear-throwers were to stone age arms: they greatly extend the power and range of our insight. In particular, I have no sympathy for those people who criticize the unrealistic simplifications of model-builders, and imagine that they achieve greater sophistication by avoiding stating their assumptions clearly. The point is to realize that economic models are metaphors, not truth. By all means express your thoughts in models, as pretty as possible (more on that below). But always remember that you may have gotten the metaphor wrong, and that someone else with a different metaphor may be seeing something that you are missing.

Question the Question

There was a limited literature on external economies and international trade before 1978. It was never, however, very influential, because it seemed terminally messy; even the simplest models became bogged down in a taxonomy of possible outcomes. What has since become clear is that this messiness arose in large part because the modelers were asking their models to do what traditional trade models do, which is to predict a precise pattern of specialization and trade. Yet why ask that particular question? Even in the Heckscher-Ohlin model, the point you want to make is something like "A country tends to export goods whose production is intensive in the factors in which that country is abundant"; if your specific model tells you that capital-abundant country Home exports capital-intensive good X, this is valuable because it sharpens your understanding of that insight, not because you really care about these particular details of a patently oversimplified model.

It turns out that if you don't ask for the kind of detail that you get in the two-sector, two-good classical model, an external economy model needn't be at all messy. As long as you ask "system" questions like how welfare and world income are distributed, it is possible to make very simple and neat models. And it's really these system questions that we are interested in. The focus on excessive detail was, to put it bluntly, a matter of carrying over ingrained prejudices from an overworked model into a domain where they only made life harder.

The same is true in a number of areas in which I have worked. In general, if people in a field have bogged down on questions that seem very hard, it is a good idea to ask whether they are really working on the right questions. Often some other question is not only easier to answer but actually more interesting! (One drawback of this trick is that it often gets people angry. An academic who has spent years on a hard problem is rarely grateful when you suggest that his field can be revived by bypassing it).

Dare to Be Silly

If you want to publish a paper in economic theory, there is a safe approach: make a conceptually minor but mathematically difficult extension to some familiar model. Because the basic assumptions of the model are already familiar, people will not regard them as strange; because you have done something technically difficult, you will be respected for your demonstration of firepower. Unfortunately, you will not have added much to human knowledge.

What I found myself doing in the new trade theory was pretty much the opposite. I found myself using assumptions that were unfamiliar, and doing very simple things with them. Doing this requires a lot of self-confidence, because initially people (especially referees) are almost certain not simply to criticize your work but to ridicule it. After all, your assumptions will surely look peculiar: a continuum of goods all with identical production functions, entering symmetrically into utility? Countries of identical economic size, with mirror-image factor endowments? Why, people will ask, should they be interested in a model with such silly assumptions—especially when there are evidently much smarter young people who demonstrate their quality by solving hard problems?

What seems terribly hard for many economists to accept is that all our models involve silly assumptions. Given what we know about cognitive psychology, utility maximization is a ludicrous concept; equilibrium pretty foolish outside of financial markets; perfect competition a howler for most industries. The reason for making these assumptions is not that they are reasonable but that they seem to help us produce models that are helpful metaphors for things that we think happen in the real world.

Consider the example which some economists seem to think is not simply a useful model but revealed divine truth: the Arrow-Debreu model of perfect competition with utility maximization and complete markets. This is indeed a wonderful model—not because its assumptions are remotely plausible but because it helps us think more clearly about both the nature of economic efficiency and the prospects for achieving efficiency under a market system. It is actually a piece of inspired, marvelous silliness.

What I believe is that the age of creative silliness is not past. Virtue, as an economic theorist, does not consist in squeezing the last drop of blood out of assumptions that have come to seem natural because they have been used in a few hundred earlier papers. If a new set of assumptions seems to yield a valuable set of insights, then never mind if they seem strange.

Simplify, Simplify

The injunction to dare to be silly is not a license to be undisciplined. In fact, doing really innovative theory requires much more intellectual discipline than working in a well-established literature. What is really hard is to stay on course: since the terrain is unfamiliar, it is all too easy to find yourself going around in circles. Somewhere or other Keynes wrote that "it is astonishing what foolish things a man thinking alone can come temporarily to believe." And it is also crucial to express your ideas in a way that other people, who have not spent the last few years wrestling with your problems and are not eager to spend the next few years wrestling with your answers, can understand without too much effort.

Fortunately, there is a strategy that does double duty: it both helps you keep control of your own insights, and makes those insights accessible to others. The strategy is: always try to express your ideas in the simplest possible model. The act of stripping down to this minimalist model will force you to get to the essence of what you are trying to say (and will also make obvious to you those situations in which you actually have nothing to say). And this minimalist model will then be easy to explain to other economists as well.

I have used the "minimum necessary model" approach over and over again: using a one-factor, one-industry model to explain the basic role of monopolistic competition in trade; assuming sector-specific labor rather than full Heckscher-Ohlin factor substitution to explain the effects of intra-industry trade; working with symmetric countries to assess the role of reciprocal dumping; and so on. In each case the effect has been to allow me to tackle a subject widely viewed as formidably difficult with what appears, at first sight, to be ridiculous simplicity.

The downside of this strategy is, of course, that many of your colleagues will tend to assume that an insight that can be expressed in a cute little model must be trivial and obvious—it takes some sophistication to realize that simplicity may be the result of years of hard thinking. I have heard the story that when Joseph Stiglitz was being considered for tenure at Yale, one of his senior colleagues belittled his work, saying that it consisted mostly of little models rather than deep theorems. Another colleague then asked, "But couldn't you say the same about Paul Samuelson"? "Yes, I could," replied Joe's opponent. I have heard the same reaction to my own work. Luckily, there are enough sophisticated economists around that in the end intellectual justice is usually served. And there is a special delight in managing not only to boldly go where no economist has gone before, but to do so in a way that seems after the fact to be almost child's play.

I have now described my basic rules for research. I have illustrated them with my experience in developing the "new trade theory" and with my more recent extension of that work to economic geography, because these are the core of my work. But I have also done quite a lot of other stuff, which (it seems to me) is also in some sense part of the same enterprise. So in the remainder of this essay I want to talk about this other work, and in particular about how the policy economist and the analytical economist can coexist in the same person.

POLICY-RELEVANT WORK

Most economic theorists keep their hands off current policy issues—or if they do get involved in policy debates, do so only after the midpoint of their career, as something that follows creative theorizing rather than coexists with it. There seems to be a consensus that the clarity and singleness of purpose required to do good theory are incompatible with the tolerance for messy issues required to be active in policy discussion. For me, however, it has never worked that way. I have interspersed my academic career with a number of consulting ventures for various governments and public agencies, as well as a full year in the U.S. government. I have also written a book, *The Age of Diminished Expectations*, aimed at a non-technical audience. And I have written a pretty steady stream of papers that are motivated not by the inner logic of my research but by the attempt to make sense of some currently topical policy debate—e.g., Third World debt relief, target zones for exchange rates, the rise of regional trading blocs. All of this hasn't seemed to hurt my research, and indeed some of my favorite papers have grown out of this policy-oriented work.

Why doesn't policy-relevant work seem to conflict with my "real" research? I think that it's because I have been able to approach policy issues using almost exactly the same method that I use in my more basic work. Paying attention to newspaper reports or the concerns of central bankers and finance ministers is just another form of listening to the Gentiles. Trying to find a useful way of defining their problems is pretty much the same as questioning the question in theory. Confronting supposedly knowledgeable people with an unorthodox view of an issue certainly requires the courage to be silly. And of course, ruthless simplification is worth even more in policy discussion than in theory for its own sake.

So doing policy-relevant economics does not, for me, mean a drastic change in intellectual style. And it has its own payoffs. Let's be honest and admit that these include invitations to fancier conferences and speaking engagements at much higher fees than an academic purist is likely to get. Let's also admit that one of the joys of policy research is the opportunity to shock the bourgeoisie, to point out the hollowness or silliness of official positions. For example, I know that I was not the only international economist to have some fun pointing out the absurdities of the Maastricht Treaty, and was not above some wicked pleasure when the Exchange Rate Mechanism crisis I and others had long predicted actually came to pass in the fall of 1992. The main payoff to policy work, though, is intellectual stimulation. Not all real-world questions are interesting—I find that almost anything having to do with taxation is better than a sleeping pill—but every couple of years, if not more often, the international economy throws up a question that gives rise to exciting research. I have been stimulated to write theory papers by the Plaza and the Louvre, by the Brady Plan, NAFTA, and European Monetary Union. All of them are papers that I think could stand on their own, even without the policy context.

There is, of course, always a risk that an economist who gets onto the policy circuit will no longer have enough time for real research. I certainly write an awfully large number of conference papers; I am a very fast writer, but perhaps it is a gift I overuse. Still, I think that the big danger of doing policy research is not so much the drain on your time as the threat to your values. It is easy to be seduced into the belief that direct influence on policy is more important than just writing papers—I've seen it happen to many colleagues. Once you start down that road, once you begin to think that David Mulford matters more than Bob Solow, or to prefer hobnobbing with the Ruritanian finance minister to talking theory with Avinash Dixit, you are probably lost to research. Pretty soon you'll probably start using "impact" as a verb.

Fortunately, while I love playing around with policy issues, I have never been able to take policymakers very seriously. This lack of seriousness gets me into occasional trouble—like the time that a gentle parenthetical joke about the French in a conference paper led to an extended diatribe from the French official attending the conference—and may exclude me from ever holding any important policy position. But that's O.K.: in the end, I would rather write a few more good papers than hold a position of real power. (Note to the policy world: this doesn't mean that I would necessarily turn down such a position if it were offered!)

REGRETS

There are a lot of things about my life and personality that I regret—if things have gone astonishingly well for me professionally, they have been by no means as easy or happy elsewhere. But in this essay I only want to talk about professional regrets.

A minor regret is that I have never engaged in really serious empirical work. It's not that I dislike facts or real numbers. Indeed, I find light empirical work in the form of tables, charts, and perhaps a few regressions quite congenial. But the serious business of building and thoroughly analyzing a data set is something I never seem to get around to. I think that this is partly because many of my ideas do not easily lend themselves to standard econometric testing. Mostly, though, it is because I lack the patience and organizational ability. Every year I promise to try to do some real empirical work. Next year I really will!

A more important regret is that while the M.I.T. course evaluations rate me as a pretty good lecturer, I have not yet succeeded in generating a string of really fine students, the kind who reflect glory on their teacher. I can make excuses for this failing—students often prefer advisers who are more methodical and less intuitive, and I all too often scare students off by demanding that they use less math and more economics. It's also true that I probably seem busy and distracted, and perhaps I am just not imposing enough in person to be inspiring (if I were only a few inches taller . . .). Whatever the reasons, I wish I could do better, and intend to try.

All in all, though, I've been very lucky. A lot of that luck has to do with the accidents that led me to stumble onto an intellectual style that has served me extremely well. I've tried, in this essay, to define and explain that style. Is this a life philosophy? Of course not. I'm not even sure that it is an economic research philosophy, since what works for one economist may not work for another. But it's how I do research, and it works for me.

THE INSTABILITY OF MODERATION

New York Times *Blog*

November 26, 2010

B rad DeLong writes of how our perception of history has changed in the wake of the Great Recession. We used to pity our grandfathers, who lacked both the knowledge and the compassion to fight the Great Depression effectively; now we see ourselves repeating all the old mistakes. I share his sentiments.

But watching the failure of policy over the past three years, I find myself believing, more and more, that this failure has deep roots—that we were in some sense doomed to go through this. Specifically, I now suspect that the kind of moderate economic policy regime Brad and I both support— a regime that by and large lets markets work, but in which the government is ready both to rein in excesses and fight slumps—is inherently unstable. It's something that can last for a generation or so, but not much longer.

By "unstable" I don't just mean Minsky-type financial instability, although that's part of it. Equally crucial are the regime's intellectual and political instability.

INTELLECTUAL INSTABILITY

The brand of economics I use in my daily work—the brand that I still consider by far the most reasonable approach out there—was largely established by Paul Samuelson back in 1948, when he published the first edition of his classic textbook. It's an approach that combines the grand tradition of microeconomics, with its emphasis on how the invisible hand leads to generally desirable outcomes, with Keynesian macroeconomics, which emphasizes the way the economy can develop magneto trouble, requiring policy intervention. In the Samuelsonian synthesis, one must count on the government to ensure more or less full employment; only once that can be taken as given do the usual virtues of free markets come to the fore.

It's a deeply reasonable approach—but it's also intellectually unstable. For it requires some strategic inconsistency in how you think about the economy. When you're doing micro, you assume rational individuals and rapidly clearing markets; when you're doing macro, frictions and ad hoc behavioral assumptions are essential.

So what? Inconsistency in the pursuit of useful guidance is no vice. The map is not the territory, and it's O.K. to use different kinds of maps depending on what you're trying to accomplish: if you're driving, a road map suffices, if you're going hiking, you really need a topo.

But economists were bound to push at the dividing line between micro and macro—which in practice has meant trying to make macro more like micro, basing more and more of it on optimization and market-clearing. And if the attempts to provide "microfoundations" fell short? Well, given human propensities, plus the law of diminishing disciples, it was probably inevitable that a substantial part of the economics profession would simply assume away the realities of the business cycle, because they didn't fit the models.

The result was what I've called the Dark Age of macroeconomics, in which large numbers of economists literally knew nothing of the hard-won insights of the thirties and forties—and, of course, went into spasms of rage when their ignorance was pointed out.

POLITICAL INSTABILITY

It's possible to be both a conservative and a Keynesian; after all, Keynes himself described his work as "moderately conservative in its implications." But in practice, conservatives have always tended to view the assertion that government has any useful role in the economy as the thin edge of a socialist wedge. When William Buckley wrote *God and Man at Yale*, one of his key complaints was that the Yale faculty taught—horrors!—Keynesian economics.

I've always considered monetarism to be, in effect, an attempt to assuage conservative political prejudices without denying macroeconomic realities. What Friedman was saying was, in effect, yes, we need policy to stabilize the economy—but we can make that policy technical and largely mechanical, we can cordon it off from everything else. Just tell the central bank to stabilize M2, and aside from that, let freedom ring!

When monetarism failed—fighting words, but you know, it really did— it was replaced by the cult of the independent central bank. Put a bunch of bankerly men in charge of the monetary base, insulate them from political pressure, and let them deal with the business cycle; meanwhile, everything else can be conducted on free-market principles.

And this worked for a while—roughly speaking from 1985 to 2007, the era of the Great Moderation. It worked in part because the political insulation of central banks also gave them more than a bit of intellectual insulation, too. If we're living in a Dark Age of macroeconomics, central banks have been its monasteries, hoarding and studying the ancient texts lost to the rest of the world. Even as the real business cycle people took over the professional journals, to the point where it became very hard to publish models in which monetary policy, let alone fiscal policy, matters, the research departments of the Fed system continued to study counter-cyclical policy in a relatively realistic way.

But this, too, was unstable. For one thing, there was bound to be a shock, sooner or later, too big for the central bankers to handle without help from broader fiscal policy. Also, sooner or later the barbarians were going to go after the monasteries too; and as the current furor over quantitative easing shows, the invading hordes have arrived.

FINANCIAL INSTABILITY

Last but not least, the very success of central-bank-led stabilization, combined with financial deregulation—itself a by-product of the revival of free-market fundamentalism—set the stage for a crisis too big for the central bankers to handle. This is Minskyism: the long period of relative stability led to greater risk-taking, greater leverage, and, finally, a huge deleveraging shock. And Milton Friedman was wrong: in the face of a really big shock, which pushes the economy into a liquidity trap, the central bank can't prevent a depression.

And by the time that big shock arrived, the descent into an intellectual Dark Age combined with the rejection of policy activism on political grounds had left us unable to agree on a wider response.

In the end, then, the era of the Samuelsonian synthesis was, I fear, doomed to come to a nasty end. And the result is the wreckage we see all around us.

TRANSACTION COSTS AND TETHERS: WHY I'M A CRYPTO SKEPTIC

July 31, 2018

I'm still on vacation, hiking and biking in various parts of Europe. I'm keeping up with the news, more or less, but am only occasionally and unpredictably in a place and condition where I can actually write something and post it.

But this is one of those times, and I thought I'd post some thoughts in advance of stuff I'll be doing after I get back. Specifically, in a couple of weeks I'm going to play Emmanuel Goldstein—the designated enemy—at a conference on blockchain and all that. Hey, if you only speak to friendly audiences, you're not challenging yourself enough. So I thought it might be worth explaining why I'm a cryptocurrency skeptic.

It comes down to two things: transaction costs and the absence of tethering. Let me explain.

If you look at the broad sweep of monetary history, there has been a clear direction of change over time: namely, one of reducing the frictions of doing business and the amount of real resources required to deal with those frictions.

First there were gold and silver coins, which were heavy, required lots of security, and consumed a lot of resources to produce.

Then came bank notes backed by fractional reserves. These were popular because they were much easier to deal with than bags of coins; they also reduced the need for physical precious metals, which, as Adam Smith said, provided "a sort of waggon-way through the air," freeing up resources for other uses.

Even so, the system still required substantial amounts of commodity money. But central banking, in which private banks held their reserves as deposits at the central bank rather than in gold or silver, greatly reduced this need, and the shift to fiat money eliminated it almost completely.

Meanwhile, people gradually shifted away from cash transactions, first toward payments by check, then to credit and debit cards and other digital methods.

Set against this history, the enthusiasm for cryptocurrencies seems very odd, because it goes exactly in the opposite of the long-run trend. Instead of near-frictionless transactions, we have high costs of doing business, because transferring a Bitcoin or other cryptocurrency unit requires providing a complete history of past transactions. Instead of money created by the click of a mouse, we have money that must be mined—created through resource-intensive computations.

And these costs aren't incidental, something that can be innovated away. As Markus Brunnermeier and Joseph Abadi point out, the high costs—making it expensive to create a new Bitcoin, or transfer an existing one—are essential to the project of creating confidence in a decentralized system.

Banknotes worked because people knew something about the banks that issued them, and these banks had an incentive to preserve their reputation. Governments have occasionally abused the privilege of creating fiat money, but for the most part governments and central banks exercise restraint, again because they care about their reputations. But you're supposed to be sure that a Bitcoin is real without knowing who issued it, so you need the digital equivalent of biting a gold coin to be sure it's the real deal, and the costs of producing something that satisfies that test have to be high enough to discourage fraud.

In other words, cryptocurrency enthusiasts are effectively celebrating the use of cutting-edge technology to set the monetary system back three hundred years. Why would you want to do that? What problem does it solve? I have yet to see a clear answer to that question.

Bear in mind that conventional money generally does its job quite well. Transaction costs are low. The purchasing power of a dollar a year from now is highly predictable—orders of magnitude more predictable than that of a Bitcoin. Using a bank account means trusting a bank, but by and large banks justify that trust, far more so than the firms that hold cryptocurrency tokens. So why change to a form of money that works far less well?

Indeed, eight years after Bitcoin was launched, cryptocurrencies have made very few inroads into actual commerce. A few firms will accept them as payment, but my sense is that this is more about signaling—look at me, I'm cutting-edge!—than about real usefulness. Cryptocurrencies have a large market valuation, but they're overwhelmingly being held as a speculative play, not because they're useful as mediums of exchange.

Does this mean that crypto is a pure bubble, which will eventually deflate to nothing? It's worth pointing out that there are other currency-like assets that don't actually get much use as money, but which people hold anyway. Gold hasn't been actual money for a very long time, yet it retains its value.

And the same can be said, to a large extent, of cash. While cash transactions are common, they account for only a small and declining fraction of the value of purchases. Yet dollar cash holdings have actually risen as a share of G.D.P. since the 1980s—a growth entirely accounted for by $50 and $100 bills.

Now, large-denomination notes aren't regularly used for payments—in fact, many stores won't accept them. So what's all that cash-holding about? We all know the answer: tax evasion, illicit activity, etc. And much of that is outside the U.S., with estimates suggesting that foreigners hold more than half of U.S. currency.

Clearly, cryptocurrencies are in effect competing for some of the same business: very few people are using Bitcoin to pay their bills, but some people are using it to buy drugs, subvert elections, and so on. And the examples of both gold and large-denomination banknotes suggest that this kind of demand could support a lot of asset value. So does this mean that crypto, even if it isn't the transformative technology its backers claim, may not be a bubble?

Well, this is where tethering—or, more precisely, its absence for cryptocurrencies—comes in.

In normal life, people don't worry about where the value of green pieces of paper bearing portraits of dead presidents comes from: we accept dollar notes because other people will accept dollar notes. Yet the value of a dollar doesn't come entirely from self-fulfilling expectations: ultimately, it's back-stopped by the fact that the U.S. government will accept dollars as payment of tax liabilities—liabilities it's able to enforce because it's a government. If you like, fiat currencies have underlying value because men with guns say they do. And this means that their value isn't a bubble that can collapse if people lose faith.

And the value of those $100 bills sitting in drug lords' lairs or whatever is in turn tethered to the value of smaller denominations back in America.

To some extent gold is in a similar situation. Most gold just sits there, possessing value because people believe it possesses value. But gold does have real-world uses, both for jewelry and for things like filling teeth, that provide a weak but real tether to the real economy.

Cryptocurrencies, by contrast, have no backstop, no tether to reality. Their value depends *entirely* on self-fulfilling expectations—which means that total collapse is a real possibility. If speculators were to have a collective moment of doubt, suddenly fearing that Bitcoins were worthless, well, Bitcoins would become worthless.

Will that happen? I think it's more likely than not, partly because of the gap between the messianic rhetoric of crypto and the much more mundane real possibilities. That is, there might be a potential equilibrium in which Bitcoin (although probably not other cryptocurrencies) remain in use mainly for black market transactions and tax evasion, but that equilibrium, if it exists, would be hard to get to from here: once the dream of a blockchained future dies, the disappointment will probably collapse the whole thing.

So that's why I'm a crypto skeptic. Could I be wrong? Of course. But if you want to argue that I'm wrong, please answer the question, what problem does cryptocurrency solve? Don't just try to shout down the skeptics with a mixture of technobabble and libertarian derp.

CREDITS

Inquiries concerning permission to reprint the following articles should be directed to The New York Times Company, c/o Pars International, 253 West 35th Street, 7th Floor, New York, NY 10001, or NYTPermissions@Parsintl.com.

Social Security Scares
Inventing a Crisis
Buying into Failure
Social Security Lessons
Privatization Memories
Where Government Excels
Ailing Health Care
Health Care Confidential
Health Care Terror
The Waiting Game
Health Care Hopes
Fear Strikes Out
Obamacare Fails to Fail
Imaginary Health Care Horrors
Three Legs Good, No Legs Bad
Obamacare's Very Stable Genius
Get Sick, Go Bankrupt, and Die
How Democrats Can Deliver on
   Health Care
Running Out of Bubbles
That Hissing Sound

Innovating Our Way to Financial
   Crisis
The Madoff Economy
The Ignoramus Strategy
Nobody Understands Debt
Depression Economics Returns
IS-LMentary
Stimulus Arithmetic (Wonkish but
   Important)
The Obama Gap
The Stimulus Tragedy
The Mythical Seventies
That Eighties Show
How Did Economists Get It So
   Wrong?
Bad Faith, Pathos, and G.O.P.
   Economics
What's Wrong with Functional
   Finance? (Wonkish)
Myths of Austerity
The Excel Depression

Jobs and Skills and Zombies

Structural Humbug

The Spanish Prisoner

Crash of the Bumblebee

Europe's Impossible Dream

What's the Matter with Europe?

The Flimflam Man

The Hijacked Commission

What's in the Ryan Plan?

Melting Snowballs and the Winter of Debt

Democrats, Debt, and Double Standards

On Paying for a Progressive Agenda

The Twinkie Manifesto

The Biggest Tax Scam in History

The Trump Tax Scam, Phase 2

Why Was Trump's Tax Cut a Fizzle?

The Trump Tax Cut: Even Worse Than You've Heard

The Economics of Soaking the Rich

Elizabeth Warren Does Teddy Roosevelt

Oh, What a Trumpy Trade War!

A Trade War Primer

Making Tariffs Corrupt Again

Graduates versus Oligarchs

Money and Morals

Don't Blame Robots for Low Wages

What's the Matter with Trumpland?

Same Old Party

Eric Cantor and the Death of a Movement

The Great Center-Right Delusion

The Empty Quarters of U.S. Politics

Capitalism, Socialism, and Unfreedom

Something Not Rotten in Denmark

Trump versus the Socialist Menace

Donald and the Deadly Deniers

The Depravity of Climate-Change Denial

Climate Denial Was the Crucible for Trumpism

Hope for a Green New Year

The Paranoid Style in G.O.P. Politics

Trump and the Aristocracy of Fraud

Stop Calling Trump a Populist

Partisanship, Parasites, and Polarization

Why It Can Happen Here

Who's Afraid of Nancy Pelosi?

Truth and Virtue in the Age of Trump

Conservatism's Monstrous Endgame

Manhood, Moola, McConnell, and Trumpism

Bait-and-Switch

Triumph of the Trivial

Is There Any Point to Economic Analysis?

The Year of Living Stupidly

Hillary Clinton Gets Gored

The Instability of Moderation

Transaction Costs and Tethers: Why I'm a Crypto Skeptic

All other inquiries concerning permission to reprint should be directed to W. W. Norton & Company, Inc.

INDEX

Page numbers in *italics* refer to charts and graphs.

Abadi, Joseph, 412
Abramoff, Jack, 283
accountability, lack of, 56
Adelson, Miriam, 364, 365
Adelson, Sheldon, 364
affinity fraud, 356–57
Affordable Care Act (A.C.A.):
    attacks on, 56–58, 59, 60, 65–66, 73,
        75, 76–78, 351–52
    as benefits enhancement program,
        211–12
    constitutionality of, 65–66
    efforts to repeal, 221, 224, 225
    federal subsidies under, 57, 66, 68,
        69, 71, 74
    financing of, 211–12
    as hybrid public-private system, 66,
        339
    impact on uninsured citizens, 56, 57,
        58, 66, 70, 367
    incrementalism (three-legged stool)
        of, 67–69, 71
    individual mandate in, 68, 69, 71,
        74, 78
    insurance exchanges in, 68, 70, 71, 318
    job growth accelerated in, 60
    Medicaid expansion under, 29, 57,
        65, 66, 68, 71, 77, 211, 367

as most conservative option, 74
negative media coverage of, 58
outreach efforts in, 71, 78
Pelosi's support of, 35–36, 55, 361, 367
popularity of, 367
and pre-existing conditions, 67, 68,
    69, 71, 73, 74, 76–77, 225
and reinsurance, 78
roads leading to, 35–37, 38–40,
    47–49, 50–52, 53–55
robust structure of, 67–69, 70–72,
    74, 361
in state-level programs, 57, 65,
    68–69, 77–78
success of, 56–58, 59–61, 66, 72, 74,
    317
threats to, 221, 224, 225, 305, 338,
    351–52, 367
universal coverage in, 51, 339
"After the Khaki Election" (Krugman),
    13–15
Age of Diminished Expectations, The
    (Krugman), 404
aggregate demand, effects of deficit
    spending on, 154
Ailes, Roger, 300
Alesina, Alberto, 158
algorithms, maximizing profits via, 357

American Academy of Actuaries, 377

American Economic Association, 203

American Medical Association
     (A.M.A.), 45, 322

American Prospect, The, 51, 300

American Recovery and Reinvestment
     Act (2009), 118–20, 193

Americans for Prosperity, 60

arbitrageurs, 146

Ardagna, Silvia, 158

Argentina, depression-level slump in
     (2002), 140

Arizona, election in, 365

Armey, Richard, 273, 274

Arrow-Debreu model, 402

assets, pricing of, 135, 136, 146, 147

Associated Press, 388

asymmetric polarization, 297

asymmetric shocks, 176–77

Atrios (Black), 157

austerity policies:
   and deleveraging, 97
   and economic slumps, 96
   in Europe, 98–99, 119, 158, 182, 185,
        188–89, 384
   "expansionary," 158, 384, 385
   and false views of debt, 97–99, 163–
        65, 203–4, 207–8
   "Myths of Austerity," 158, 160–62, 165
   and tipping point, 164–65

automation, 288–90

Axios, 359

bad faith, conservative politics dom-
     inated by, 7, 8, 10, 75, 149–51,
     332–33

"Bad Faith, Pathos, and G.O.P.
     Economics," 125

Baily, Martin, 127

Baker, Dean, 169

Bangladesh, 243–44

banking system:
   unregulated "shadow" of, 9
   vulnerability to panics, 82, 89

banknotes, 411, 412, 413

Bank of England, 103, 128

Barnhart, Jo Anne, 26

Barrasso, John, 57

Bartley, Robert, 271, 276

Batchelder, Lily, 239

Beck, Glenn, 356

behavioral finance, 145–46

benefits enhancement, 210, 211–12

Berlin Wall, fall of, 188, 358

Bernanke, Ben, 82, 130, 140, 141
   and financial crisis (2007–2008), 89,
        147
   on income inequality, 282, 283

bin Salman, Mohammed, 371

bipartisanship, 198

Bitcoin, 411–14

Black, Duncan, 157

Blackwater affair, 299

Blanchard, Olivier, 130, 139, 194,
     203–5

Blasey Ford, Christine, 345, 346

Bloomberg, Michael, 306

Boehner, John, 362

Bonfire of the Vanities (Wolfe), 262, 270

bothsidesism, 297–98, 375, 378

Bowles, Erskine, 198, 199, 203, 218

Bowyer, Jerry, 44

"Bridge Too Far, A" (Krugman), 175–77

Britain:
   Brexit, 158
   budget surpluses of, 154

currency of, 180
economy of, 180
hard-money policy in, 185
health care in, 45, 47, 48
retirement system in, 22–24
Brunnermeier, Markus, 412
bubbles:
  ends of, 87
  see also specific bubbles
Buckley, William, 408
budget, balancing, 6
budget deficits, 96, 104, 105, 107, 120,
    157–58, 179
  "deficit scolds," 194, 207, 209
  deficit spending, 153, 218
budget surplus, 154
Bureau of Labor Statistics, 87
Bush, George H. W., 306
Bush, George W., 276, 381
  and election (2000), 387
  on health care, 47
  as movement conservative, 299, 301
  and national security, 306
  and taxes, 215–16, 229, 299
Bush, Jeb, 60, 381
Bush (W.) administration:
  authoritarianism of, 301
  bait-and-switch tactics of, 378–79, 387
  compared to that of Trump, 9, 13
  corruption of, 343
  disdain for rule of law, 301
  dishonesty of, 9, 25, 26–27, 93, 343,
    377–78, 389
  functions outsourced by, 299–300
  general incompetence of, 300
  and income distribution, 271
  and Iraq war, 13, 26, 27, 299, 343,
    381

reliance on elite consensus, 14
on Social Security privatization,
    14–15, 22–24, 25–27, 28–29, 32,
    302, 306, 361, 377, 378
tax cuts by, 16–17, 20, 26, 50
torture authorized by, 300
voting rights curtailed by, 300
business decisions, 227–28

California:
  health care in, 77
  housing bubble in, 84
  taxes in, 216, 229
Canada:
  health care in, 36, 45, 47, 48–49
  imports from, 253, 255
  unions in, 290
Cantor, Eric, 302–4, 386
cap and-trade system, 339
Capital Asset Pricing Model (CAPM),
    135–36
capital gains:
  on houses, 87, 274
  and income inequality, 273–74
  inflation component of, 273
capitalism, voter confusion about, 320
capital market, 228
Capitol Hill Baby-Sitting Co-op, 137–38
carbon emissions, tax on, 339
Carter, Jimmy, 276
Cato Institute, 22, 23, 317, 320
caution, risk of, 104, 106, 107, 116–17
Cavuto, Neil, 44
Census data, 262–65, *263*
  capital gains omitted from, 264
  Current Population Survey, 263, 264
  and income distribution, 265–66, *266*
  top-coding, 264, 265

Center for a Responsible Federal
  Budget (CRFB), 193
central banks, 103–4, 124, 128, 133,
  181, 182, 409–10
centrists, 308
  belief in symmetry between left and
    right, 28, 29, 309
  double standards of, 208–9
  influence of, 28
  and public opinion, 298, 306
Century Foundation, 22
CEOs, compensation for, 259, 262, 265
Chandler, Raymond, *The Simple Art of
  Murder,* 327
Charity Watch, 388
Chávez, Hugo, 324
Cheney, Dick, 300, 381
Chicago School, 131, 143–44
child care, proposals on, 210, 211, 212
Chile, retirement system in, 22, 23
China:
  economy of, 324
  U.S. trade with, 252, 254, 255
cholera, 81
Civil Rights Act (1964), 53
civil rights movement, 346
classless society, myth of, 285
climate change, 327–28
  and alternative energies, 340
  and corruption, 337
  deniers of, 329–31, 332–34, 335–37,
    365
  and fossil fuels, 333, 336
  global temperatures in, 330
  greenhouse gases as a cause of, 330,
    335, 339–40
  and Green New Deal, 328, 338–40
  "hockey stick" graph on, 328, 336

politicization of, 4
positive incentives in, 340
transition industries in, 340
and tropical storms, 330
Climategate, 336
Clinton, Bill:
  Gingrich's attacks on, 362
  and health care (1993), 35, 37, 50,
    378
  and income inequality, 271
  smear tactics against, 380
  and taxes, 7, 215
Clinton, Hillary:
  and election (2016), 376, 388–89
  and health care, 50, 51–52
  and income inequality, 291
  smear tactics against, 380
  Trump vs., 336, 343
Clinton Foundation, 388
"Closing the Skills Gap" (Dimon and
  Seltzer), 166–68
Coal and Steel Community (1952), 175
coal-fired power plants, 331
coal mining, 289, 340
Cochrane, John H., 131, 138, 143
cockroach ideas, 329
Cohen, Michael, 359
Cohn, Jonathan, 300
coins: gold and silver, 411, 412
college graduates, earnings of, 282, 283
Collins, Susan, 360
Comey, James, 336, 343
*Coming Apart: The State of White
  America, 1960–2010* (Murray),
  285–86
Commission on Economic Security
  (1934), 26
Common Market (1959), 175

Commonwealth Fund, 48
competition:
  imperfect, 400
  perfect, 402
"confidence fairy," belief in, 158, 160,
  161
Congressional Budget Office (CBO),
  19, 29, 54, 59, 195–96
  budget and economic outlook of,
    115–16
  Green Book of, 265
  and income inequality, 265–66, *266*,
    272–74, 285
  and Ryan plan, 201, 202
Conscience of a Conservative, The
  (Goldwater), 300
conservatism:
  ambition of practitioners, 151
  bad faith of, 7, 8, 10, 75, 149–51,
    332–33
  and bipartisanship, 198
  compassionate conservatism, 378
  confusion about socialism in, 323
  democracy rejected by, 369
  disinterest in good government, 300
  and income inequality, 261–62, 266,
    271–75
  and Keynesian economics, 124
  moral and intellectual decline of, 262
  movement conservatism, 8, 297–98,
    299–301, 302–4, 307, 343, 368
  Orwellian instincts in, 281
  permanent rule by, 13
  Republican, *see* Republican Party
  taking credit for growth, 275–76
  uses and abuses of statistics by, 262
  wing-nut welfare as safety net for,
    303

conservative professional economists,
  149–51
conspiracy theories, 150, 337, 343,
  345–46, 365
Constitution, U.S., 301
containerization, 289
Cornyn, John, 346
corporate profits, 228, 232–33
corporate taxes:
  avoidance vs. evasion of, 349
  cuts in, 201, 202, 218, 221, 222, 227,
    229, 230, 231–33, *232*, 351
  and stock buybacks, 227, 230
corporations:
  "bringing money home," 230
  cooking their books, 228, 230–31, *231*
  global, 231–32
  profits to foreign nationals, 232–33
  and trade war, 371
  unrestricted power for, 318
corruption:
  and Bush administration, 343
  and climate change, 337
  in Europe, 358
  in financial services, 92, 93
  in highly unequal societies, 283, 324,
    349–50, 358
  and Republican Party, 335–37, 338,
    343, 358
  in trade policy, 246, 247, 254, 255
  of Trump administration, 70, 246,
    331, 338, 343, 349, 350
"Cost of Bad Ideas, The" (Krugman),
  123–25
Council of Economic Advisers, and
  CEA calculation, 271–72
Cox, Christopher, 93
credit, 89, 90, 104

"Cruelty Caucus, The" (Krugman),
    65–66
Cruz, Ted, 57, 225
Cruz amendment, 69
cryptocurrencies, 411–14
Crystal, Graef, 265
    In Search of Excess, 262
Cuccinelli, Ken, 336
currency, 412–14
    fiat, 412, 414
    optimum currency areas, 177
Customs and Border Protection, 371

debt:
    and austerity policies, 97–99, 163–
        65, 203–4, 207–8
    fear of, 107, 116
    and G.D.P., 154, 204–5, 205
    interest rates on, 204, 211
    magic threshold of, 158, 385
    overrated as issue, 194, 206, 208
    problematic, 153
    and sustainable growth rate, 153–54,
        204
    and taxes, 154, 222–23, 224–26
    tipping point of, 165
    and total wealth, 154
    Trump's SOTU on, 207–9
    winter of, 203–6
"debt scolds," 204, 205, 206
"deficit scolds," 194, 207, 209
deficit spending, 153, 218
deleveraging, 97
DeLong, Brad, 131, 143–44, 270, 316, 407
democracy:
    threats in Europe to, 188, 189, 344,
        346, 358, 359
    threats in U.S. to, 366, 367–69

Democratic Party:
    basic values of, 366
    center-left position of, 28, 306, 310
    and civil rights, 310
    future plans for, 338
    and Green New Deal, 338–40
    and health care, 36, 55, 77, 78
    House majority of, 338
    impact in state governments, 77, 78
    as loose coalition of interest groups,
        297, 368
    and midterm elections, 76, 194, 338,
        344, 367
    policy analysis by, 73
    social democratic aspect of, 313–14,
        321
    and Social Security, 29, 30
    subpoena power of, 338
De-Moralization of Society
    (Himmelfarb), 285–86
Denmark, economy of, 184, 239, 313,
    317, 319–21, 323
deregulation, 370, 371, 409
derivatives, 135
"Developing a Positive Agenda"
    (Krugman), 35–37
Dew-Becker, Ian, 283
Diamond, Peter, 234–35, 236
diminishing marginal utility, 235
Dimon, Jamie, 166
dishonesty, power of, 324
"Dismal Science, The" (Krugman),
    393–94
Dixit, Avinash K., 396–98, 405
dollar, international value of, 228
Donors Trust, 333
"Don't Blame Robots for Low Wages"
    (Krugman), 260, 288–90

dot-com bubble, 90

double talk, political, 222, 225–26

Dow 36,000 (Gleason and Hassett), 84, 86

Draghi, Mario, 181–83

dumping, and tariffs, 252

Duncan, Greg, 277

economic analysis, importance of, 383–84, 386, 400

economic freedom, 317–18, *317*

economic geography, 398–99, 400, 403

economic growth:
  (1982–1984), 215
  long-term, 275–76
  post–World War II, 219, 234
  so-so, 315
  taking credit for, 275–76
  and taxes, 236–37, *236*

economic models:
  Arrow-Debreu model, 402
  CAPM, 135–36
  Heckscher-Ohlin, 400–401, 403
  importance of, 400
  as metaphors, 400, 402
  minimalist, 403
  monopolistic competition models, 396–98
  and neoclassical theory, 140
  purposes of, 112

economic policy, failure of, 407

economics:
  behavioral, 146
  easy questions in, 6
  golden era of, 130–31
  Keynesian, *see* Keynesian economics
  mathematics in, 131
  monetary, 176

"neoclassical," 132, 133, 139–40, 147
  and politics, 149–51
  "positive" vs. "normative," 1
  real vs. theoretical ideal in, 145–47
  supply-side, 128, 275–76, 299

economic theory:
  development of, 128–29, 132–34
  policy-relevant work, 404–6
  rules for research, 401–2

economies, external, 400

economies of scale, 396, 400

economy, interwoven: my spending = your income; your spending = my income, 96, 97, 157

education:
  earnings of college graduates, 282, 283
  for-profit colleges, 370
  and income inequality, 260, 282, 283
  jobs in knowledge-intensive industries, 292
  and unemployment, 166–67

Education Department, U.S., 248

Edwards, John, 50–51, 380, 381

efficient-market hypothesis, 134, 135–36, 141, 145–46

80-20 fallacy, 282, 284

Eisenhower, Dwight D., 219, 239, 381

election (2000), 387

election (2004), 13–14

election (2016), 13, 343, 372, 375, 387–89

election (2020), 227, 347, 361

electricity generation, greenhouse gases from, 339–40

electric vehicles, 340

Elmendorf, Douglas, 161

empiricists, 399–400

employers, relying on good will of,
    315, *316*
employment, *see* jobs; unemployment
energy, renewable, 331, 339–40
entitlement reform, 189, 223, 225, 240
environmental issues, 333, 371
Environmental Protection Agency
    (EPA), 248, 368
Erdogan, Recep Tayyip, 346
Estonia, slumps in, 162
euro, 99, 176–77, 178–79, 181–83,
    184–86, 187–89
Europe:
  common currency (euro), 99,
    176–77, 178–79, 181–83, 184–86,
    187–89
  dark forces in, 188
  fiscal austerity in, 98–99, 119, 158,
    182, 185, 188–89, 384
  housing bubbles in, 182
  national rivalries in, 176
  as net lender to the world, 98
  post–World War II recovery of, 175,
    187
  post–World War I war debts of, 254
  run on fantasy economics, 184–86
  threats to democracy in, 188, 189,
    344, 346, 358, 359
  white nationalist right in, 343
European Central Bank, 103, 128, 181,
    182
European Commission, 176
European project, 175, 183, 188
European Union, 175, 181–83
  effects of possible trade war against,
    247
  and elections, 188
  see also Europe

Excel, coding error, 163, 164
Exchange Rate Mechanism crisis, 405
executive compensation, 259, 262, 265
externalities, 132
extremism, profiting from, 357

fads and fashions, 160
"fake news," 364, 375–76
false equivalence, 375
Fama, Eugene, 135, 141, 146
family income:
  adjusted (AFI), 273
  median, 267–70, *268*, 272
family size, and income inequality,
    272–73
family values, 260, 285–87
Federal Reserve:
  asset holdings of, 104
  bonds purchased by, 1
  in Great Moderation years, 142
  and housing bubble, 83, 85
  and income distribution, 270
  and interest rates, 106–7, 110, 118,
    215
  and monetary policy, 128–29, 140,
    144
  "money-printing" by, 96, 105, 133
  and money supply, 110, 112, 124,
    133
  and recessions, 118, 133, 142, 215,
    275
  Republican attacks on, 180
  and unemployment, 150
  wealth study of, 274
fiat money, 412, 414
Fidesz (Hungarian Civic Alliance),
    189, 358
finance, dysfunctional, 147

financial advisers, fees of, 31
financial crises, predictability of, 140–42
financial crisis (1929–1941), *see* Great Depression
financial crisis (1990s), in Asia, 81–82, 89, 103, 140, 164
financial crisis (2008):
    aftermath of, 1, 9–10, 103–5, 131–32, 146, 147–48, 150
    and budget deficits, 157
    buildup of, 89–91, 130–31, 136, 157
    Great Recession (2007–2009), 157, 407
    and international trade, 252
    and Obama stimulus plan, 115–17, 118
    surprise of, 103
    and unemployment, 157
financial innovation, risk in, 90–91
financial markets:
    credit in, 89
    "efficient-market" theory, 134, 135–36, 141, 145–46
    imperfect, 131, 132
financial services industry, 92–94, 371
financial stability, threats to, 98
Finland, economy of, 176–77, 184
fiscal policy, 129, 153
fiscal responsibility, 107
"Fiscy Awards," 193–94
Five Star Movement, 188
"Flimflam Man, The" (Krugman), 194, 195–97
Florida:
    economic freedom in, 317, *317*, 318
    health care in, 318
    housing bubble in, 84, 181

Local Government Investment Pool, 90
    voting in, 364–65, 381–82
food stamps, 120
Ford, Christine Blasey, 345, 346
foreign trade, *see* international trade
fossil fuels, 333, 336
Fox News, 226, 303, 307, 356–57, 368
France, health care in, 39, 45, 47, 48
Frank, Barney, 282
Frank, Thomas, *What's the Matter with Kansas?*, 302
Freedom House, 358
Friedman, Milton, 124, 134, 140, 146, 150, 409–10
    and monetarism, 133
    neoclassical revival led by, 133
    "A Theoretical Framework for Monetary Analysis," 144
Frum, David, *Trumpocracy*, 369
"functional finance" doctrine, 152–54

G.D.P. (gross domestic product):
    and balance on current account, 231, *232*
    and debt, 154, 204–5, *205*
    dollar value of, 204
    and IS-LM, 109–10, *111*
    and Okun's Law, 113
    and tax evasion, 413
General Agreement on Tariffs and Trade (GATT, 1947), 250–51
General Motors, 39
General Theory of Employment, Interest and Money, The (Keynes), 132–33
geography, economic, 398–99, 400, 403
Georgia, Republican Party in, 359, 369

Germany:
  and the euro, 182–83
  government debt in, 98
  health care in, 48
  public debt of, 179
Gertler, Mark, 147
"Getting Real about Rural America"
    (Krugman), 7
Gilded Age, 2, 3
Gingrich, Newt, 53, 54, 55n, 196, 362
Glassman, James K., 84
Gleckman, Howard, 116, 202
"Globaloney and the Backlash"
    (Krugman), 243–45
global temperatures, 330
global warming:
  evidence for, 336, 365
  impacts of, 332
  see also climate change
God and Man at Yale (Buckley), 408
gold, retaining its value, 413, 414
gold and silver coins, 411, 412
goldbuggery, 385
Goldin, Claudia, 270
Goldman Sachs, 170
Goldstein, Emmanuel, 411
Goldwater, Barry, 300–301
  The Conscience of a Conservative,
    300
G.O.P., see Republican Party
Gordon, Robert, 283
Gore, Al, 376, 387
government:
  and central banks, 133
  cutting spending in, 96, 98, 104, 105,
    158, 185, 196, 202, 203
  expansion of, 4, 5, 124, 133
  and health care, 36–37, 116

reduction in size of, 300
right-wing partisans in, 368
separate from private sector, 96
shutdowns of, 362
small, 315
technocratic dream for, 5
trade surplus of, 243
where it excels, 30–32, 181
government activism:
  halo effect on, 4
  stimulus, 107–8
government bonds, purchase of, 104
government debt, 97–99, 104
  effects of, 6
  interest rates on, 89
  private debt vs., 97, 118, 157
  and recessions, 124, 142
government spending, economic
    growth driven by, 227
government stimulus:
  multiplier effect of, 116
  Obama plan, 104, 107–8, 113–14,
    115–17, 118–20, 131, 193, 206,
    362
"Graduates Versus Oligarchs"
    (Krugman), 260, 282–84
Graham, Lindsey, 360
Gramlich, Edward, 91
Grassley, Charles, 54, 346
Great Depression, 81, 103, 106, 115,
    157, 407
  as economy's adjustment to change,
    134, 139
  and Federal Reserve, 133, 140
  and interest rates, 143
  Keynes on, 137
  loss of faith in the market system,
    123, 131, 132

as problem of inadequate demand, 124, 138, 139, 144

and unemployment, 131, 215

Great Moderation, 130, 142, 409

Great Recession (2007–2009), 157, 407

"Great Slump of 1930, The" (Keynes), 137

Great Unraveling, The (Krugman), 9

Greece:

austerity in, 163–65, 188

budget crisis (2009), 158

economy of, 153, 160, 178, 179, 184, 185–86, 188

elections in, 99

and euro, 99, 176, 186, 187

loans to, 182

unemployment in, 182

Green Book, 265

greenhouse gases, 330, 335, 339–40

Green New Deal, 208–9, 211, 328, 338–40

Greenspan, Alan:

and the Fed, 140

and financial crisis, 94, 136

and housing bubble, 83, 84, 91, 141

and income inequality, 283

and interest rates, 161

and Social Security, 17, 19, 20

Gross, Bill, 89

"Growth in a Time of Debt" (Reinhart and Rogoff), 163–65

"Gullibility of the Deficit Scolds, The" (Krugman), 193–94

gun violence, 2

halo effect, 4

hard-money policy, 185

Hassett, Kevin, 84

Hastert, Dennis, 362, 363

Hastert rule, 362

Hawley, Josh, 225

Health and Human Services Department, 57, 368

health care, 35–37, 340

basic facts about, 38–40

competitiveness of, 40

costs of innovation in, 38–39

deductibility of health benefits, 199

failed Clinton plan (1993), 35, 37, 50, 378

government spending on, 116

inefficiency of, 39–40

and midterm election, 367

as morality issue, 44

private sector in, 31, 39–40

rising costs of, 17, 36, 38, 40, 200

scare tactics in, 44–45, 47, 49, 51, 54, 313

and socialized medicine, 43, 52

special interests in, 37, 45, 46, 48, 52, 67

Trump's sabotage of, 351–52, 367, 371

see also Affordable Care Act; Medicaid; Medicare

healthcare.gov, 77

health coverage:

comparison shopping for, 43

competition in, 68

"death spiral" in, 68, 70, 71

employer-provided, 36, 37, 39, 61, 67, 71, 212, 286, 317, 339

government efficiency in, 30–31

government provision for, 36–37, 212

individual mandate for, 68, 69, 71, 313, 324

health coverage (*continued*)
  insurance exchanges in, 68, 70, 71
  for lower-income families, 221, 305
  minimum standards for, 68, 71
  necessity of, 36, 68
  for pre-existing conditions, 67, 68,
    69, 71, 73, 74, 225, 307
  single-payer system, 36–37, 51, 67,
    324, 339
  universal, 4, 35, 36, 42, 44–45, 46,
    47–49, 50–52, 313, 317, 321, 339
  V.H.A. system of, 40, 41–43
Heckscher-Ohlin model, 400–401, 403
Heller, Dean, 75, 225
Helpman, Elhanan, 398
Hersh, Seymour, 300
Hertel-Fernandez, Alexander, 305, 306
high development theory, 399
"Hijacked Commission, The"
    (Krugman), 194, 198–200
Himmelfarb, Gertrude, *The
    De-Moralization of Society,* 285–86
Hofstadter, Richard, "The Paranoid
    Style in American Politics," 346
honesty and dishonesty, 7–8, 324
Hoover, Herbert, 161
Horton, Willie, 306
House Ways and Means Committee, 265
housing:
  construction spending, 88, 90
  Flatland vs. Zoned Zone in, 86–87,
    88
  and Nimbyism, 291
  owners' equivalent rent, 87
  trust in the market, 141
housing bubble, 83–85, 86–88, 93
  aftermath of, 88, 118, 119
  bursting of, 82, 86, 90, 118, 141, 182

economic effects of, 142
and efficient-market theory, 141
in "sand states," 170
and subprime mortgages, 90–91, 136
"How Did Economists Get It So
    Wrong?" (Krugman), 123, 130–48
Howdy Doody Show, The (TV), 218
"How I Work" (Krugman), 395–406
  origins, 395–99
  policy-relevant work, 404–6
  regrets, 406
  rules for research, 399–404
"How Top Executives Live" (*Fortune*),
    219
HSBC, 349
Hubbard, Glenn, 278
Hubbard study, 278–79
Hull, Cordell, 244
Hungary:
  aid to, 189
  Fidesz (Hungarian Civic Alliance)
    in, 189, 358
  one-party autocracy in, 188, 189,
    344, 346, 358, 359
  white nationalism in, 346
hurricane relief, 225
hysteresis, 206

IBM, 215
Iceland, financial crisis of, 162, 187
ignoramus strategy, 95–96
illiberalism, 358
immigration, and Republican Party, 303
income distribution:
  bottom 20 percent of, 272
  Census data about, 262–66, *263, 266*
  median family income, 267–70, *268,*
    272, 275

and productivity, 268–69, 272, 273
redistribution, 221–23
regression toward the mean, 280
income inequality, 1–2, 238–39, 240,
  259–60, 348–49
  and capital gains, 273–74
  CBO figures, 265–66, *266*, 272–74,
    285
  and CEA calculation, 271–72
  deconstructing the debate about,
    261–81
  deniers of, 259, 261, 262, 271–75
  and education, 260, 282, 283
  executive compensation in, 259, 262,
    265
  and family size, 272–73
  and income mobility, 262, 277
  "Krugman calculation" in, 267–70,
    268, 272, 273, 274, 276
  misperceptions of, 260
  and oligarchy, 283
  and polarization, 291
  political implications of, 270–71
  in pre-tax income, 271
  regional divergence in, 260
  and sample size, 274
  significance of growth in, 280–81
  and social changes, 287
  sources of data on, 262
  and technology, 260, 288–90
  women's wages, 286
  "*WSJ* calculation" of, 279–80
income mobility, 276–78
  blender model, 276–77, 280
  and income inequality, 262, 277
  and middle class, 277, *278*
"Increasing Returns and Economic
  Geography" (Krugman), 6, 393

infant mortality, *317*
inflation:
  averting, 81
  causes of, 96, 133
  effects of, 225
  in the 1980s, 128–29, 215
  in the 1970s, 126–27, 128, 129
  and unemployment, 124, 383
In Search of Excess (Crystal), 262
"Instability of Moderation, The"
  (Krugman), 394
intellectual stimulation, 405
interest rates:
  cuts in, 83, 107
  on debt, 204, 211
  and deficit reduction, 208
  effects of changes in, 228
  and employment, 153, 208
  Fed policy of, 106–7, 110, 118, 215
  and financial crises, 89, 96, 104, 105,
    106
  and housing bubble, 141
  and IS-LM, 109
  "liquidity preference" approach to,
    109–11
  "loanable funds" approach to, 109–11
  on mortgages, 199
  and private borrowing and spend-
    ing, 104
  and recessions, 124, 142, 215
  rise in, 161
  on U.S. Treasuries, 205
  zero, 111–12, *111*, 142–43, 153
Interior Department, U.S., 248
Internal Revenue Service (IRS), 350
international diplomacy, 244
International Monetary Fund, 97–98,
  208

international trade, 243–45, 249–53
    arbitration in, 252
    backlash from, 244–45
    conflicts of interest in, 246–47
    and corporate assets, 249
    and corruption, 246, 247, 254, 255–56
    free trade, 249
    literature on, 400
    political realism in, 251–52
    producer interests vs. consumer
        interests in, 250
    protectionism, 247, 250, 252
    reasons for agreements in, 246, 247,
        249–50, 255
    in recent history, 250–51, *251*, 255–56
    role of executive branch in, 250,
        252–53, 255–56
    as rules-based system, 244, 245, 247,
        250–51, 252, 254–55, 256
    tariffs, 244, 246–48, 252–53, 254–56
    trade war, 353, 361, 371–72
    and U.S. credibility, 256
investment:
    as accounting fiction, 228–29
    debt-financed, 212
    lure of personal wealth in, 93
    Madoff's Ponzi scheme in, 92–94
    negative, 230–31, *231*
    overseas, 228
    private, 204, 205, 208
    progressive expenditure, 210–11
    public "shovel-ready" projects, 116,
        133, 205–6, *206*
    rate of return on, 205
    uses of the term, 7
investment-savings, liquidity-money
    (IS-LM), 109–12, *111*
invisible bond vigilante, 160–61

Iran-Contra, 300
Iraq war:
    based on false premises, 13, 26, 343,
        381
    failed reconstruction in, 299
    support from Very Serious People,
        157
    unpopularity among voters, 27
Ireland:
    austerity-with-growth in (1980s),
        161
    banks in, 179
    and Europe, 178
    foreign investment in, 228
    and recover, 183
irrational behavior, 132, 146
Irrational Exuberance (Shiller), 84
Irwin, Neil, 315, 316
"IS-LMentary" (Krugman), 103, 109–
    12, *111*, 125
Israeli stabilization (1985), 127
Italy:
    economy of, 188
    elections in, 188
    Mussolini regime in, 346
"It Can't Happen, It's a Bad Idea, It
    Won't Last" (Jonung and Drea),
    184–85
"It's Baaack: Japan's Slump and the
    Return of the Liquidity Trap"
    (Krugman), 9, 82

Japan:
    Bank of Japan, 104
    financial crisis in, 81–82, 103, 116,
        164
jargon, avoiding, 7
Jensen, Michael, 135

jobs:
  creation of, 120, 293
  cuts in, 107, 120
  employment benefits, 286, 317
  full employment, 96, 114
  health insurance covered in, 39
  involuntary part-time employment,
    60
  in knowledge-intensive industries, 292
  monopsony power in, 316–17
  new geography of, 292
  and real earnings, *316*
  taken by robots, 288–89
  work opportunities for less-educated
    men, 286, 292
  see also unemployment
Johnson, Lyndon B., 53, 54, 55*n*
Johnston, David Cay, 350
Jones, Alex, 356, 357
Journal of Money, Credit and Banking,
  137
JPMorgan Chase, 163

Kaiser Family Foundation, 39, 58
kakistocracy, 350
Kamin, David, 239
Kansas:
  education in, 293
  taxes in, 216, 229, 293
Kavanaugh, Brett, 345, 346, 352
Kentucky, health care in, 68
Kerry, John, 366, 380, 381, 382
Kerry, Teresa Heinz, 380, 381
"ketchup economists," 136, 141
Keynes, John Maynard, 81, 123, 134,
  135, 143, 394, 402
  The General Theory of Employment,
    Interest and Money, 132–33

"The Great Slump of 1930," 137
Keynesian economics:
  and business cycle, 276
  and Capitol Hill Baby-Sitting Co-op,
    137–38
  and dysfunctional finance, 147
  free-market, 124, 125, 133, 394
  macroeconomics, 123, 407–8
  as "moderately conservative," 4, 123,
    133, 408
  New Keynesian views, 129, 139–40,
    143, 145, 147
  and the 1980s, 129
  opponents of, 4, 95, 124, 133–34, 143
  re-embracing, 147–48
"khaki election," use of term, 13
Khashoggi, Jamal, 330
Kinsley, Michael, 126
Kiyotaki, Nobuhiro, 147
Kleiman, Mark, 48
Klein, Ezra, 51, 356
Klein, Joe, 29
Koch brothers, 60, 303, 331, 336, 355
Kocherlakota, Narayana, 384
Kristol, Irving, 299
"Krugman calculation," 267–70, *268,*
  272, 273, 274, 276
K Street project, 283
Kudlow, Larry, 330
Kydland, Finn, 139

Laffer curve, 385
Lancaster, Kelvin, 398
Langone, Ken, 95, 96
language:
  avoiding jargon, 7
  specialized, 393–94
  writing in clear English, 6–7

Latvia, slumps in, 162
Lazear, Eddie, 384
Lehman Brothers, 123, 146, 157
Leonhardt, David, 5
Lerner, Abba, 152–54
liberalism, 324
  death of, 13
liberal professional economists, 149, 150
libertarians, 5
life expectancy, 199
liquidity, 89, 90
  IS-LM, 109–12
liquidity trap, 112
Logic of Collective Action, The (Olson), 354–55
London market, banks lending in, 89
"London Whale" venture, 163
Longman, Phillip, 42
Lucas, Robert, 128, 130, 131, 138–39, 143

Maastricht Treaty, 405
macroeconomics:
  business cycle vs. long-term growth in, 275–76
  and Capitol Hill Baby-Sitting Co-op, 137–38
  Dark Age of, 131, 408, 409
  as divided field, 123–25, 136–37
  false peace in (1985–2007), 142
  Keynesian, 123, 407–8
  rational-expectation, 128
  "saltwater" vs. "freshwater" schools in, 123, 124–25, 138–39, 140, 142, 143, 144
macroeconomics analysis, 103–5, 138
Madhouse Effect, The (Mann), 333
Madoff, Bernard, 92–94
Maduro, Nicolás, 239

Manafort, Paul J., Jr., 359
Mankiw, N. Gregory, 139
Mann, Michael E., 328, 336–37
  The Madhouse Effect, 333
marginal product, 235
marginal utility, diminishing, 235
market disruption, 251
market economy, unregulated, 315–18, 323
marketing scams, 354, 355–56, 357
markets:
  compared to casinos, 134, 135
  competitive, 235, 236
  efficient-market hypothesis, 134, 135–36
  free, 408, 409
  global, 228
  instability of, 146, 147
  monopoly power in, 228, 236
  monopsony power in, 316–17
  1930s disrespect for, 134
  perception of demand, 228
  perfect, 131, 132, 138, 139, 144–45, 148
Market Structure and Foreign Trade (Helpman and Krugman), 398
Mars Orbiter, crash of, 163
Marxism, 2, 123
Massachusetts:
  health care in, 51, 54
  per-capita income in, 292
McCain, John, 73, 320, 335, 365
McCarthy, Joseph, 301
McConnell, Mitch, 104, 114, 224, 225, 307, 370
McCulley, Paul, 83
McKinley, William, 353
McKinsey Global Institute, "Debt and (Not Much) Deleveraging," 97

media:
  biases in, 375, 381
  and conspiracy theory, 375
  credibility of, 375
  cynicism representing contempt for, 226
  failings of, 376
  and "fake news," 364, 375–76
  and freedom of the press, 347
  hesitation to call out lies, 226
  innuendo reported as fact by, 388–89
  intimidation of, 300
  mainstream, 56
  manipulated by conservatives, 75, 336, 368
  Murdoch empire, 297–98
  negative coverage of Affordable Care Act, 58
  party line followed by, 226, 368
  Pelosi attacked by, 362, 363
  "populism" misunderstood by, 351, 353
  propaganda outlets of, 226
  right-wing, 56
  on tax cuts, 216
  trivialization by, 381
  and Trumpism, 343, 347
Medicaid:
  and budget projections, 29
  expansion under Affordable Care Act, 29, 57, 65, 66, 68, 71, 77, 211, 367
  government efficiency in, 31
  poor citizens covered by, 36, 61
  popularity of, 306
  state cuts to, 69, 293
  threats to, 202, 223, 224, 309
Medicare:
  administration's lies about, 225
  attempts to privatize, 363
  and budget projections, 29
  buy-in option for, 77
  creation of, 43, 54
  drug legislation of, 42–43
  government efficiency in, 31
  and health care costs, 17, 38
  increasing spending on, 240, 310
  and innovation in health care, 38–39
  popularity of, 306, 322
  senior citizens covered by, 36, 39, 61
  threats to, 16, 17, 31, 45, 196, 201, 223, 224, 363
  in U.S. vs. Canada, 48–49
  see also health coverage
Medicare Advantage program, 196
  voucher scheme for, 196, 202
Medicare for All, 51, 67, 74, 211, 212, 321, 324, 339
Mencken, H. L., 147
mercantilism, 250
Merkel, Angela, 98
microeconomics, 407, 408
middle class:
  cutting benefits for, 30, 196, 309
  and financial managers, 92–94
  and income distribution, 266, 273
  and income mobility, 277, 278
  raising taxes on, 199
Mildenberger, Matto, 305, 306
Minskyism, 409
Mississippi, income inequality in, 291–92
Mnuchin, Steven, 322
moderation, instability of, 407–10
  financial instability, 409–10
  intellectual instability, 407–8
  political instability, 408–9

Modern Monetary Theory (MMT), 125, 152, 154, 203
monetarism, 133, 409
monetary economics, 176
monetary policy, 128–29, 140, 143, 144, 153
money:
  conventional (currency), 412–14
  cryptocurrency, 411–14
  dollar cash holdings, 413
  dollar notes, 413–14
  fiat currencies, 414
  speculative, 413
  as store of value, 112
"Money and Morals" (Krugman), 260, 285–87
money managers, 92–94
money supply, central banks' control of, 110, 112, 124, 133
"Monopolistic Competition and Optimum Product Diversity" (Dixit and Stiglitz), 396–98
monopoly power, 228, 236
monopsony power, 316–17
Moore, John, 147
Moore, Michael, 44, 45
Moore, Roy, 309
Moretti, Enrico, *The New Geography of Jobs*, 292
mortgage rates, 87
mortgages, subprime, 90–91, 136
"Most Important Thing, The" (Krugman), 327–28
motives, talk about, 8
Moulton, Seth, 76
movement conservatism, 297–98, 302–4, 307
  definition of, 302

keeping zombie ideas alive via, 8
and Republican Party, 297, 299–301, 302, 368
and Tea Party, 303
white resentment as basis of, 343
"Movement Conservativism" (Krugman), 297–98
Moynihan, Daniel Patrick, 5
Mueller, Robert, 307
Mueller investigation, 360
Mulford, David, 405
Mulligan, Casey, 144
Mulvaney, Mick, 207, 225
Murdoch, Rupert, 297, 375
Murphy, Kevin, 279
Murray, Charles, *Coming Apart: The State of White America, 1960–2010*, 285–86
Mussolini, Benito, 346
"Myths of Austerity" (Krugman), 158, 160–62, 165

NAFTA, 372
NAIRU (non-accelerating-inflation rate of unemployment), 114
NASA, 163
National Association of Realtors, 84
National Climate Assessment, 332, 336
National Commission on Fiscal Responsibility and Reform, 198–200
nationalism, 343
National Older Women's League, 198
National Review, The, 301
national security:
  and elections, 306
  and tariffs, 251, 253, 255
NATO, 244

neoclassical economics, 132, 133, 139–40, 147

neoliberal ideology, 315

Netherlands, economy of, 184

New Deal, 107, 293, 308

New Geography of Jobs, The (Moretti), 292

New Hampshire, economic freedom in, 317, *317*

New Jersey, health care in, 76, 78

New Keynesian views, 129, 139–40, 143, 145, 147

New York:
  health care in, 74, 318
  infant mortality in, 317, *317*
  Medicaid expanded in, 318

New York Times, The, 348, 349

Nicaragua, and Iran-Contra, 300

Nimbyism, 291

Nixon administration, and media, 300

Nordhaus, William, 396

Norman, Victor, 398

"normative" economics, 1

Northam, Ralph, 308, 309

North Carolina:
  health care in, 77
  Republican Party in, 359

Norway, economy of, 323

Obama, Barack:
  conservatives vs., 150, 208, 302, 320, 362
  on health care, 53–55, 66, 339, 361
  and international trade, 252
  and taxes, 216, 219, 229

Obama administration:
  on debt and unemployment, 208
  "hijacked" commission of, 198–200

and revenue growth, 225

stimulus plan of, 104, 107–8, 113–14, 115–17, 118–20, 131, 193, 206, 362

Obamacare, see Affordable Care Act

O'Brien, Michael, 126

Ocasio-Cortez, Alexandria (AOC), 234, 236, 237, 320–21

Occupy Wall Street, 285

O'Connor, Reed, 367, 369

oil shocks, 126

Oklahoma, tax cuts in, 293

Okun's Law, 113

oligarchy, 283, 349, 350

Olson, Mancur, The Logic of Collective Action, 354–55

Operation Coffee Cup (1961), 322

optimum currency areas, 177

Palin, Sarah, 54

Panama Papers, 349

Pangloss, Doctor (fict.), 135, 140

"paperclip maximizers," 357

"Paranoid Style in American Politics, The" (Hofstadter), 346

parasites, 354–57

Paulson, Henry, 91

PBS Newshour, 169–71

Pelosi, Nancy:
  achievements of, 361–63
  and Affordable Care Act, 35–36, 55, 361, 367
  and financial reform, 362
  as House Speaker, 76, 344, 362, 363
  on "monstrous endgame," 367, 369
  on Social Security, 15, 35, 306, 361
  and stimulus plan, 362
  and trade agreement, 372
  on the wall as "manhood thing," 370

Pence, Mike, 73
pensions:
    defined benefit, 14
    defined contribution, 14–15
    401(k)-type plans, 31–32
    private, decline of, 31–32
Perlstein, Rick, 302, 354, 355
Perot, H. Ross, 245
personal savings rate, 88
Peterson, Pete, 193
Piketty, Thomas, 219
    Capital in the 21st Century, 238
Pimco bond fund, 83, 89
Pizzagate, 375
Poland:
    Law and Justice Party in, 358
    threats to democracy in, 188, 189,
        344, 346, 358, 359, 360
    white nationalism in, 346
polarization, 5–9, 291, 297–98, 356
policy discussion, absence of, 13
political action, 355–56
political realism, 251–52
politicization:
    pressures from the right, 3–4
    and racism, 4–5, 226, 301, 307,
        308–10, 360
    roots of, 2–5
PolitiFact, 386
Ponzi scheme, 92–93
population, aging of, 16
population density, 87
population growth, 225, 271, 272
"populism," use of term, 351–53
Portugal, economy of, 178
"positive" economics, 1
post-truth politics, 61
poverty:
    and cuts in benefits, 30

    of elderly, 23–24
    and health care, 47, 66
precious metals, 411
Prescott, Edward, 139
productivity, 283
    and income distribution, 268–69,
        272, 273
    slowdown in, 267, 289
    and technology, 289
    and wages, 289
professional conservative economists,
    149
profit, appearance of, 92–93
progressive expenditure, categories of,
    210–11
propagandists, 149
protectionism, 353
prudence, downside of, 104, 106,
    107–8, 117
"public good," use of term, 354–55
public goods, 30
public health, 355
public works, spending on, 116, 133,
    143, 205–6, *206*
punditry:
    author's rules for, 5–9
    honesty about dishonesty, 7–8
    staying with easy stuff, 6
    talking about motives, 8–9
    writing in English, 6–7
Putin, Vladimir, 371

racism:
    and hate-mongering, 54
    interracial marriages, 215
    and politicization, 4–5, 226, 301,
        307, 308–10, 360
Rajan, Raghuram, 136
Rampell, Catherine, 5

Rand, Ayn, *Atlas Shrugged,* 219
rationality:
 assumption of, 134, 138, 139, 144–45, 148
 investor irrationality, 135
 limitations of, 131, 132
Rawls, John, 3
Reagan, Ronald:
 and economic growth, 262, 275–76
 and health care, 45, 53, 322
 as icon of conservative purity, 300, 302
 and supply-side economics, 271
 and taxes, 7, 19, 215, 299
 and Voting Rights Act, 300
Reagan administration:
 and income inequality, 271
 and Iran-Contra, 300
 and private contractors, 300
"real business cycle" theory, 139
real estate:
 housing bubble, 82, 83–85, 86–88
 land-use restrictions, 87
recessions:
 causes of, 138–39, 185
 central banks' roles in, 103–4, 124, 133
 demand-side view of, 139
 desirability of, 144, 147
 "double-dip" (1979–1982), 215
 effects of, 126–27
 fears of, 81–82
 and fiscal policy, 140, 141, 215, 275
 and government debt, 124, 142
 and printing money, 4, 104, 105
 and unemployment insurance claims, 106
Reciprocal Trade Agreements Act (1934), 250, 252, 254–55
"Red-Baiting in the 21st Century" (Krugman), 313–14

red ink, fear of, 107, 116
Regan, Trish, 319, 320
regulation, minimal, 315
Reid, Harry, 28, 29
Reinhardt, Uwe, 35
Reinhart, Carmen, 158, 163
Repealing the Job-Killing Health Care Law Act (2011), 59
Republican Party:
 campaign (2020), 313
 center-right delusion of, 305–7
 climate denial of, 337, 365
 conspiracy theorizing by, 345–46, 365
 corruption in, 335–37, 343, 358, 368
 dark side of, 334, 336, 368
 democracy undermined by, 367–69
 double standards of, 208, 209
 double talk of, 225–26
 economic doctrine of, 229
 facts or logic ignored by, 28, 237, 366
 "Flimflam Man" of, 194, 195–97, 362
 frauds promoted by, 74–75, 224–26
 and health care, 65–66, 69, 70, 71–72, 73–75, 76–77, 309, 338
 hostility to science, 335, 337
 and immigration, 303
 IRS defunded by, 350
 lying by, 225–26
 and movement conservatism, 8, 297–98, 299–301, 302–4, 307, 343, 368
 one-party rule sought by, 358–60
 paranoid style in, 345–47
 and party loyalty, 67, 150–51, 226, 368
 policy analysis shunned by, 73–74, 77
 power plays by, 359–60, 369
 privatization of public assets as goal of, 338
 racism of, 226
 radicalization of, 189, 298, 309

Republican Party (*continued*)
  realities of, 197
  state governments controlled by,
    65–66, 68, 77
  and Supreme Court, 345, 346, 352
  tax plans of, 222, 224–26, 236, 309
  Trumpism of, 335–37, 343, 345–46,
    359–60, 370–72
  voter preferences vs., 309
  workable ideas lacking in, 69, 74
retirement, economics of, 15, 22,
    23–24, 31–32, 362
retirement accounts:
  private, 17, 19, 22–24
  real rate of return on, 23
Return of Depression Economics, The
    (Krugman), 82
Reynolds, Alan, 273, 274
Ricardo, David, 289
risk:
  elimination of, 81
  in financial innovation, 90–91
  reward vs., 135
Rivlin, Alice, 263
Roach, Stephen, 83, 85
Roberts, David, 307
Roberts, Paul Craig, 273, 274, 279
Robin, Corey, 315–16
robot, defined, 288
Rodgers, Cathy McMorris, 60
Rogers, Will, 297
Rogoff, Ken, 158, 163
Romer, Christina, 234, 236
Romer, David, 139
Romney, Mitt, 51–52, 54, 219, 320
Roosevelt, Franklin D.:
  and balanced budget, 107
  on health care, 46

and reciprocal trade act, 247, 250,
    252, 254
and Social Security, 25, 26
Roosevelt, Theodore, 239
Roosevelt (FDR) administration, and
    international trade, 244
rule of law:
  disdain of, 252, 256, 301, 347
  interpretation and enforcement of,
    367–68
rules for research, 399–404
  dare to be silly, 401–2, 404
  listen to the gentiles, 399–400, 404
  question the question, 400–401, 404
  simplify, simplify, 402–4
Russia, and trade, 256
Ryan, Jack, 381
Ryan, Paul, 28, 203, 219, 363
  as flim-flam man, 194, 195–97, 362
  and Medicare, 225
  and Ryan plan, 193–94, 195–97,
    201–2
  super PAC of, 225

Saez, Emmanuel, 219, 234–35, 236,
    238–39
safety-net programs, 4, 224, 313, 317,
    320, 321, 323, 370
Samuelson, Paul, 124, 403, 407, 408,
    410
San Diego, housing in, 87
"sand states," unemployment in, 170
Santorum, Rick, 303
Sawhill, Isabel, 280
Scaife, Richard Mellon, 380
Schultz, Howard, 212, 308, 310
Schumer, Chuck, 93
Schumpeter, Joseph A., 132, 134, 395

Schwartz, Anna, 133
SeaWorld, 352
secular stagnation, 206
Securities and Exchange Commission,
    93
segregationists, 346
Seltzer, Marlene, 166
Senate, role of, 368
September 11, 2001, attacks, aftermath
    of, 13
Sessions, Pete, 59
Shapiro, Ben, 354, 355, 356, 357
Shiller, Robert, 84, 136, 141, 146
Shleifer, Andrei, 146
Sicko (movie), 44–45
silver and gold coins, 411, 412
"silver-loading," 71
Simple Art of Murder, The (Chandler),
    327
Simpson, Alan, 198, 199, 203, 218
Sinema, Kyrsten, 365
"Skewing of America, The"
    (Krugman), 259–60
"skills gap," 159, 166–68, 290
Slemrod, Joel, 277
Smith, Adam, 132, 138, 411
Smith, Noah, 95
smoking, dangers of, 333, 334
Smoot-Hawley Tariff Act (1930), 247
snake oil, peddling, 357
Snow, John, 81
social democracy, 313–14, 317, 320–
    21, 323
social dysfunction, indicators of, 286
socialism, 219, 313–14, 316, 319–21,
    322–24
social justice, 3
social media, *see* media

Social Security:
    cuts in benefits, 17, 32
    expansion of, 30, 32, 212, 240
    financial condition of, 16–17, 20,
        28–29
    guaranteed benefits of, 24
    historic success of, 21, 22, 24, 31–32
    importance to voters, 14, 26, 31, 306
    as independent entity, 20
    "Life Expectancy for Social Security"
        (Web site), 26
    percentage of revenues going to ben-
        efits, 22
    politicization of, 25–27
    privatization of, 14–15, 19–21,
        22–24, 25–27, 28–29, 32, 35, 302,
        306, 361, 377, 378
    retirement age for, 199
    supported by dedicated tax on pay-
        roll earnings, 19
    threats to, 16–18, 198, 199, 200, 223,
        224
    Trump administration's lies about,
        225
    trust fund of, 20
Social Security Act (1934), 26
Solow, Bob, 396, 405
Soros, George, 345, 346, 365
Soviet Union:
    central planning by, 323
    economy of, 324
    fall of, 177
Spain:
    anti-establishment forces in, 99
    economy of, 178–80, 184
    and euro, 177, 178–79, 181, 187, 188
    housing bubble in, 181
    internal devaluation in, 179

Spain (*continued*)
   loans to, 182
   public debt of, 179
   unemployment in, 182, 184
speculation:
   destructive, 135
   short-term, 133
stagflation (1970s), 124, 133
Stalin, Joseph, 239, 324
"State of Macro, The" (Blanchard), 130
statistics, uses and abuses of, 262
Stein, Herbert, 271
Stiglitz, Joseph E., 5, 396–98, 403
"Stimulus Arithmetic" (Krugman),
   104, 113–14
stock market bubble, 83, 84, 86
Stokes, Leah, 305, 306
Stone Center for the Study of
   Socioeconomic Inequality
   (CUNY), 259
Stross, Charlie, 357
sugar, import quotas on, 250
Summers, Larry, 136, 145–46
"Sum of All Fears, The" (Krugman), 81
supply-side economics, 128, 275–76, 299
Supreme Court, U.S.:
   on Affordable Care Act, 65, 68, 77
   Kavanaugh appointment to, 345,
     346, 352
   moral authority destroyed, 345, 360
   partisanship in, 346
sustainable growth rate, 153–54, 204
Sweden, economy of, 239, 323
Switzerland, health care in, 37
system overhaul, 210, 212

tanning parlors, tax on, 211
tariffs, 244, 246–48, *251*, 252–53, 254–56

taxes:
   carbon tax, 339
   corporate, *see* corporate taxes
   cutting, 8, 16–17, 19, 20, 116–17,
     199, 201, 215–17, 218–20, 224–
     26, 227–29, 230–33, 231–33, *232*,
     236–37, 306–7, 351, 361, 370,
     371
   and debt, 154, 222–23, 224–26
   economic effects of, 7, 222–23, 224–
     26, 233, 236–37
   incentive effects of, 154
   and income inequality, 238–39
   low, 315
   on middle class, 221–23
   and monopoly power, 236
   narrow-gauge, 211
   optimal top rates of, 234–35
   on payroll, 212
   political trade-offs in, 153
   on pollution, 339
   progressive taxation, 238–40, 323
   raising, 185, 196, 199, 219, 229, 380
   tariffs, 244, 246–48, *251*, 252–53,
     254–56
   temporary breaks, 222
   top marginal income tax rates,
     236–37, *236*
   Trump's frauds, 348–50
   value-added, 154, 212
   on the wealthy, *see* wealthy
   on working class, 20, 221–23
tax evasion, 349–50, 413, 414
tax liabilities, 414
tax loopholes, 93, 349
Tax Policy Center, 196, 202, 283
tax reform, 26, 198–99
Tea Party, 53–54, 303

technology, and income inequality, 260, 288–90

Tennessee, health care in, 68

tethering, 413–14

Thatcher, Margaret, 22, 23, 128

"That Eighties Show" (Klugman), 124

"Theoretical Framework for Monetary Analysis, A" (Friedman), 144

Thompson, Fred, 47, 52

tobacco companies, 333, 334

Toles, Tom, 333

torture, 300

totalitarianism, 324

trade theory, 399–400, 401, 403

trade war, 353, 361, 371–72
   see also international trade

transcription costs, 411–14

transportation, greenhouse gases from, 339–40

Treasury, U.S.:
   on income gains, 279–81
   Office of Tax Analysis, 278
   partisan functions of, 26
   and Social Security, 16

Trichet, Jean-Claude, 161

"Triumph of Macroeconomics, The" (Krugman), 103–5

Trotsky, Leon, 324

trucking industry, 290

Trump, Donald:
   attacks on media by, 347
   attitude toward truth, 364–66
   belligerent ignorance of, 246, 307, 337, 345, 346–47, 352
   campaigning, 309, 370
   contempt for rule of law, 252, 256, 347
   corruption of, 335–37, 338, 343, 349, 350, 368, 389
   and cronyism, 256, 343
   as deal-maker, 348–50
   election of (2016), 13, 343, 372, 375, 387–89
   family history of, 348–49
   foreign dictators admired by, 346–47, 365, 371
   humiliating others, 352–53
   and inequality, 260, 291
   and international trade, 245, 246, 247–48, 249, 252–53, 254–56, 353, 361
   laziness of, 352
   as liar, 348, 353, 364, 365
   on manhood, 370, 371, 372
   on neo-Nazis as "very fine people," 365
   and populism, 351–53
   and racism, 246, 310, 360
   and Republican Party, 335–37, 359, 372
   scandals about, 388–89
   and socialism, 322–23
   State of the Union address (2019), 207–9, 322
   supporters scammed by, 353, 372, 389
   and taxes, 216, 221–23, 224–26, 227–29, 230–33, 306–7, 308, 350, 361, 371
   tax returns of, 359
   tough-guy posturing by, 334, 346–47, 370–72
   and 2020 election, 227, 347, 361
   and the wall, 370, 371

Trump, Fred (father), 348

Trump administration:
   anti-science views of, 332
   as anti-worker, 351–53
   appointments to, 352

Trump administration (*continued*)
  bad faith of, 151, 332, 365
  charlatans and cranks in, 149, 151,
    329, 331, 333
  climate change deniers in, 329–31,
    332–34, 335–37
  and collapse of freedom, 187
  compared to that of G. W. Bush, 9,
    13
  and conspiracy theories, 150, 337,
    343, 345, 365
  corruption of, 70, 246, 331, 338, 343,
    349, 350
  depravity of, 332–33, 334
  and "fake news," 375–76
  and health care, 70, 71, 75, 77–78,
    308, 351–52
  and immigration, 387
  investigations of, 347, 359
  labor policy of, 352
  lying by, 225
  political disaster, 158
  and tax scam, 221–23, 224–26
  trade war of, 353, 361, 371–72
  the worst and the dimmest in, 151
Trump family, investments of, 371
Trumpism, 335–37, 343, 345–46, 347,
  359–60, 370–72
Trumpocracy, (Frum), 369
Trump Organization, contributions
  to, 371
Trump University, 388, 389
trust:
  collapse of, 90, 145
  in economic theory, 132, 134
truth, 364–66
Turkey, Erdogan regime in, 346
Twinkie Era, 218–20

"Ultimate Zombie, The" (Krugman),
  215–17
unemployment:
  and austerity, 164, 203
  causes of, 81, 96, 133, 139, 144, 158–59
  and consumer spending cuts, 107
  cyclical, 170–71, *170*, 383
  and deficit reduction, 208
  and education, 166–67
  and the Fed, 150
  and "full" employment rate, 96, 114,
    153, 205, 383, 408
  and government stimulus, 113, 115,
    144
  and Great Depression, 131, 215
  and income levels, 275
  and inflation, 124, 383
  and interest rates, 153, 208
  long-term, 167
  NAIRU, 114
  "natural" level of, 133
  by occupation, 170–71, *170*
  and Okun's Law, 113
  rates of, 106, 108
  and recessions, 133, 157, 215
  and "skills gap," 159, 166–68, 290
  structural, 169–71, 383–84, 385
  and wages, 179
  in winter of debt, 203
unemployment insurance, 106
unfair practices, and tariffs, 251–52,
  255
unions:
  bargaining power of, 218–19, 220,
    289
  decline of, 289–90
  vs. monopsony power, 317
United Nations (U.N.), 244

United States:
  central bank of, *see* Federal Reserve
  democracy in danger in, 366, 367–69
  unnecessary misery in, 321
Urban Institute, 57, 279, 280

values, 3
Venezuela:
  economic disaster in, 313, 317, 319,
    323, 324
  nationalization of industry in, 323
"Very Serious People" (Krugman),
  157–59, 160, 189, 375
Veterans Health Administration
  (V.H.A.), lean and efficient system
  of, 40, 41–43
Victorian Era, virtues of, 286
Vishny, Robert, 146
Voltaire, on the best of all possible
  worlds, 135
Voting Rights Act, 300

wage gap, 286
wage-price spiral, 126, 127
wage stagnation, 92, 168, 288, 289
Wallace, George, 310
Wall Street Journal, The, 271, 273,
  279–80
Warren, Elizabeth, 210, 211–12, 238–
  40, 309
Washington Post, The, 303
wealth distribution:
  historical estimates of, 270
  and income inequality, 274–75, 282,
    284
Wealth of Nations, The (Smith), 132
wealthy:
  and capital gains, 273

concentration of, 238, 349
conservatives, 149
cutting taxes on, 4, 7, 20, 30, 51, 69,
  196, 199, 200, 201, 215–17, 218–
  20, 221–23, 224, 227, 229, 236–37,
  308, 309, 351, 355, 370, 371
donors to Republican Party, 370
exploding incomes of, 92, 283
health coverage for, 36, 39
idolizing of, 94
incentive effects on, 235
and income distribution, 265–66,
  266, 267, 269–70, 273; *see also*
  income inequality
income from assets, 221, 233
income from earnings, 349
increasing taxes on, 66, 211–12, 220,
  238–40, 307, 309, 310, 324, 380
as Masters of the Universe, 270
and monopoly power, 236
optimal tax rates on, 235–37, *236*
"stealth politics" of, 240
tax avoidance vs. evasion by, 349–50
as too rich, 274–75
and Trumpism, 343
Weigel, Dave, 28
welfare, 126
West Virginia, Republican Party in,
  359
What's the Matter with Kansas?
  (Frank), 302
*When Work Disappears: The World
  of the New Urban Poor* (Wilson),
  286–87
"Where Did the Productivity Growth
  Go?" (Dew-Becker and Gordon),
  283
Whitaker, Matthew, 333

white nationalism, 343, 346, 360

"Why Not the Worst?" (Krugman), 343–44, 350

wildfire, growing risks of, 332

Will, George, 381

Wilson, William Julius, 292
    When Work Disappears; The World of the New Urban Poor, 286–87

wing-nut welfare, 303

Wisconsin, Republican Party in, 369

Wolfe, Tom, *Bonfire of the Vanities,* 262, 270

Wolff, Edward, 270

working class:
    anti-worker bias in politics, 290, 318, 351–53
    falling incomes of, 96, 244
    family values of, 286
    and health care, 352
    and income inequality, 259–60, 272, 273
    and "skills gap," 167–68
    stagnating wages of, 92, 168, 288, 289
    tax increases on, 20, 221–23
    and trade war, 372
    and unions, 218, 289–90, 317
    work opportunities available to, 286–87, 292

World Trade Organization (WTO), 247, 252

World War I, war debts from, 254

World War II:
    postwar economic growth, 219, 234
    postwar trading system, 244, 250
    wage controls in, 270

Wren-Lewis, Simon, 5, 385–86

"*WSJ* calculation," 280

Yellen, Janet, 97

Yunus, Muhammad, 388

Zandi, Mark, 113

"zero lower bound" interest rates, 142–43, 153

zombie ideas:
    on climate change, 4
    cutting taxes on the rich, 4, 215–17
    eating people's brains, 3–4
    and health care, 216
    on impossibility of universal health coverage, 4
    invasion of, 259
    in movement conservatism, 8
    and racism, 4

Zucman, Gabriel, 238–39, 349